The Complete
PLAIN WORDS

BY

SIR ERNEST GOWERS

Author of Plain Words *and*
An ABC of Plain Words

LONDON
HER MAJESTY'S STATIONERY OFFICE
1954

Published . .   . . *September, 1954*

Crown Copyright Reserved

PUBLISHED BY HER MAJESTY'S STATIONERY OFFICE

To be purchased from

York House, Kingsway, LONDON, W.C.2   423 Oxford Street, LONDON, W.1
P.O. Box 569, LONDON, S.E.1
13a Castle Street, EDINBURGH, 2   1 St. Andrew's Crescent, CARDIFF
39 King Street, MANCHESTER, 2   Tower Lane, BRISTOL, 1
2 Edmund Street, BIRMINGHAM, 3   80 Chichester Street, BELFAST
or from any Bookseller

Price 5s. od. net

Printed in Great Britain under the authority of HER MAJESTY'S STATIONERY OFFICE
by The Campfield Press, St. Albans.

Preface

THIS book is in the main a reconstruction of my two previous books, *Plain Words* and *ABC of Plain Words*. Both these, as I explained in the prefaces to them, were written at the invitation of the Treasury as a contribution to what they were doing to improve official English. The first was by way of an introduction to the subject; the second was designed as a work of reference. When my publishers told me last year that the time was ripe for a new edition of *Plain Words*, I thought it would be well to round off the venture by weaving into the new edition material from the *ABC*. I could then say all I had to say in one volume, and, by giving it the index which the original edition lacked, could make it serve as a book of reference, and so do away with the need for a separate book with the layout, inevitably unattractive, of a series of unrelated topics arranged alphabetically.

I am not a grammarian, and *The Complete Plain Words*, like its predecessors, makes no claim to be a grammar of the English Language, though for reasons I have explained in the text, I felt bound, reluctantly and diffidently, to give one chapter (VIII) to some points of grammar and one (IX) to punctuation. Apart from these two chapters, this book is wholly concerned with what is described in one of the quotations that head the first chapter as the choice and arrangement of words in such a way as to get an idea as exactly as possible out of one mind into another. Even so I must not be credited with too high an ambition: the scope of the book is circumscribed by its being intended primarily for those who use words as tools of their trade, in administration or business.

I have made full use of this opportunity to revise what I wrote before by alteration, by omission, and especially by the addition of new matter. In doing so I have profited from reading books on kindred subjects since published, and I tender my grateful acknowledgment to their authors. They are among the books listed in the bibliography on page 200. But above all I am indebted to the many correspondents from all parts of the English-speaking world who have been good enough to respond to my invitation to send me suggestions, criticisms and specimens. I have thanked them all individually by letter, and I should have liked to print a list of their names here as a perpetual token of my gratitude for their kindness. But they are too numerous. Many of them, if they read this book, will recognise passages in it as their own contributions, and I would ask them to treat this discovery as conveying a message of special thanks from me to them.

But I must make one or two exceptions to the anonymity of my gratitude. Kind letters from fellow-workers in the same field gave me particular pleasure: among these were Mr. Ivor Brown, Mr. V. H. Collins, Dr Rudolph Flesch, Mr. Frank Jones and Mr. Henry Strauss, M.P. And I must record my deep obligation to that master-craftsman of the English language, my friend Mr. G. M. Young: the frequency with which references to him occur in the following pages imperfectly reflects the debt I owe him for his encouragement and advice. I must also repeat the thanks I expressed in my previous prefaces to Dr. Wyn Griffith for continuing to allow me to draw on his wise counsel, and to him and to my brother, Sir William Gowers, for being good enough to read the proofs and making many valuable suggestions. Finally I am most grateful to Sir Gordon Welch, lately Controller of the Stationery Office, and to Mr. H. G. Carter of that Office, for the keen interest they have shown in this book and the great trouble they have taken over its preparation.

Contents

I

Prologue

Do but take care to express yourself in a plain, easy Manner, in well-chosen, significant and decent Terms, and to give a harmonious and pleasing Turn to your Periods; study to explain your Thoughts, and set them in the truest Light, labouring as much as possible, not to leave them dark nor intricate, but clear and intelligible.

CERVANTES. *Preface to Don Quixote*

The final cause of speech is to get an idea as exactly as possible out of one mind into another. Its formal cause therefore is such choice and disposition of words as will achieve this end most economically.

G. M. YOUNG

THE purpose of this book is to help officials in their use of written English as a tool of their trade. I suspect that this project may be received by many of them without any marked enthusiasm or gratitude. "Even now", they may say, "it is all we can do to keep our heads above water by turning out at top speed letters in which we say what we mean after our own fashion. Not one in a thousand of the people we write to knows the difference between good English and bad. What is the use of all this highbrow stuff? It will only prevent us from getting on with the job."

But what is this job that must be got on with? Writing is an instrument for conveying ideas from one mind to another; the writer's job is to make his reader apprehend his meaning readily and precisely. Do these letters always say just what the writer means? Nay, does the writer himself always know just what he means? Even when he knows what he means, and says it in a way that is clear to him, is it always equally clear to his reader? If not, he has not been getting on with the job. "The difficulty", said Robert Louis Stevenson, "is not to write, but to write what you mean, not to affect your reader, but to affect him precisely as you wish." Let us take one or two examples given later in this book to illustrate particular faults, and, applying this test to them, ask ourselves whether the reader is likely to grasp at once the meaning of

Prices are basis prices per ton for the representative-basis-pricing specification and size and quantity.

or of

Where particulars of a partnership are disclosed to the Executive Council the remuneration of the individual partner for superannuation

> purposes will be deemed to be such proportion of the total remuneration of such practitioners as the proportion of his share in partnership profits bears to the total proportion of the shares of such practitioner in those profits.

or of

> The treatment of this loan interest from the date of the first payment has been correct—i.e. tax charged at full standard rate on Mr. X and treated in your hands as liability fully satisfied before receipt.

or of

> The programme must be on the basis of the present head of labour ceiling allocation overall.

or, to take an example from America, so as to show that this is not the only country in which writers sometimes forget that what has a meaning for them may have none for their readers, of

> The non-compensable evaluation heretofore assigned to you for your service-connected disability is confirmed and continued.*

All these were written for plain men, not for experts. What will the plain man make of them? The recipients of the last three may painfully and dubiously reach the right conclusions—the taxpayer that no more money is wanted from him, the builder that he is unlikely to get more labour than has been allocated to him, and the veteran that there is still no disability pension for him. But the recipient of the first example will be unable to unlock the secret of the jargon without a key, and what the second will make of the explanation given to him is anyone's guess. Yet the writers may be presumed to have known exactly what they meant; the obscurity was not in their thoughts but in their way of expressing themselves. The fault of writing like this is not that it is unscholarly but that it is inefficient. It wastes time: the reader's time because he has to puzzle over what should be plain, and the writer's time because he may have to write again to explain his meaning. A job that needed to be done only once has had to be done twice because it was bungled the first time.

Professional writers realise that they cannot hope to affect their readers precisely as they wish without care and practice in the proper use of words. The need for the official to take pains is even greater, for if what the professional writer has written is wearisome and obscure the reader can toss the book aside and read no more, but only at his peril can he so treat what the official has tried to tell him. By proper use I do not mean grammatically proper. It is true that

---

*Quoted in *Time*, 7th May, 1947.

there are rules of grammar and syntax, just as in music there are rules of harmony and counterpoint. But one can no more write good English than one can compose good music merely by keeping the rules. On the whole they are aids to writing intelligibly, for they are in the main no more than the distillation of successful experiments made by writers of English through the centuries in how best to handle words so as to make a writer's meaning plain. Some, it is true, are arbitrary. One or two actually increase the difficulty of clear expression, but these too should nevertheless be respected, because lapses from what for the time being is regarded as correct irritate the educated reader, and distract his attention, and so make him the less likely to be affected precisely as you wish. But I shall not have much to say about text-book rules because they are mostly well known and well observed in official writing.

The golden rule is not a rule of grammar or syntax. It concerns less the arrangement of words than the choice of them. "After all," said Lord Macaulay, "the first law of writing, that law to which all other laws are subordinate, is this: that the words employed should be such as to convey to the reader the meaning of the writer." The golden rule is to pick those words and to use them and them only. Arrangement is of course important, but if the right words alone are used they generally have a happy knack of arranging themselves. Matthew Arnold once said: "People think that I can teach them style. What stuff it all is. Have something to say and say it as clearly as you can. That is the only secret of style." That was no doubt said partly for effect, but there is much truth in it, especially in relation to the sort of writing we are now concerned with, in which emotional appeal plays no part.

This golden rule applies to all prose, whatever its purpose, and indeed to poetry too. Illustrations could be found throughout the gamut of purposes for which the written word is used. At the one end of it we can turn to Shakespeare, and from the innumerable examples that offer themselves choose the lines

> Kissing with golden face the meadows green,
> Gilding pale streams with heavenly alchymy

which, as a description of what the rising sun does to meadows and rivers on a "glorious morning", must be as effective a use of thirteen words as could be found in all English literature. At the other end we can turn (for the golden rule can be illustrated from official writing in its observance as well as in its breach) to the unknown member of the staff of the General Post Office who by composing the notice that used to be displayed in every post office

> Postmasters are neither bound to give change nor authorised to demand it

used twelve words hardly less efficiently to warn customers of what must have been a singularly intractable dilemma. At first sight there seems little in common between the two. Their purposes are different; one is descriptive and emotional, the other instructional and objective. But each serves its purpose perfectly, and it is the same quality in both that makes them do so. Every word is exactly right; no other word would do as well; each is pulling its weight; none could be dispensed with. As was said of Milton's prose in the quotation that heads Chapter VI, "Fewer would not have served the turn, and more would have been superfluous".

It is sometimes said that the principle of plain words can be overdone. That depends on a writer's purpose. If what he wants is to use words to conceal his thoughts and to leave a blurred impression on the minds of his readers, of course it can; and there may be occasions when prudence prompts him to do so. Even those who want to express their thoughts sometimes prefer to do so not too plainly. That rare artist in words, C. E. Montague, once amused himself by tilting against exaggerated lucidity. He said:

> Even in his most explicit moments a courteous writer will stop short of rubbing into our minds the last item of all that he means. He will, in a moderate sense of the term, have his non-lucid intervals. At times he will make us wrestle a little with him in the dark before he yields his full meaning.

That again depends on what the writer's purpose is, and on who his reader will be. As Samuel Butler said, "It takes two to say a thing —a sayee as well as a sayer, and the one is as essential to any true saying as the other". I recall an old story of an Indian official who on finding his British superior laboriously correcting a letter he had drafted to a brother Indian official, remarked "Your honour puts yourself to much trouble correcting my English and doubtless the final letter will be much better literature; but it will go from me Mukherji to him Bannerji, and he Bannerji will understand it a great deal better as I Mukherji write it than as your honour corrects it". But the writers for whom this book is intended are not addressing a small group whose idiosyncrasies must be studied. They have the whole adult population as their readers. In other words the sayees are mostly plain, simple, not highly educated people. And the things the sayers have to say are in the main concerned with telling the sayees what they may or may not do and what they are or are not entitled to. There is no room here for experiments with hints and nuances. No doubt these writers do in fact sometimes make us

wrestle with them in the dark before yielding their full meaning—
sometimes indeed no amount of wrestling will make them yield it.
But it is charitable to suppose that this is by accident, and not, as
when Montague's writer does it, by design. Just as those servants of
the Crown whose weapon is the sword have had to abandon the gay
trappings of regimental uniforms and assume the dull monotony of
battledress, so those who wield the pen must submit to a similar
change; the serviceable is now more needed than the ornamental.
"That the hurry of modern life has put both the florid and the
polished styles out of fashion, except for very special audiences, is
not to be deplored if this leads to a more general appreciation of the
capacity of the plain style. By 'plain' we do not mean bald but
simple and neat."*

Moreover you need to choose the right words in order that you
may make your meaning clear not only to your reader but also to
yourself. The first requisite for any writer is to know just what
meaning he wants to convey, and it is only by clothing his thoughts
in words that he can think at all. "What a man cannot state he
does not perfectly know, and conversely the inability to put his
thoughts into words sets a boundary to his thought. . . . English is
not merely the medium of our thought; it is the very stuff and
process of it."* And the less one makes a habit of thinking, the less
one is able to think: the power of thinking atrophies unless it is
used. The following was written about politicians, but it is true of
all of us:

> A scrupulous writer in every sentence that he writes will ask
> himself . . . What am I trying to say? What words will express it?
> . . . And he probably asks himself . . . Could I put it more shortly?
> But you are not obliged to go to all this trouble. You can shirk it by
> simply throwing open your mind and letting the ready-made phrases
> come crowding in. They will construct your sentences for you—even
> think your thoughts for you to a certain extent—and at need they will
> perform the important service of partially concealing your meaning
> even from yourself.†

"Go to all this trouble" is not an overstatement. Few common
things are more difficult than to find the right word, and many
people are too lazy to try. This form of indolence sometimes betrays
itself by a copious use of inverted commas. "I know this is not quite
the right word", the inverted commas seem to say, "but I can't be
bothered to think of a better"; or, "please note that I am using this
word facetiously"; or, "don't think I don't know that this is a

---

Report of the Departmental Committee on the Teaching of English in England. H.M.
Stationery Office, 1921.
†George Orwell in *Horizon*, April, 1947.

cliché". If the word is the right one, do not be ashamed of it: if it is the wrong one, do not use it. The same implied apology is often made in conversation by interposing "shall I say?" or by ending every sentence with phrases such as "or something" or "sort of thing". Officials cannot do that, but in them the same phenomenon is reflected in an unwillingness to venture outside a small vocabulary of shapeless bundles of uncertain content—words like *position, arise, involve, in connexion with, issue, consideration* and *factor*—a disposition, for instance, to "admit with regret the position which has arisen in connection with" rather than to make the effort to tell the reader specifically what is admitted with regret. Clear thinking is hard work, but loose thinking is bound to produce loose writing. And clear thinking takes time, but time that has to be given to a job to avoid making a mess of it cannot be time wasted and may in the end be time saved.

It is wise therefore not to begin to write until you are quite certain what you want to say. That sounds elementary, but the elementary things are often the most likely to be neglected. Some, it is true, can never be sure of clarifying their thoughts except by trying to put them on paper. If you are one of these, never be content with your first draft; always revise it. Within the Service, authoritative advice has varied in its emphasis on the need for revision. In the Foreign Office a memorandum on draft-writing, after recommending simplicity, continued:

> It is a commonplace that this simplicity does not always come in a first draft even to the greatest stylists. Redrafting takes time, and I know that members of departments have little enough time to spend on it in these days. But it is up to them, for heads of departments and under-secretaries have still less time to spare. . . .

The Ministry of Health ended a similar memorandum:

> I do not expect our letters to be models of the best English prose, and I do not want the time taken in answering letters (which is already too long) to be increased still further by unnecessary labour in the preparing, and, still less, the polishing of drafts. . . . But it is clear that there are ways of saying what is meant in shorter, plainer and better English [than the examples given].

These pieces of advice are not irreconcilable. They relate to rather different types of communication. Both are no doubt wise. But I am sure that you should fear more the danger of putting out slipshod work by omitting to revise it than that of delaying public business by excessive polishing. Very few can write what they mean and affect their readers precisely as they wish without revising their first attempt. There is a happy mean between being content with the first thing that comes into your head and the craving for perfection that makes a Flaubert spend hours or even days on getting a single sentence to his satisfaction. The article you are paid to produce need not be polished but it must be workmanlike.

The official must use the written word for many different purposes —for Parliamentary Bills, Statutory Orders and other legal documents, for despatches to Her Majesty's representatives abroad, for reports of commissions and committees, for circulars to Local Authorities and similar bodies, for departmental instructions, for minute writing, for correspondence with other departments and with the public, and for explaining the law to the millions for whom it now creates complicated personal rights and obligations and whose daily lives it orders in countless ways. Whatever the purpose, the object of the writer will be the same—to make the reader take his meaning readily and precisely. But a choice has sometimes to be made between the simplicity that conveys some meaning readily and the elaboration necessary to convey a precise one. In the first of the categories mentioned—Parliamentary Bills, Statutory Orders and other legal documents—precision is so important that these form a class apart, with which this book is not concerned. But there is so much confused thinking on this subject, even among people who ought to know better, that it will be as well to begin with a digression explaining why it is outside my present scope.

II

A Digression on Legal English

Even where the Counsel in chambers is merely "advising on a case" or drawing up a conveyance of property, he is really thinking of what view the court and the judges will take of his advice or his draftsmanship if any dispute arises on them. . . . The supreme test in every case is: "Will this stand the scrutiny of the Court?"

STEPHENS. *Commentaries on the Laws of England*

THE peculiarities of legal English are often used as a stick to beat the official with. They are cited (to quote a typical comment) to show that "it would be a herculean task to teach the Civil Service to write its own language creditably". The style in which Acts of Parliament are written is contemptuously called "official jargon". That the style has peculiarities cannot be denied, but if it is jargon*—an arguable question—its species is the legal not the official. It is written by lawyers, not by civil servants (in the sense in which the critics use the term), and its peculiarities arise from causes exactly opposite to those of the peculiarities alleged against officials. Those of the one come from a desire to convey a precise meaning; those of the other—so it is said—come too often from a reluctance to convey any meaning at all. The only difference between the language of Acts of Parliament and that of private legal documents is that in the skilled and experienced hands of Parliamentary Counsel its inevitable peculiarities are less obtrusive and ungraceful than they are in the hands of the ordinary private practitioner. Such as they are, they are caused by the necessity of being unambiguous. That is by no means the same as being readily intelligible; on the contrary, the nearer you get to the one the further you are likely to get from the other.

The reason why certainty of meaning must be the paramount aim is clear enough. These documents impose obligations and confer rights, and neither the parties to them nor the draftsmen of them have the last word in deciding exactly what those rights and obligations are. That can only be settled in a Court of Law on the words

---

*The proper meaning of *jargon* is writing that employs technical words not commonly intelligible. *Catachresis*, for instance, is grammarians' jargon for using a word in a wrong sense. When grammarians call writing jargon merely because it is verbose, circumlocutory and flabby, they themselves commit the sin of catachresis that they denounce in others.

8

of the document. If anyone is to be held irrevocably to meaning what he says, he must be very careful to say what he means. And words are an imperfect instrument for expressing complicated concepts with certainty; only mathematics can be sure of doing that. As Dr. Glanville Williams has pointed out in this connexion, "words have a penumbra of uncertainty". He writes:

> The ordinary man is not usually troubled with these perplexities. It does not matter to the seaman whether an anchor is or is not called part of a vessel. A chemist does not need to answer the question, yes or no, does a rolled-gold watch come within the description gold. Biologists may find difficulty with their classification, but nothing turns on the question whether they classify a creature under one head or another: it is simply a question of verbal expediency. With the lawyer it is different. The lawyer, like the theologian, is faced with a number of texts that he regards as authoritative and that are supposed to settle any question that can conceivably arise. Each text was once drawn up by someone who presumably meant something by it; but once the document has left its author's hands it is the document that matters, not any unexpressed meaning that still remains in the author's mind. For the lawyer the words of the document are authoritative as words and there is no possibility of obtaining further information from the author, either because the author is dead or because of the rules of evidence precluding reference to him.*

It is accordingly the duty of a draftsman of these authoritative texts to try to imagine every possible combination of circumstances to which his words might apply and every conceivable misinterpretation that might be put on them, and to take precautions accordingly. He must avoid all graces, not be afraid of repetitions, or even of identifying them by *aforesaids*; he must limit by definition words with a penumbra dangerously large, and amplify with a string of near-synonyms words with a penumbra dangerously small; he must eschew all pronouns when their antecedents might possibly be open to dispute, and generally avoid every potential grammatical ambiguity. (An application for quashing a New Towns Order turned on the true antecedent of a *thereto*.) All the time he must keep his eye on the rules of legal interpretation and the case-law on the meaning of particular words, and choose his phraseology to fit them. (Previous judicial interpretations of the word *money* compelled the beneficiaries under a will to take a case to the House of Lords in order to establish that *money* meant what everyone knew the testatrix had intended it to mean.) No one can expect pretty writing from anyone thus burdened. A well-meant attempt was made by the Minister in charge of the Bill that became the Workmen's Compensation Act 1906 to make perfectly clear to ordinary

---

* "Language and the Law", *Law Quarterly Review*, April, 1945.

people what sort of accidents gave rise to a right to compensation; he insisted on using the simple words "arising out of and in the course of" the employment. Simplicity proved to have been bought at such cost in precision that those words must have caused more litigation than any other eight words on the Statute Book. Halsbury's *Laws of England* takes more than 38 pages to explain the phrase and cite the cases on it.

To illustrate the difference between ordinary phraseology that makes its meaning plain and legal phraseology that makes its meaning certain, let us take an example at random. I open the volume of Statutory Rules and Orders for 1945, and, turning over the pages until I find a short one, alight on the "Rags (Wiping Rags) (Maximum Charges) (Amendment) Order". In the summer of 1945, it appears, the President of the Board of Trade, moved perhaps by compassion for those who follow what must be a spiritually un-satisfying occupation, decided to increase the profit allowed for washing wiping rags. The Order effecting this (if we omit the common-form provisions about the Interpretation Act and the Short Title) runs as follows:

> The Rags (Wiping Rags) (Maximum Charges) Order 1943 (as amended) shall have effect as if in Article 1 thereof for the figure "8" where it occurs in the last line there were substituted the figure "11½".

This by itself conveys no meaning at all to anybody. Because the same is true of so many Orders, instructions have been given to all Departments that every Order submitted to Parliament must be accompanied by an explanatory memorandum. In this case the explanatory memorandum was as follows:

> This Order permits launderers of wiping rags to add 11½ per cent to the charges they were making during the week beginning the 31st August, 1942, for such work.

That is a statement immediately intelligible. Why could not the Order itself be equally lucid? Because, although the explanatory memorandum is probably enough to tell most people all that they want to know, it is not precise enough to give unmistakable guidance in doubtful cases or to support a prosecution for its breach. What is a "wiping rag", and what are "charges"? Both need definition, and both are elaborately defined in the original Order. Why then, it may be asked, did not the amending Order repeat these definitions, and so make all clear? Because the definitions are so complicated that re-enactment of the Order as amended would have been far from making the meaning of the Order immediately clear. Research would have been necessary to find out what was old and what was new. If the whole of the old Order had been reprinted with the substitution of 11½ for 8 not only would there have been a waste of paper, but everyone would have had to look through both old and new Orders with minute attention, only to discover in the end that the only change was in the figure. Moreover the two volumes of Statutory Rules and Orders for 1945 already contain no fewer than 3,000 pages. No one would ask for more. To complete the picture, here are the definitions of "charges" and "wiping rags" in the original Order:

(i) basic charge means in relation to the services to which this Order applies,

(*a*) the charge made for such services in the ordinary course of the business in the course of which those services were being performed during the week beginning 31st August, 1942, in accordance with the method of charge then in being in relation to that business for performing such services; or

(*b*) the charge made for such services in the ordinary course of a substantially similar business during the said week, in accordance with the method of charge then in being in relation to that business for performing such services;

Provided that in any case in which a person who performs such services proves that such services were being performed in the course of his own business during the said week, "basic charge" shall only have the meaning specified in sub-paragraph (*a*) of this paragraph.

"Rags" means any worn-out, disused, discarded or waste fabric or material made wholly or mainly from wool, cotton, silk, rayon or flax or from any mixture thereof.

"Wiping rags" means rags each one of which is not less than 144 square inches in size and has been trimmed and washed and is suitable for use as a wiping rag.

This may provoke the comment that the washing of wiping rags can hardly be worth such lavishness of words. But that is beside the point. The point is that the law, whatever it is about, must be certain; and if it is necessary for the law to concern itself with washing wiping rags, it must be no less certain here than anywhere else. If anyone thinks that he can draft more simply and no less certainly, I advise him to try his hand and then ask an expert whether he can find any loopholes. I have seen even eminent members of the Bar humbled by that test. Drafting is more a science than an art; it lies in the province of mathematics rather than of literature, and its practice needs long apprenticeship. It is prudently left to a specialised legal branch of the Service. The only concern of the ordinary official is to learn to understand it, to act as interpreter of it to ordinary people, and to be careful not to let his own style of writing be tainted by it, a subject to which we will return. These remarks are therefore a digression from my main subject; their purpose is to expose the confusion of thought of those who criticise officials because Acts of Parliament are not written in readily intelligible English. Even Eric Partridge slips into it when he quotes in his *Usage and Abusage*, under the heading *Officialese*, an article in a newspaper making game of this extract from the Shops (Sunday Trading Restriction) Act, 1936:

> . . . the following provisions of this Act shall extend only to shops, that is to say, those provisions of section six and section eight which relate to the approval by occupiers of shops of orders made under those sections, the provisions of paragraph (*e*) of subsection (1) of section seven and the provisions of paragraph (*a*) of section twelve.

If example were needed to prove that legal language cannot be elegant or luminous, this would serve well enough.* But that needs no proof; everyone knows it. To a reader with the Act before him (and he cannot expect to understand it unless he has) the meaning that this subsection conveys is precise: it says unambiguously that certain provisions of the Act apply to trading only in shops and that all the others apply to trading not only in shops, but also in any place that is not a shop. The trouble in this case arose not from any obscurity in the words quoted, but from the penumbra round the word *place* used in another section. The Court held that it was not as large as the draftsman had thought. He had naturally assumed that, when he had covered both sales in shops and sales in places that are not shops, he had left nothing outside. But he was wrong. He forgot the stop-me-and-buy-one man. The Court held that the ice-cream vendor's tricycle is neither a shop nor a place; and the bit of ground on which it happens to be standing is not a place either. His sales are therefore outside both categories, and he escapes the meshes of the Act. This curious instance of the waywardness of words shows how hard it is for the draftsman to foresee every possible path down which the judicial mind may be led by what he writes, and also provides another illustration of the truth that legal ambiguities are caused more often by over-simplicity of diction than by over-elaboration.

The official has therefore two good defences against a charge of failing to draft a law in literary English: one that he did not draft it, and the other that if it had been so drafted it would not have served its purpose.   .   .   .   .   .

After the publication of the first edition of *Plain Words* several correspondents, especially from America, took me to task for having

---

*If all the commas are left out, as they are in *Usage and Abusage*, it is made to look even harder to understand than it really is.

been too indulgent to legal draftsmen; they maintained that I exaggerated the difficulty of being precise without being obscure, and that there was much room for improvement in the drafting of statutory documents. I did not mean to imply that there was none; my concern was to show that legal draftsmen must not be judged by the same standards as officials. By way of redressing the balance a little I will borrow from a correspondent of the *Spectator* a remarkable example of the reaction a legal draftsman may provoke in his reader:

My attention has been called (I have just invented this serviceable phrase) to Statutory Rules and Orders 1943 No. 1216, issued by the Ministry of Supply. You can buy it from the Stationery Office for a penny. Its operative clause runs thus:

1. The Control of Tins Cans Kegs Drums and Packaging Pails (No. 5) Order, 1942(*a*), as varied by the Control of Tins Cans Kegs Drums and Packaging Pails (No. 6) Order, 1942(*b*), the Control of Tins Cans Kegs Drums and Packaging Pails (No. 7) Order, 1942(*c*), the Control of Tins Cans Kegs Drums and Packaging Pails (No. 8) Order, 1942(*d*), and the Control of Tins Cans Kegs Drums and Packaging Pails (No. 9) Order, 1942(*e*), is hereby further varied in the Third Schedule thereto (which is printed at p. 2 of the printed (No. 6) Order), in "Part II. Commodities other than Food", by substituting for the reference "2A" therein, the reference "2A(1)"; and by deleting therefrom the reference "2B".

This is excellent news, that will gladden the heart of every public-spirited citizen. Why the Ministry of Supply could not leave it at that is unimaginable. Jettisoning gratuitously the sound and time-honoured principle that a Government Department never explains, it adds—quite incredibly—an Explanatory Note, which reads:

The above Order enables tinplate to be used for tobacco and snuff tins other than cutter-lid tobacco tins.

What is to be said of this unwarrantable insult to the national intelligence? What kind of people do they think we are? Do they suppose we can't read plain English? (The *Spectator*, 17 Sept., 1943.)

III

The Elements

Essentially style resembles good manners. It comes of endeavouring to understand others, of thinking for them rather than yourself—of thinking, that is, with the heart as well as the head. . . . So (says Fénelon) . . . "your words will be fewer and more effectual, and while you make less ado, what you do will be more profitable".

QUILLER-COUCH. *The Art of Writing*

HAVING thus cleared the decks we can return to the various other purposes for which official writing has to be used. The relative importance of these, in quantity at any rate, has been changed by the immense volume of modern social legislation and the innumerable statutory controls necessitated by the war and its consequences. Official writing used to consist mostly of departmental minutes and instructions, inter-departmental correspondence, and despatches to Governors and Ambassadors. These things still have their places. But in volume they must have been left far behind by the vast output now necessary for explaining the law to the public. The man in the street is still supposed to know the law without being told, and ignorance is no excuse for breaking it. That was all very well in the days when he had little more concern with the law than an obligation to refrain from committing the crimes prohibited by the decalogue; he had then no need to have its niceties explained to him. Today his daily life is conditioned by an infinity of statutory rights and obligations. Even if the laws that define them were short, simple and intelligible, their number alone would prevent him from discovering by his own study what those rights and obligations were.

Consider for instance the small shopkeeper. Like everyone else, he must have a working knowledge of the legislation governing his and his employees' tax liability, and of those that determine his and their duties and rights in respect of the National Health and Insurance Services. But that for him is only the beginning. He must also know that, on pain of committing a criminal offence, he must not (subject to certain rather complicated exceptions) keep his shop open later than a certain hour on four days in the week, a different hour on the fifth, and yet a different one on the sixth, or open it at all on Sundays; that he must give his assistants a half-holiday every week; that, if an assistant is under 18, his hours of work are limited by statute and his right to a weekly half-holiday is slightly different; that if the assistant is a girl she must be given a seat and allowed to sit on it; that the ventilation, lighting and temperature of his shop, as well as its sanitary accommodation, must at all times be "suitable and sufficient", and that if he sells food he must take various precautions against its becoming contaminated. That is a lot to expect anyone to learn for himself from a study of the statutes at large. The same is true of almost every walk of life.

The official must be the interpreter. Now this is a task as delicate as it is difficult. An official interpreting the law is looked on with suspicion. It is for the legislature to make the laws, for the executive to administer them, and for the judiciary to interpret them. The official must avoid all appearance of encroaching on the province of the Courts. For this reason it used to be a rule in the Service that when laws were brought to the notice of those affected by them the actual words of the statute must be used; in no other way could the official be sure of escaping all imputation of putting his own interpretation on the law. Here then we have a dilemma. If the official is tied to the words of the law, and if, as we have seen, the words of the law must be obscure in order to be precise, how is the man in the street to be helped to understand it?

No doubt much can be done by selection and arrangement, even though the words used are those of the Act. But something more than that is needed to carry out the exhortation given by a President of the Board of Trade to his staff: "Let us get away entirely from the chilly formalities of the old-style correspondence which seemed to come from some granite monolith rather than from another human being". And so the old rule is yielding to the pressure of events. It never was quite so important as it was made out to be, if only because, in most of the subjects that call particularly for simple explanation, a protection from bureaucracy readier than recourse to the Courts is given to the citizen. In theory he was amply protected by the Courts as the sole authoritative interpreter of the law. But in practice the man of small means will suffer much rather than embark on legal proceedings which the State, for the sake of the principle involved in them, may think it necessary to take to the House of Lords. For this reason 150 years ago Pitt tempered the first Income Tax Act by providing that assessments were to be made not by officials but by local committees of taxpayers. This precedent was followed in the Old Age Pensions Act of 1908, the National Insurance and Unemployment Insurance Acts of 1912, and all modern social legislation. In all these things the ordinary citizen has a ready means of securing, without any expense, that the exact nature of his rights and duties are defined neither by an official nor by the Courts but by a body of his fellow citizens.

This has lessened the need of the official to adhere scrupulously to the words of an Act at a time when he finds it more and more difficult to be helpful otherwise than by departing from them. A new technique is being developed for those pamphlets and leaflets that are necessary to explain the law to the man in the street in such matters as P.A.Y.E. and National Insurance. Its guiding principles are to use the simplest language and avoid technical terms, to employ the second person freely, not to try to give all the details of the law relevant to the subject, but to be content with stating the essentials, to explain, if these are stated in the writer's words and not the words of the Act, that they are an approximation only, to tell the reader where he can find fuller information and further advice, and always to make sure that he knows what are his rights of appeal. This technique is being closely studied in the Departments concerned by experts who have nothing to learn from me.

But there is another part of this subject: the answering of letters from individual correspondents about their own cases. These answers cannot be written, like the pamphlets and leaflets, by people who are experts both in the subject matter and in English composition, and here I shall have some advice to give. They need in some respects a special technique, but the principles of it are the same as those of all good writing, whatever its purpose. We have here in its most elementary form—though not on that account its least difficult —the problem of writing what one means and affecting one's reader precisely as one wishes. If therefore we begin our study of the problems of official English by examining the technique of this part of it, that will serve as a good introduction to the rest of the book, for it will bring out most of the points that we shall have to study more closely later. It is in this field of an official's duties more than in any other that good English can be defined simply as English which is readily understood by the reader. To be clear is to be efficient; to be obscure is to be inefficient. Your style of letter-writing is to be judged not by literary conventions or grammatical niceties but by whether it carries out efficiently the job you are paid to do.

But "efficiency" must be broadly interpreted. It connotes a proper attitude of mind towards your correspondent. He may not care about being addressed in literary English, but he will care very much about being treated with sympathy and understanding. It is not easy nowadays to remember anything so contrary to all appearances as that officials are the servants of the public; and the official must try not to foster the illusion that it is the other way round. So your style must not only be simple but also friendly, sympathetic and natural, appropriate to one who is a servant, not a master.

Let us now try to translate these generalities into some practical rules.

(1) Be sure that you know what your correspondent is asking before you begin to answer him. Study his letter carefully. If he is obscure, spare no trouble in trying to get at his meaning. If you conclude that he means something different from what he says (as he well may) address yourself to his meaning not to his words, and do not be clever at his expense. Get into his skin, and adapt the atmosphere of your letter to suit that of his. If he is troubled, be sympathetic. If he is rude, be specially courteous. If he is muddle-headed, be specially lucid. If he is pig-headed, be patient. If he is helpful, be appreciative. If he convicts you of a mistake, acknowledge it freely and even with gratitude. But never let a flavour of the patronising creep in as it did into this letter received by a passenger who had lost his ticket:

> In the circumstances you have now explained, and the favourable enquiries made by me, I agree as a special case and without prejudice not to press for payment of the demand sent you . . . and you may consider the matter closed.
> I would however suggest that in future you should take greater care of your railway tickets to obviate any similar occurrence.

Follow the admirable advice given in this instruction by the Board of Inland Revenue to their staff:

> There is one golden rule to bear in mind always: that we should try to put ourselves in the position of our correspondent, to imagine his feelings as he writes his letters, and to gauge his reaction as he receives ours. If we put ourselves in the other man's shoes we shall speedily detect how unconvincing our letters can seem, or how much we may be taking for granted.

(2) Begin by answering his question. Do not start by telling him the relevant law and practice, and gradually lead up to a statement of its application to his case. By doing this you keep him on tenter-hooks and perhaps so befuddle him that by the time he gets to the end he is incapable of grasping what the answer is. Give him his answer briefly and clearly at the outset, and only then, if explanation is needed, begin your explanation. Thus he will know the worst, or the best, at once, and can skip the explanation if he likes.

(3) So far as possible, confine yourself to the facts of the case you are writing about. Avoid any general statement about the law. If you make one, you are likely to find yourself in this dilemma: that if you want to be strictly accurate you will have to use technical

terms and legal diction that your correspondent will not understand, and if you want to be simple and intelligible you will have to qualify your statement so copiously with hedging phrases like *normally*, *ordinarily*, *in most cases* and *with some exceptions*, that your correspondent will think you are keeping something up your sleeve, and not being frank with him.

(4) Avoid a formal framework, if you can. This is a difficult subject and those who supervise correspondence of this kind are still groping for a satisfactory standard practice. How are we to "get away from the chilly formalities of the old style"?

Over the years when the "old style" became set, official correspondence consisted mostly of interdepartmental communications. Custom required, and still requires, these to be in form letters from the Permanent Head of one Department to his opposite number in another. They begin invariably with a mention of the subject about to be dealt with and of the letter, if any, that is being answered. The opening words of the letter must be "I am directed by (say) the Secretary of State for Foreign Affairs", and throughout the letter turns of phrase must be used (e.g. "I am to ask you to submit to the Lords Commissioners of the Treasury") which serve as reminders that, for present purposes, both he who writes and he who is written to are in themselves things of naught; they merely form a conduit along which the thoughts of their political chiefs may be exchanged. It is no doubt right that officials and the public should be reminded constantly that ministerial responsibility is the keystone of our democracy. But, however appropriate this style may be for formal letters on subjects about which the Minister may possibly have been personally consulted, it will not do for the sort of letter we are now concerned with. It is too flagrantly unreal; everyone knows that these letters are sent on the authority of comparatively junior officials, exercising a delegated responsibility within prescribed limits. Besides, it is quite impossible to weave into a framework of this sort the spirit of friendliness we **have** seen to be desirable.

There are two difficulties. One is how to start. The other is to whom to attribute the sentiments, opinions and decisions that the letter contains. As to the first, everyone's inclination is to follow tradition at least to the point of beginning all replies "In reply to (or 'with reference to') your letter of . . . ". That brings us to our first difficulty. If we are forbidden to follow our natural inclination to continue "I am directed", as we have seen we must be, how are we to go on?

In detail the possibilities are infinite, but the main forms are few. "I have (or 'I am') to inform you" used to be—perhaps still is—the most common. But it is unsatisfactory, not to say silly, with its mysterious suggestion of some compulsion working undisclosed in the background. "I would inform you" is another popular variant. It is passable, but not to be commended, for its archaic use of *would* in the sense of "I should like to" makes it stiff, as though one were to say "I would have you know". "I should inform you", in the sense of "it is my duty to inform you" is also tolerable and sometimes useful. But it will not do always; it is less suitable for beginning than for picking up something at the end ("I should add", "I should explain however"). "I beg to inform you" will not do. (*See* p. 25). "I regret to inform you" and "I am glad to inform you" will do nicely when there is anything to be glad or sorry about but that is not always. "In reply to your letter . . . I wish to inform you" (which I have seen) is crushingly stiff; this also is almost like saying "I would have you know". The passive ("you are informed",) has an aloofness that ought to rule it out. There remains the device of plunging straight into saying what you have to say without any introductory words. But this will not do as a continuation of "In reply to your letter". What is in reply to the letter is not the information but the giving of it. It is nonsense to say "In reply to your letter of . . . the Income Tax Law on personal allowances has been changed".

Must we then conclude that in this type of letter we ought to abandon the stock opening "In reply to your letter" unless we can continue naturally with "I am glad to tell you", or "I am sorry to have to tell you", or some such phrase? Perhaps. Nothing would be lost. There are plenty of other ways of beginning that will not lead us into the same difficulties. The trouble about "In reply to your letter" is that it forms the beginning of a sentence which we must finish somehow. If we turn it into a complete sentence we shake off those shackles.

This must be done with discretion; some attempts are unfortunate. For instance:

> With reference to your claim. I have to advise you that before same is dealt with. . . .

There is no need to start with an ejaculatory and verbless clause. All that was needed was to begin: "Before I can deal with your claim". Or again:

> Your letter is acknowledged, and the following would appear to be the position.
> Receipt of your letter is acknowledged. It is pointed out. . . .

Here again is the inhuman third person. A better way of saying what these two were trying to say is "Thank you for your letter. The position is (or the facts are) as follows . . . ".

I believe that a common opening formula during the war was:

> Your letter of the . . . about. . . . We really cannot see our way. . . .

I am told that this is fortunately dying out, perhaps because it is becoming less difficult to see our way.

Another not very happy effort is:

> I refer to recent correspondence and to the form which you have completed. . . .

There is a faint air of bombast about this: it vaguely recalls Pistol's way of talking ("I speak of Africa and golden joys"). Probably "Thank you for the completed form" would have been an adequate opening.

There are however many possible ways of turning "with reference to your letter" into a complete sentence without getting ourselves into trouble.

> I have received your letter of . . .
> Thank you for your letter of . . .
> I am writing to you in reply to your letter of . . .
> You wrote to me on such-and-such a subject
> I have looked into the question of . . . about which you wrote to me

and so on. All enable you to say what you have to say as a direct statement without any preliminary words like "I have to say" or "I would say".

There remains the second question. To whom are you to attribute the opinions and decisions which, having got over the first hurdle, you then proceed to deliver? In a large and increasing class of letters the answer is simple. These are the letters sent from those provincial offices of a Ministry that are in the charge of an official who has a recognised status and title and who signs the letters himself. Such are Inspectors of Taxes, Collectors of Customs, the Regional Controllers of various Departments, Telephone Managers and others. Everyone knows that these officers exercise a delegated authority; those who draft the letters for them to sign can use the first person, and all is plain sailing.

But a great many letters, sent from other branches of Government Departments, are signed not by someone of known status and authority, but by some unknown person in the hierarchy, who may or may not have consulted higher authority before signing; that is a matter of domestic organisation within the Department and is nobody else's business. To whom are the opinions and decisions conveyed in these letters to be attributed? It cannot be the Minister himself; we have ruled that out. There are four other possibilities. One is that the letter should be written in the first person, and that the official who signs it should boldly accept responsibility. The second is that responsibility should be spread by the use of the first person plural. The third is that it should be further diluted by attributing the decisions and opinions to "the Department". The fourth is that responsibility should be assigned to a quarter mystically remote by the use throughout of the impersonal passive. To illustrate what I mean, let us take what must to-day be a common type of letter, one turning down an application:

> I have considered your application and do not think you have made out a case.
> We have considered your application and do not think you have made out a case.
> The Department has (or have) considered your application and does (or do) not think you have made out a case.
> Your application has been considered and it is not thought that you have made out a case.

I cannot pretend to be an authoritative guide on the comparative merits of these; no doubt every Department makes it own rules. But there are three things that seem to me important.

First, in letters written in the first person be careful to avoid giving the impression that an all-powerful individual is signifying his pleasure. If the letter grants what is asked for, do not say that you are making a "concession". If it refuses a request never say, as in the example given, *I* do not think you have made out a case. Imply that your duty is not yourself to be your correspondent's judge, but merely to decide how the case before you fits into the instructions under which you work.

Secondly, it is a mistake to mix these methods in one letter unless there is good reason for it. If you choose an impersonal method, such as "the Department", you may of course need to introduce the first person for personal purposes such as "I am glad" or "I am sorry" or "I should like you to call here", "I am glad to say that the Department has . . .". But do not mix the methods merely for variety, saying *I* in the first paragraph, *we* in the second, *the Department* in the third and *it is* in the fourth. Choose one and stick to it.

Thirdly, do not use the impersonal passive, with its formal unsympathetic phrases such as "it is felt", "it is regretted", "it is appreciated". Your correspondent wants to feel that he is dealing with human beings, not with robots. How feeble is the sentence, "It is thought you will now have received the form of agreement" compared with "I expect you will have received the form of agreement by now".

(5) Be careful to say nothing that might give your correspondent the impression, however mistakenly, that you think it right that he should be put to trouble in order to save you from it. Do not use paper stamped "Date as postmark". This will be read by many recipients as meaning: "I am much too important and busy a person to remember what the date is or to put it down if I did; so if you want to know you must pick the envelope out of the waste-paper basket, if you can find it, and read the date on the postmark, if you can decipher it. It is better that you should do this than that I should be delayed in my work even for a moment". Do not ask him to give you over again information he has already given you unless there is some good reason for doing so, and, if there is, explain the reason. Otherwise he will infer that you think it proper that he should have to do what is perhaps quite a lot of work to save you the trouble of turning up a back file.*

(6) Use no more words than are necessary to do the job. Superfluous words waste your time and official paper, tire your reader and obscure your meaning. There is no need, for instance, to begin each paragraph with phrases like *I am further to point out, I would also add, you will moreover observe.* Go straight to what you have to say, without precautionary words, and then say it in as few words as are needed to make your meaning clear.

(7) Keep your sentences short. This will help both you to think clearly and your correspondent to take your meaning. If you find you have slipped into long ones, split them up.

> If he was not insured on reaching the age of 65 he does not become insured by reason of any insurable employment which he takes up later, and the special contributions which are payable under the Act by his employer only, in respect of such employment, do not give him any title to health insurance benefits or pension, and moreover a man is not at liberty to pay any contributions on his own account as a voluntary contributor for any period after his 65th birthday.

This sentence is a long one. It contains three statements of fact

---

*It does not seem to me to be reasonable that anyone who asks for something to which he is legally entitled should be required to do more than to provide once, and once only, the information necessary to establish his right. To demand that forms shall be furnished in triplicate, or that an applicant, having written his name, address and identity number in Section A, should write them again in Section B, is to force a member of the public to act as unpaid copyist for someone whom he pays to do that sort of thing for him. But that reflection takes me outside the scope of this book.

linked by the conjunction *and*. Because this is its form, the reader is never quite sure until he has read further whether any of these statements has been completed, and he probably has not taken any of them in when he has finished. He then re-reads the sentence and picks up the statements one by one. If they had been separated by fullstops (after *later* and *pension*) and the *ands* omitted, he would have grasped each at first reading. The fullstops would have seemed to say to him: "Have you got that? Very well; now I'll tell you something else".

(8) Be compact; do not put a strain on your reader's memory by widely separating parts of a sentence that are closely related to one another. Why, for instance, is this sentence difficult to grasp on first reading?

> A deduction of tax may be claimed in respect of any person whom the individual maintains at his own expense, and who is (i) a relative of his, or of his wife, and incapacitated by old age or infirmity from maintaining himself or herself, or (ii) his or his wife's widowed mother, whether incapacitated or not, or (iii) his daughter who is resident with him and upon whose services he is compelled to depend by reason of old age or infirmity.

The structure of the sentence is too diffuse; the reader has to keep in mind the opening words all the way through. It ends by telling him that a deduction of tax may be claimed "in respect of any person whom the individual maintains at his own expense and who is his daughter", but "his daughter" is separated from "who is" by no fewer than 32 words. This sentence, taken from a leaflet of Income Tax instructions, was later rewritten, and now runs as follows:

> If you maintain a relative of yourself or your wife who is unable to work because of old age or infirmity, you can claim an allowance of. . . . You can claim this allowance if you maintain your widowed mother, or your wife's widowed mother, whether she is unable to work or not. If you maintain a daughter who lives with you because you or your wife are old or infirm, you can claim an allowance of. . . .

Why is the new version so much easier to grasp than the old? Partly it is because a sentence of 81 words has been split into three, each making a statement complete in itself. But it is also because a device has been employed that is a most useful one when an official writer has to say, as he so often has, that such-and-such a class of people who have such-and-such attributes, and perhaps such-and-such other attributes, have such-and-such rights or obligations. The device is to use conditional clauses in the second person instead of relative clauses in the third—to say: *if* you belong to such-and-such a class of people, and *if* you have such-and-such attributes, you have such-and-such a right or obligation. The advantage of this is that it avoids the wide separation of the main verb from the main subject; the subject *you* comes immediately next to the verb it governs, and in this way you announce unmistakably to your reader: "I have finished describing the class of people about whom I have something to tell you, and I shall now say what I have to tell you about them".

(9) Do not say more than is necessary. The feeling that prompts you to tell your correspondent everything when explaining is commendable, but you will often help him more by resisting it, and confining yourself to the facts that will enable him to understand what has happened.

> I regret however that the Survey Officer who is responsible for the preliminary investigation as to the technical possibility of installing a telephone at the address quoted by any applicant has reported that owing to a shortage of a spare pair of wires to the underground cable (a pair of wires leading from the point near your house right back to the local exchange and thus a pair of wires essential for the provision of telephone service for you) is lacking and that therefore it is a technical impossibility to install a telephone for you at. . . .

This explanation is obscure partly because the sentence is too long, partly because the long parenthesis has thrown the grammar out of gear, and partly because the writer, with the best intentions, says far more than is necessary even for a thoroughly polite and convincing explanation. It might have run thus:

> I am sorry to have to tell you that we have found that there is no spare pair of wires on the cable that would have to be used to connect your house with the exchange. I fear therefore that it is impossible to install a telephone for you.

(10) Explain technical terms in simple words. You will soon become so familiar with the technical terms of the law you are administering that you will feel that you have known them all your life, and may forget that to others they are unintelligible. Of this fault I can find no English example to equal the American one already quoted:

> The non-compensable evaluation heretofore assigned to you for your service-connected disability is confirmed and continued.

This means, I understand, that the veteran to whom it is addressed has been judged to be still not entitled to a disability pension.

I am indebted for the following example to a friend in the Board of Inland Revenue, who also supplies the comment.

Example:
> I have pleasure in enclosing a cheque for £ . . . , a supplementary repayment for. . . . This is accounted for by the fact that in calculating

the untaxed interest assessable the interest on the loan from Mr. X was treated as untaxed, whereas it should have been regarded as received in full out of taxed sources—any liability thereon being fully satisfied. The treatment of this loan interest from the date of the first payment has been correct—i.e. tax charged at the full standard rate on Mr. X and treated in your hands as a liability fully satisfied before receipt.

Comment :

"There is matter for an essay in this letter! The occasion was the issue of an unexpected cheque, and the sender thought that some kind of an explanation was needed to reassure the recipient. It is a very difficult matter to explain, very technical, and an honest attempt has been made. The major fault is one of over-explanation, in technical language.

"What the occasion called for was a simple explanation of the fact, and not a complete justification of the whole process. If the writer had said:

> In calculating the amount of repayment due to you, the interest you received on the money you lent to Mr. X was included in those items of your income which had not already been taxed. This was wrong. Mr. X has paid the tax on this interest, and you are not liable to pay tax on it again,

then the recipient would have been satisfied. The writer could add: 'We did not make this mistake in earlier years, and you have been repaid all the tax due to you for those years', instead of his last sentence. 'Treated in your hands as a liability' is a queer way of describing an asset, and the loan was, of course, *to* Mr. X, not from him. 'Interest-on-the-loan' is treated confusingly as a composite noun."

(11) Do not use what have been called the "dry meaningless formulae" of commercialese. Against some of these a warning is not needed: officials do not write *your esteemed favour to hand* or address their correspondents as *your good self*. But some of these formulae occasionally appear. *Same* is used as a pronoun (on which *see* p. 148), *enclosed please find* is preferred to *I enclose*, and foolish *begs* are common. The use of *beg* in this way is presumably to be accounted for by a false analogy with the reasonable use of *I beg* as a polite introduction to a contradiction, "I beg to differ", that is "I beg your leave to differ". There is no reason why one should apologise, however faintly, for acknowledging a letter or remaining an obedient servant. *Per* should not be permitted to get too free with the English language. Such convenient abbreviations as *m.p.h.* and *r.p.m.* are no doubt with us for good. But generally it is well to confine *per* to its own language

—e.g. *per cent, per capita, per stirpes, per contra,* and not to prefer *per day* to *a day,* or *per passenger train* to *by passenger train,* or *as per my letter* to *as I said in my letter.*

Even for phrases in which *per* is linked to a Latin word, there are often English equivalents which serve at least as well, if not better. A letter can equally well be signed *AB for CD* as *CD per pro AB.* £100 *a year* is more natural than £100 *per annum. Per se* does not ordinarily mean anything more than *by itself* or *in itself.*

Another Latin word better left alone is *re.* This is the ablative case of the Latin word *res.* It means *in the matter of.* It is used by lawyers for the title of lawsuits, such as "*In re* John Doe deceased". It has passed into commercialese as an equivalent of the English preposition *about.* It has no business there, or in officialese. It is not needed either in a heading ("re your application for a permit"), which can stand without its support, or in the body of a letter, where an honest *about* will serve your purpose better. Avoid that ugly and unnecessary symbol *and/or* when writing letters; it is fit only for forms and lists and specifications and things of that sort. It can always be dispensed with. Instead of writing (say) "soldiers and/or sailors" we can write "soldiers or sailors or both". Finally, the widespread dislike now felt for commercialese seems to extend to *inst, ult* and *prox,* and there is no obvious reason for preferring these Latin abbreviations to the name of the month, which is also capable of abbreviation and has the advantage over them of conveying an immediate and certain meaning.

A correspondent has sent me the following example of the baleful influence of commercialese:

> Payment of the above account, which is now overdue at the date hereof, appears to have been overlooked, and I shall be glad to have your remittance by return of post, and oblige.
>   Yours faithfully,

The superfluous *at the date hereof* must have been prompted by a feeling that *now* by itself was not formal enough and needed dressing up. The word *oblige* is grammatically in mid-air. It has no subject, and is firmly cut off by a fullstop from what might have been supposed to be its object, the writer's signature.

The fault of commercialese is that its mechanical use has a bad effect on both writer and reader—the writer because it deadens his appreciation of the meaning of words, the reader because he feels that the writer's approach to him lacks sincerity.

(12) Use words with precise meanings rather than vague ones. Since, as we have seen, you will not be doing your job properly unless you make your meaning readily understood, this is an elementary

duty. Yet habitual disregard of it is the commonest cause of the abuse and raillery directed against what is called officialese. Every entrant into the service comes equipped with a vocabulary of common words of precise meaning adequate for all ordinary purposes. But when he begins to write as an official he has a queer trick of forgetting them and relying mainly on a smaller vocabulary of less common words with a less precise meaning. It is a curious fact that in the official's armoury of words the weapons readiest to hand are weapons not of precision but of rough and ready aim; often, indeed, they are of a sort that were constructed as weapons of precision but have been bored out by him into blunderbusses.* They have been put in the front rack of the armoury; he reaches out for a word and uses one of these without troubling to search in the racks behind for one that is more likely to hit the target in the middle. For instance, the blunderbuss *integrate* is now kept in front of *join, combine, amalgamate, coordinate* and other words, and the hand stretching out for one of these gets no farther. *Develop* blocks the way to *happen, occur, take place* and *come*. *Alternative* (a converted weapon of precision) stands before many simple words such as *different, other, new, fresh, revised. Rehabilitate* and *recondition* are in front of others, such as *heal, mend, cure, repair, renovate* and *restore. Involve* throws a whole section of the armoury into disuse, though not so big a one as that threatened by *overall*; and rack upon rack of simple prepositions are left untouched because before them are kept the blunderbusses of vague phrases such as *in relation to, in regard to, in connexion with* and *in the case of*.

It may be said that it is generally easy enough to guess what is meant. But you have no business to leave your reader guessing at your meaning, even though the guess may be easy. That is not doing your job properly. If you make a habit of not troubling to choose the right weapon of precision you may be sure that sooner or later you will set your reader a problem that is past guessing.

(13) If two words convey your meaning equally well, choose the common one rather than the less common. Here again official tendency is in the opposite direction, and you must be on your guard. Do not prefer *regarding, respecting* or *concerning* to *about*, or say *advert* for *refer*, or *state, inform* or *acquaint* when you might use the word *say* or *tell. Inform* is a useful word, but it seems to attract adverbs as prim as itself, sometimes almost menacing. In *kindly inform me* the politeness rings hollow; all it does is to put a frigid and magisterial tone into your request. *Perhaps you will inform me* means

---

*The O.E.D. defines this word as "A short gun with a large bore, firing many balls or slugs, and capable of doing execution within a limited range without exact aim".

C

generally that you have *got* to inform me, and no "perhaps" about it, and I suspect the consequences may be serious for you. *Furthermore* is a prosy word used too often. It may be difficult to avoid it in cumulative argument (moreover . . . in addition . . . too . . . also . . . again . . . furthermore) but prefer one of the simpler words if they have not all been used up. Do not say *hereto, herein, hereof, herewith, hereunder,* or similar compounds with *there* unless, like *therefore,* they have become part of everyday language. Most of them put a flavour of legalism into any document in which they are used. Use a preposition and pronoun instead. For instance:

> With reference to the second paragraph thereof. (With reference to its second paragraph.)
> I have received your letter and thank you for the information contained therein. (contained in it.)
> I am to ask you to explain the circumstances in which the gift was made and to forward any correspondence relative thereto. (. . . any correspondence about it.)

To take a few more examples of unnecessary choice of stilted expressions, do not say *predecease* for *die before, ablution facilities* for *wash basins, it is apprehended that* for *I suppose, capable of locomotion* for *able to walk, will you be good enough to advise me* for *please tell me, I have endeavoured to obtain the required information* for *I have tried to find out what you wanted to know, it will be observed from a perusal of* for *you will see by reading.* The reason why it is wrong for you to use these starchy words is not that they are bad English; most of them are perfectly good English in their proper places. The reason is twofold. First, some of the more unusual of them may actually be outside your correspondent's vocabulary and convey no meaning at all to him. Secondly, their use runs counter to your duty to show that officials are human. These words give the reader the impression that officials are not made of common clay but are, in their own estimation at least, beings superior and aloof. They create the wrong atmosphere; the frost once formed by a phrase or two of this sort is not easily melted. If you turn back to the example given under Rule (8) you will see how careful the writer of the revised version has been about this. The word *individual* (a technical term of income tax law to distinguish between a personal taxpayer and a corporate one) was unnecessary and has disappeared. *Deduction of tax* is translated into *allowance, incapacitated* into *unable to work, is resident with* into *lives with,* and *by reason of old age or infirmity* into *because you are old or infirm.*

Here is an example of words deliberately and effectively chosen for their simplicity:

If a worker's clothing is destroyed beyond all hope of repair by an accident on his job his employer can apply to us for the coupons needed to replace it. This does not mean of course that anyone can get coupons if his boots fall to pieces through ordinary wear or if he just gets a tear in his trousers.

"If he just gets a tear in his trousers" not only conveys a clearer meaning than (say) "If his garments suffer comparatively minor damage and are capable of effective reconditioning". It also creates a different atmosphere. The reader feels that the writer is a human being and not a mere cog in the bureaucratic machine—almost that he might be quite a good chap.

In the same way these opening words of a booklet issued by the Ministry of Agriculture for farmers are well calculated to make the reader feel that here is someone who knows what he is talking about and can explain it to others:

> WHY KEEP BOOKS? There are several very good reasons why the farmer, busy man as he is, should keep proper records of his business. It is the only way in which he can find out how much profit he has made, and how one year's profit compares with another. It helps him to manage his farm efficiently, and shows him how the various operations compare in outlay and in receipts.

I have called this chapter "The Elements" because in it I have suggested certain elementary rules—"be short, be simple, be human" —for officials to follow in the duties that I have described as "explaining the law to the millions". The rules apply no less to official writing of other kinds, and they will be elaborated in Chapters V to VIII, in which much of what has been said in this chapter will be expanded. I can claim no novelty for my advice. Similar precepts were laid down for the Egyptian Civil Service some thousands of years ago:

> Be courteous and tactful as well as honest and diligent.
> All your doings are publicly known, and must therefore
> Be beyond complaint or criticism. Be absolutely impartial.
> Always give a reason for refusing a plea; complainants
> Like a kindly hearing even more than a successful
> Plea. Preserve dignity but avoid inspiring fear.
> Be an artist in words, that you may be strong, for
> The tongue is a sword. . . . .

If we may judge from the following letter, those brought up in this tradition succeeded in avoiding verbiage. The letter is from a Minister of Finance to a senior civil servant:

> Apollonius to Zeno, greeting. You did right to send the chickpeas to Memphis. Farewell.

IV

Correctness

My Lord, I do here, in the name of all the learned and polite persons of the nation, complain to Your Lordship as First Minister, that our Language is extremely imperfect; that its daily improvements are by no means in proportion to its daily corruptions; that the pretenders to polish and refine it have chiefly multiplied abuses and absurdities; and that in many instances it offends against every part of grammar.

SWIFT

WE will now turn to the implications of the remark I made on p. 3. "Lapses from what for the time being is regarded as correct irritate the educated reader, and distract his attention; and so make him less likely to be 'affected precisely as you wish'." We shall have to add a fourth rule to the three with which we finished the last chapter—be correct. It applies to both vocabulary and grammar; this chapter is concerned with vocabulary only, and grammar will be the subject of Chapter IX.

Correctness of vocabulary seems once to have been enforced more sternly on officials than it is now. More than two centuries ago the Secretary to the Commissioners of Excise wrote this letter to the Supervisor of Pontefract.

> The Commissioners on perusal of your Diary observe that you make use of many affected phrases and incongruous words, such as "illegal procedure", "harmony", etc., all of which you use in a sense that the words do not bear. I am ordered to acquaint you that if you hereafter continue that affected and schoolboy way of writing, and to murder the language in such a manner, you will be discharged for a fool.*

To us the punishment seems disproportionate to the offence, though the same penalty today might prove gratifying to those who think we have too many officials. But we can have nothing but admiration for the sentiment of the letter or for the vigorous directness of its phrasing. It serves moreover to illustrate a difficulty presented by this precept. What is correctness, and who is to be the judge of it? It cannot be the same now as it was then. A Collector of Customs and Excise today might certainly use the expression "illegal procedure" without being called in question; he might even

---

*Quoted in *Humour in the Civil Service*, by John Aye. Universal Publications, 1928.

refer to the harmony of his relations with the Trade without running much risk. On the other hand it would not do for him to say, as the Supervisor of Pontefract might have said, that the Local Bench were an indifferent body, meaning that they performed their duties with impartiality, or that he prevented the arrival of his staff at his office, meaning that he always got there first.

English is not static—neither in vocabulary nor in grammar, nor yet in that elusive quality called style. The fashion in prose alternates between the ornate and the plain, the periodic and the colloquial. Grammar and punctuation defy all the efforts of grammarians to force them into the mould of a permanent code of rules. Old words drop out or change their meanings; new words are admitted. What was stigmatised by the purists of one generation as a corruption of the language may a few generations later be accepted as an enrichment, and what was then common currency may have become a pompous archaism or acquired a new significance.

Eminent men with a care for the language, from Dean Swift* to Lord Wavell,† have from time to time proposed that an Authority should be set up to preserve what is good and resist what is bad. "They will find", said Swift, "many words that deserve to be utterly thrown out of the language, many more to be corrected, and perhaps not a few long since antiquated, which ought to be restored on account of their energy and sound." "They should issue", said Lord Wavell, "a monthly journal of words that required protection and a pillory of misused words, and so on." Swift's plea, which was made in the form of a letter to the Lord Treasurer, came to nothing. This, Lord Chesterfield drily observed, was not surprising, "precision and perspicuity not being in general the favourite objects of Ministers". Dr. Johnson thought the task hopeless:

> Academies have been instituted to guard the avenues of the languages, to retain fugitives and to repulse invaders; but their vigilance and activity have been vain; sounds are too volatile and subtile for legal restraints, to enchain syllables and to lash the wind are equally the undertakings of pride, unwilling to measure its desires by its strength.

In our own day we have seen a Society for Pure English, with leaders as eminent as Henry Bradley, Robert Bridges and Logan Pearsall Smith, inviting the support of all those who "would preserve all the richness of differentiation in our vocabulary, its nice grammatical usages and its traditional idioms, but would oppose whatever is slipshod and careless and all blurring of hard-won distinctions, and

---

Proposal for correcting, improving and ascertaining the English Tongue.
†Letter from Lord Wavell to Mr. Ivor Brown quoted in *Ivor Brown's Book of Words.*

oppose no less the tyranny of schoolmasters and grammarians, both in their pedantic conservatism and in their enforcing of new-fangled rules". But it is now defunct.

Dr. Johnson was right, as usual. One has only to look at the words proposed by Swift for inclusion in his *Index Expurgatorius* to realise how difficult, delicate and disappointing it is to resist new words and new meanings. He condemns, for instance, *sham, banter, mob, bully* and *bamboozle*. A generation later Dr. Johnson called *clever* a "low word" and *fun* and *stingy* "low cant". Should we not have been poorer if Swift and Johnson had had their way with these? There is no saying how things will go. The fight for admission to the language is quickly won by some assailants and long resistance is maintained against others. The word that excited Swift to greatest fury was *mob*, a contraction of *mobile vulgus*. Its victory was rapid and complete. So was that of *banter* and *bamboozle*, which he found hardly less offensive. And if *rep* for *reputation* proved ephemeral, and *phiz* for *physiognomy* never emerged from slang status, and is now dead, that is not because Swift denounced them, but because public opinion disliked them or got tired of them. *Nice* in the sense in which it is ordinarily used today in conversation has not yet established itself in literary English, though we know from the rather priggish lecture that Henry Tilney gave to Catherine Morland about it in *Northanger Abbey* that it was trying to get over the barrier nearly a hundred and fifty years ago. *Reliable* was long opposed on the curious ground that it was an impossible construction; an adjective formed from *rely* could only be *reli-on-able*. I remember noticing as a junior in the India Office many years ago that John Morley as Secretary of State struck it out of a draft dispatch and wrote in *trustworthy*. That must have been almost the last shot fired at it. The objection to it was a survival of the curious theory, widely held in pre-Fowler days, and not yet wholly exorcised, that no sentence could be "good grammar", and no word a respectable word, if its construction violated logic or reason. (I shall have more to say about this reign of pedantry when we consider grammar in Chapter IX). It is not the habit of the English to refrain from doing anything merely because it is illogical; in any case it was less illogical to accept *reliable* than to strain at it after swallowing *available* and *objectionable*.

Some words gatecrash irresistibly because their sound is so appropriate to the meaning they are trying to acquire. *Spiv* is a recent example. *Blurb*, Professor Weekley tells us, was described by Robert Bridges as "an admirable word, quite indispensable". *Haver* does not mean *vacillate* (it means *blather*), but almost everyone south of the Border thinks it does: there is no withstanding its suggestion of simultaneous hovering and wavering. The dictionaries do not yet recognise this, but doubtless they will soon bow to the inevitable; for, as Sir Alan Herbert has reminded us, "modern dictionaries are pusillanimous works, preferring feebly to record what has been done than to say what ought to be done".* Vidkun Quisling won instant admission to the company of the immortals who, like the Earl of Sandwich, Mr. Joseph Aloysius Hansom, General Shrapnel and Captain Boycott, have given their names to enrich the language. There has been stout resistance against certain words that attacked the barrier in the nineteenth century with powerful encouragement from Dickens—*mutual, individual, phenomenal* and *aggravate. Mutual* in the sense of *common*, pertaining to both parties, as in *Our Mutual Friend*, goes back to the sixteenth century, according to the O.E.D., but is "now regarded as incorrect". Perhaps the reason why it is so difficult to restrain the word to its "correct" meaning is the ambiguity of *common*. "Our common friend" might be taken as a reflection on the friend's manners or birth. The use of *individual* that is unquestionably correct is to distinguish a single person from a collective body, as it is used in the Income Tax Acts to distinguish between a personal taxpayer and a corporate one. But its use as a facetious term of disparagement (like the French *individu*) used to be common and still lingers. That was how Mr. Jorrocks understood it when Mr. Martin Moonface described him as an "unfortunate individual", and provoked the retort "You are another indiwidual". *Phenomenal* to the purists means nothing more than "perceptible to the sense", and a *phenomenon* is an occurrence so perceptible; they would say that Mr. Vincent Crummles ought to have called his daughter not "the infant phenomenon" but "the juvenile prodigy". Over *aggravate* the long-drawn-out struggle still continues between those who, like Dickens, use it in the sense of *annoy* and those who would confine it to its original sense of *make worse*. About all these words the issue is still in the balance, but as *aggravating* for *annoying* and *phenomenal* for *prodigious* have unimpeachable contemporary authority—the one of Professor Trevelyan and the other of Professor Weekley—these two at least may claim victory to be in sight.†

---

*When this book was first published a Scottish friend wrote to me: "As a Scot I wept bitter tears over your defeatist attitude in the matter of *haver*. I think it is utterly damnable that a perfectly honest word with a clearly defined meaning should be taken by 'havering bodies' and given a meaning, quite arbitrarily, which violates all its past history. . . . I deplore your weak-kneed acquiescence."

†"But Archbishop Tenison, though much out of favour with the Queen, outlived her in a most aggravating manner, so that Lambeth was never available for a Tory or a High Churchman." *Blenheim*, p. 171.

"English finds itself in possession of a phenomenal number of unrelated words identical in form and sound." *Something about Words*, p. 5.

Today the newcomers are mostly from the inventive and colourful minds of the Americans. The gates have been opened wide for them by film, radio and comic. We have changed our outlook since Dean Alford declared eighty years ago that the way the Americans corrupted our language was all of a piece with the character of that nation "with its blunted sense of moral obligation and duty to men". Yet we still have defenders of our tongue who scrutinise these immigrants very closely. That is as it should be, for some of them are certainly undesirables. But we ought not to forget how greatly our language has been enriched by the vigorous word-making habit of the Americans. Bridges' tribute to *blurb* might be applied to other more recent acquisitions, *gatecrasher, debunk, cold war, baby-sitter, stockpile, bulldoze, commuter* and many others. Nor do I see why anyone should turn up his nose at *teenager*, for it fills a gap usefully. We have no word that covers both sexes in what it is fashionable to call that "age-bracket", except *adolescents*, which vaguely suggests what I believe the psychologists call "imbalance", *juveniles*, which has been tainted by its association with delinquency, and *young persons*, which, though adopted by the law, retains a flavour of primness inappropriate to the young person of today: we are no longer in danger of feeling, as Mr. Podsnap did, that "the question about everything was, would it bring a blush to the cheek of the young person?" But these things are matters of taste, and one's own taste is of no importance unless it happens to reflect the general.

It is around new verbs that the battle now rages most hotly. New verbs are ordinarily formed in one of three ways, all of which have in the past been employed to create useful additions to our vocabulary. The first is the simple method of treating a noun as a verb; it is one of the beauties of our language that nouns can be so readily converted into adjectives or verbs. This was the origin, for instance, of the verb *question*. The second is what is called "back-formation", that is to say, forming from a noun the sort of verb from which the noun might have been formed if the verb had come first. In this way the verb *diagnose* was formed from *diagnosis*. The third is to add *ise** to an adjective, as *sterilise* has been formed from *sterile*. All these methods are being used today with no little zest. New verbs for something that is itself new (like *pressurise*) cannot be gainsaid. *Service* is a natural and useful newcomer in an age when almost everyone keeps a machine of some sort that needs periodical attention. But it provides an interesting example of the way these new verbs take an ell, once you give them an inch. *Service* is already trying to oust *serve*, as in

*On the question whether this should be *ise* or *ize* see p. 175.

A large number of depots of one sort or another will be required to service the town,

and

To enable a Local Authority to take advantage of this provision it is essential that sites should be available, ready serviced with roads and sewers.

The credentials of *to contact* are still in dispute between those who, like Sir Alan Herbert, think it a "loathsome" word and those who hold, with Ivor Brown, that it can claim indulgence on the ground that "there is no word which covers approach by telephone, letter and speech, and *contact* is self-explanatory and concise". If I were to hazard a prophecy, it would be that *contact* will win, but for the present it still excites in some people the same feeling as used to be aroused by split infinitives, *very pleased's* and *those kind of things* in the days when the observance of grammarians' shibboleths was regarded as the test of good writing. So do *feature, glimpse, position, sense* and *signature* when used as verbs, though all have long since found their way into the dictionaries. So do the verbs *loan, gift* and *author*, though these were verbs centuries ago, and are only trying to come back again after a long holiday, spent by *loan* in America, by *gift* in Scotland and by *author* in oblivion. Whatever may be the fate of these, we shall not be disposed to welcome such a word as *reaccessioned*, used by a librarian of a book once more available to subscribers. To *underground* (of electric cables) seems at first sight an unnecessary addition to our vocabulary of verbs when *bury* is available, but an editor to whom a protest was made retorted that *bury* would not have done because the cables were "live".

But these words are merely skirmishers. The main body of the invasion consists of verbs ending in *ise*. "There seems to be a notion", says Sir Alan Herbert, "that any British or American subject is entitled to take any noun or adjective, add *ise* to it, and say, "I have made a new verb. What a good boy am I." Among those now nosing their way into the language are *casualise* (employ casual labour), *civilianise* (replace military staff by civil), *diarise* (enter in a diary), *editorialise* (make editorial comments on), *finalise* (put into final form), *hospitalise* (send to hospital), *publicise* (give publicity to). All these except *diarise* are new enough not to have been included in the Shorter Oxford English Dictionary, published in 1933, or (except *hospitalise*) in the 1928 edition of Webster's International Dictionary. The reason for inventing them seems to be to enable us to say in one word what would otherwise need several. Whether that will prove a valid passport time alone can show.* If the words I

---

*A remarkable experiment in this direction is the American verb to *nolle prosse*. meaning to enter a writ of *nolle prosequi*.

have listed were all, they might eventually be swallowed, though with many wry faces. But they are by no means all; a glut of this diet is being offered to us (*trialise, itinerise* and *reliableise* are among the specimens sent to me), and we are showing signs of nausea. It is perhaps significant that at the Coronation of Queen Elizabeth II the word *Inthroning* was substituted for the first time for the word *Inthronisation,* used in all previous Coronations. This may be symptomatic of a revolt against the ugliness of *ise* and still more of *isation,* which Sir Alan Herbert has compared to lavatory fittings, useful in their proper place but not to be multiplied beyond what is necessary for practical purposes.

Another popular way of making new words is to put *de, dis* or *non* at the beginning of a word in order to create one with an opposite meaning. *De* and *dis* are termed by the O.E.D. "living prefixes with privative force". "Living" is the right word; they have been living riotously of late. Anyone, it seems, can make a new verb by prefixing *de* to an existing one. Some years ago Sir Alan Herbert made a collection of some remarkable creations of this sort, and included them in his *index expurgatorius* of "septic verbs". Among them were *debureaucratise, decontaminate, dedirt, dehumidify, deinsectize, deratizate derestrict, dewater, dezincify.* The Ministry of Food, I am told, once fixed maximum prices for *defeathered* geese.

Some of these, it is to be hoped, may prove to be freaks of an occasion and will be seen no more. But there is a class which has come to stay, whether we like it or not. This comprises *decontaminate, derestrict* and *derequisition.* Their origin is the same: they all denote the undoing of something the doing of which called for—or at any rate was given—a special term. If to affect with gas is to *contaminate,* to enforce a speed limit is to *restrict,* and to commandeer a house is to *requisition,* then the cancellation of those things will inevitably be *decontaminate, derestrict* and *derequisition,* whether we like it or not, and it is no use saying that they ought to be *cleanse, exempt* and *release,* or any other words that are not directly linked with their opposites. But some people will still wince on reading that the Ministry of Transport have decided to detrunk a road, as though it were an elephant, and on hearing that witnesses in a postponed trial have been dewarned.

Most of the new *dis*-words since the war have been invented by economists (several by *The Economist* itself). *Disincentive* and *disinflation,* received at first with surprised disapproval, seem to have quite settled down. It is recognised that the old-fashioned opposites of *incentive* and *inflation—deterrent* and *deflation—*will not do: we need special words for that particular form of deterrent that discourages men from working hard, and for that process of checking inflation which is something less than deflation. On the heels of these new arrivals come *diseconomy* and *dissaving*.

> It would yield economies that would far outweigh the diseconomies that are the inevitable price of public ownership and giant size.
>
> Some 13.4 million of the 22 million income earners . . . kept their spending in such exact step with their incomes that they saved or dissaved less than £25 in that year.

Will these be accepted also on the ground that in the first no positive word—neither *extravagance* nor *waste* nor *wastefulness* would express the writer's meaning so well as *diseconomies*, and that in the second *dissaved* is the only way of expressing the opposite of *saved* without a clumsy periphrasis that would destroy the nice balance of the sentence. Perhaps; it is at least certain that these words spring from deliberate and provocative choice and not from mental indolence. What is deplorable is that so many of those who go in for the invention of opposites by means of "living prefixes with privative force" do not know when to stop. It becomes a disease. *Disincentive* replaces *deterrent*; then *undisincentive* ousts *incentive*, and then *disincentive* itself has to yield to *non-undisincentive*. No wonder Mr. G. V. Carey is moved to write to *The Times*:

> I have long been waiting for somebody to dispel my growing bewilderment at the modern expression of affirmative and negative (or should I say "disaffirmative"?) in English. I had always imagined that the opposite of "harmony" was "discord", not "disharmony"; of "incentive", "deterrent"; and so on. But at the present rate of distortion of our language it looks as though we shall soon be talking about "black and disblack", "good and disgood".

In the "newspeak" which George Orwell pictured as the language of 1984 *very bad* has become *doubleplusungood*.

The same warning is needed about the prefix *non*. To put *non* in front of a word is a well-established way of creating a word with the opposite meaning. *Non-appearance, non-combatant, nonconformist* and *non-existent* are common examples. But the lazy habit of using *non* to turn any word upside-down, so as not to have the trouble of thinking of its opposite, is becoming sadly common. "Institutions for the care of the *non-sick*" presumably means something different from "institutions for the care of the healthy", but the difference is not apparent. Sir Alan Herbert remarked some years ago that no one would think of saying *non-sober* when he meant drunk. I cannot feel sure that that is still true. I should have said that this trick was of recent origin if Mr. G. M. Young had not sent me an eighty-year-old example of it that would hold its own against any modern rival.

Sir John Simon, F.R.S., the eminent surgeon who later became a Government official, giving evidence before the Royal Commission on the Sanitary Laws in 1869, referred to "a disease hereditarily transmissible and spreading among the non-fornicative part of the population". Mr. Young says he was surprised to come across this, because Simon was a man of culture and a friend of Ruskin. "It just shows", he adds unkindly, "what Whitehall can do."

Yet another favourite device for making new words is the suffix *ee*. This is an erratic suffix, not conforming wholly to any rule. But in its main type it serves to denote the object of a verb, generally the indirect object, as in *assignee*, *referee* and *trustee*, but sometimes the direct object, as in *examinee*, *trainee* and *evacuee*. It therefore makes for confusion of language if the suffix is used to form a word meaning the subject of the verb. *Escapee* is worse than useless; we already have *escaper*. When unskilled labour is used to "dilute" skilled labour, the unskilled ought to be called not *dilutees*, as they are officially termed, but *dilutors*. The skilled are the *dilutees*. Apart from misuse such as this, we are getting too many *ee* words; they are springing up like weeds. Their purpose seems to be the same as that of many of our new verbs: to enable us to use one word instead of several. But we have got on very well for quite a long time without such words as *expellee*, *persecutee* and *amputee*.

While the age-long practice of creating new words has quickened its tempo, so has the no less ancient habit of extending the meaning of established words. Here again we ought to examine the novelties on merits, without bias. The main test for both is whether the new word, or the new meaning, fills a need in the vocabulary. If it is trying to take a seat already occupied—as the new verbs *decision* and *suspicion* are squatting in the places of *decide* and *suspect*, and the enlarged meanings of *anticipate* and *claim* in those of *expect* and *assert*—they are clearly harming the language by "blurring hard-won distinctions". Still more are words like *overall* and *involve* open to that charge: they are claiming the seats of half a dozen or more honest words. But those that claim seats hitherto empty may deserve admittance. *Stagger*, for example, has recently enlarged its meaning both logically and usefully in such a phrase as *staggered holidays*. *Deadline* (originally a line around a military prison beyond which a prisoner might be shot) has done the same in taking over the task of signifying a limit of any sort beyond which it is not permissible to go. Nor do I see why purists should condemn the use of *nostalgic* not only for a feeling of homesickness but also by the emotion aroused by thinking of the days that are no more. An appeal to etymology is not conclusive. When a word starts straying from its derivative meaning it may often be proper, and sometimes even useful, to try to restrain it; there are many now who would like to restrain the wanderlust of *alibi* and *shambles*. The ignorant misuse of technical terms excites violent reactions in those who know their true meanings. The popular use of *to the nth degree* in the sense of *to the utmost* exasperates the mathematician, who knows that strictly the notion of largeness is not inherent in *to the nth* at all. The use of *by and large* in the sense of *broadly speaking* exasperates the sailor, who knows that the true meaning of the phrase—alternately close to the wind and with the wind abeam or aft—has not the faintest relation to the meaning given to it by current usage. But there is a point where it becomes idle pedantry to try to put back into their etymological cages words and phrases that escaped from them many years ago and have settled down firmly elsewhere. To do that is to start on a path on which there is no logical stopping-point short of such absurdities as insisting that the word *anecdote* can only be applied to a story never told before, whereas we all know that it generally means one told too often. As Sir Clifford Allbutt used to remind his students, "the word *apostate* means for us far more than an *absentee* or a *dissenter*, and a *muscle* more than a *little mouse*; *monks* rarely live alone; *rivals* contend for more than water rights, and *hypocrites* are no longer confined to the theatre."

Sometimes words appear to have changed their meanings when the real change is in the popular estimate of the value of the ideas they stand for. *Imperialism*, which Lord Rosebery defined as "a greater pride in Empire, a larger patriotism", has fallen from its pedestal. *Academic* is suffering a similar debasement owing to the waning of love of learning for its own sake and the growth of mistrust of intellectual activities that have no immediate utilitarian results. In music, according to the music critic of *The Times*, the word "has descended from the imputation of high esteem to being a withering term of polite abuse", in spite of Stanford's attempt to stop the rot by defining the word as "a term of opprobrium applied by those who do not know their business to those who do". A change in popular sentiment may also account for a confusing enlargement of the meaning of *afford*. "Can we afford to do it?" asks one of our legislators in a debate on some expensive project, meaning "have we the financial resources to do it?" "Can we afford not to do it?" retorts another, meaning "can we face the consequences of not doing it?" Unless this means "Shall we not have to spend more money in some other way if we do not do it?" the arguments are not in the same plane, and will never meet.

Public opinion decides all these questions in the long run; there is little that individuals can do about them. Our national vocabulary is a democratic institution, and what is generally accepted will ultimately be correct. I have no doubt that if anyone should read this book in fifty years' time he would find current objections to the use of certain words in certain senses as curious as we now find Swift's denunciation of *mob*. Lexicographers soon find this out. I have quoted Dr. Johnson; seventy years later Noah Webster said the same thing in different words:

> It is quite impossible to stop the progress of language—it is like the course of the Mississippi, the motion of which at times is scarcely perceptible yet even then it possesses a momentum quite irresistible. Words and expressions will be forced into use in spite of all the exertions of all the writers in the world.

The duty of the official is, however, clear. Just as it has long been recognised that, in salaries and wages, the Civil Service must neither walk ahead of public opinion nor lag behind it, but, in the old phrase, be "in the first flight of good employers", so it is the duty of the official in his use of English neither to perpetuate what is obsolescent nor to give currency to what is novel, but, like a good servant, to follow what is generally regarded by his masters as the best practice for the time being. Among his readers will be vigilant guardians of the purity of English prose, and they must not be offended. So the official's vocabulary must contain only words that by general consent have passed the barrier, and he must not give a helping hand to any that are still trying to get through, even though he may think them deserving.

> For last year's words belong to last year's language
> And next year's words await another voice.

The sentence that is right, adds Mr. Eliot, is one

> . . . where every word is at home,
> Taking its place to support the others,
> The word neither diffident nor ostentatious,
> An easy commerce of the old and the new,
> The common word exact without vulgarity,
> The formal word precise but not pedantic,
> The complete consort dancing together.*

I will end this chapter on correctness in words with a list of some words and phrases often used in senses generally regarded as incorrect. At the end of Chapters VII and VIII are lists of other words and phrases that are apt to be used unsuitably rather than incorrectly. It is not easy to decide which words should be assigned to the

---

*T. S. Eliot, *Little Gidding*. Faber & Faber, 1943.

"incorrect" category and which to the "unsuitable", and I do not suppose that all readers will agree with my classification: so many words are trying to arrogate new meanings that opinions may well differ about which have succeeded and which not. Even if my choice is right now, it will almost certainly be out-of-date before long.

For instance, as this book goes to the publisher, I am shaken to find that the very first word in the list is used in *The Times Literary Supplement* in the sense that I condemn.* But in spite of this high authority I cannot bring myself to move the word from the "incorrects" to the "inexpedients".

. . . . .

ALIBI

> There is still a minority of our membership which has failed to recognise its new responsibilities. It is not sufficient to point to certain shortcomings of the National Coal Board to create an alibi.
>
> Members of the timber trade, like members of any other trade, are glad of any alibi to explain any particular increases in price.
>
> Either we accept the bare facts or we go down to a lower standard of living. The day of alibis is gone.

Alibi is used in these examples, in the sense of *excuse*, or of an admission of guilt with a plea of extenuating circumstances, or of throwing the blame on someone else. But *alibi* is the Latin for *elsewhere*. To plead an alibi is to rebut a charge by adducing evidence that the person charged was elsewhere at the time of the act alleged against him. "Oh Sammy Sammy vy vornt there an alleybi?" cried old Mr. Weller at the conclusion of *Bardell* v. *Pickwick* (in which it was not disputed that Mrs. Bardell had been found in Mr. Pickwick's embrace) and so furnished a classic example of the confusing properties of this word. The mischief is that if this novel use establishes itself language will lose precision; we shall be left without a word to signify the true meaning of *alibi*. The vogue of detective stories is no doubt responsible for the corruption. So many of them rely on an alibi for their plot that ignorant readers think the word will do for any means of rebutting a charge.

ALTERNATE(LY) and ALTERNATIVE(LY)

These are sometimes confused. *Alternate(ly)* means by turns. *Alternative(ly)* means in a way that offers a choice. "The journey may be made by rail or alternately by road" means, if it means anything, that every other journey may be made by road. It does

---

*"This alibi [the legend that Ruskin had married not for his own gratification but to please his parents] dwindles . . . in the breath of passion exhaled by the love letters." *The Times Lit. Supp.*, 3rd July 1953.

not mean as the writer intended, that for every journey the traveller has a choice between the two means of transport. Conversely "alternatively they sat and walked in the moonlight, talking of this and that" cannot have been intended to mean that they sat and walked in the moonlight as an alternative to doing something else; what must have been intended is that they sat and walked alternately. *Alternate* can also be a verb meaning, in popular language, to "take it in turns".

A PRIORI

Do not say *a priori* when you mean *prima facie*; in fact you can probably get on without either.

> Several countries most advanced from a medical point of view have for the last 20 years done without this drug, "a fact", says the Board, "which is sufficient to show that there is an *a priori* case for its total abolition".

No—it does not. To argue *a priori* is to argue from assumed axioms and not from experience. The argument here rests on the 20-year experience of several countries, and so is an argument *a posteriori*.

Prima facie, which is what the writer probably had in mind, means on a first impression, before hearing fully the evidence for and against.

BEG THE QUESTION

This does not mean, as is commonly supposed, to evade a straight answer to a question. It means to form a conclusion by making an assumption which is as much in need of proof as the conclusion itself. Logicians call this *petitio principii*. "Thus to say that parallel lines will never meet because they are parallel is simply to assume as a fact the very thing you profess to prove" (Brewer). A single word can be used in a question-begging way. *Reactionary, victimisation, aggression, imperialism* and *warmonger* are examples.

COMPRISE

A body comprises (or consists of) the elements of which it is composed (or constituted); in the first example, for instance, Op. 77 comprises the quartets, not the other way round. *Compose* or *constitute* or *form* should have been used in these examples.

> The two quartets comprising Haydn's Op. 77.
> The smaller Regional Hospitals which comprise a large proportion of those available to Regional Boards.
> The twelve Foreign Ministers who comprise the Atlantic Treaty Council.

The O.E.D. recognises *comprise* in the sense of *compose*, but calls it "rare". In the interests of precision it should remain so. The difference between *comprise* and *include* is that *comprise* is better when all the components are enumerated and *include* when only some of them are.

CONSEQUENTIAL

Consequential has now only two meanings in common use. It retains that of *self-important*, and in legal language it signifies a secondary and incidental result, especially in the phrases *consequential damages* and *consequential amendments*. For all other purposes *consequent* is the adjective of *consequence*. Thus a Minister might say, "This amendment is consequent on a promise I gave on second reading" and "This amendment is consequential on one accepted yesterday".

DEFINITIVE

This word differs from *definite* by importing the idea of finality. A definite offer is an offer precise in its terms. A definitive offer is an offer which the person making it declares to be his last word.

DESIDERATE

Desiderate is a rather pedantic word. It is not, as some think, a formal synonym of *desire*, or *ask for*.

> One influential deputation desiderated State management [of licensed premises in New Towns]."

Desiderate means more than *desire*. It means to feel the want of, to miss, to think long for, as the Irish say. Mrs. Gummidge desiderated the old 'un. But the influential deputation cannot have been feeling like that about something that existed only in their hopes.

DISINTERESTED

Disinterested means "unbiased by personal interest" (O.E.D.). It is sometimes used wrongly for *uninterested* (i.e. not interested). A Minister recently said in the course of a speech in Parliament:

> I hope that [what I have said] will excuse me from the charge of being disinterested in this matter.

A public man dealing with public business can never be "charged" with being disinterested, as if it were a crime. It is his elementary duty always to be so.

FACTITIOUS

Factitious means "engineered" in the derogatory sense of that word, i.e. not naturally or spontaneously created. It is easily confused with *fictitious*, which means sham, counterfeit, unreal. A factitious thing may be genuine; a fictitious thing cannot.

D

Feasible

This word means *practicable, capable of being done*. It should not be used as a synonym for *probable* or *plausible*.

I.E.

This is sometimes used (by confusion with e.g.) to introduce an example. It stands for (*id est*) "that is", and introduces a definition, as one might say "we are meeting on the second Tuesday of this month, i.e. the tenth". E.g. (*exempli gratia*) means "for the sake of example" and introduces an illustration, as one might say "let us meet on a fixed day every month, e.g. the second Tuesday".

Infer

It is a common error to use *infer* for *imply*:

> Great efforts were made to write down the story, and to infer that the support was normal. . . . I felt most bitter about this attitude . . . for . . . it inferred great ignorance and stupidity on the part of the enemy.

A writer or speaker *implies* what his reader or hearer *infers*. The difference is illustrated thus by Sir Alan Herbert:

> If you see a man staggering along the road you may infer that he is drunk, without saying a word; but if you say "Had one too many?" you do not infer but imply that he is drunk.

There is authority for *infer* in the sense of *imply*, as there is for *comprise* in the sense of *compose*. But here again the distinction is worth preserving in the interests of the language.

Leading Question

This does not mean, as is widely supposed, a question designed to embarrass the person questioned. On the contrary, it means a question designed to help him by suggesting the answer—a type of question not permitted when a witness is being examined by the counsel who called him.

Mitigate

Mitigate for *militate* is a curiously common malapropism. An example is:

> I do not think that this ought to mitigate against my chances of promotion.

Practical and Practicable

Practical, with its implied antithesis of *theoretical*, means useful in practice. *Practicable* means capable of being carried out in action.

That which is practicable is often not practical. Anything that is possible of accomplishment by available means may be called practicable. Only that which can be accomplished successfully or profitably under given circumstances may be called practical.

(WESEEN, *Words Confused and Misused.*)

PRESCRIPTIVE RIGHT

This does not mean the same as indefeasible right. Prescriptive right is a technical term of the law. It means a right founded on "prescription," that is to say on long and unchallenged custom. It has no greater sanctity than any other sort of right; on the contrary, it is likely to be more questionable than most.

PROTAGONIST

This word is not the opposite of *antagonist* (one who contends with another); the pair must not be used as synonyms of *supporter* and *opponent*, the *pros* and the *antis*. *Protagonist* has nothing to do with the Latin word *pro*: its first syllable is derived from a Greek word meaning *first*, and it means literally the principal actor in a play; hence it is used for the most prominent personage in any affair. It is not necessarily associated with the advocacy of anything, although it often happens to be so in fact. When we say that Mr. Willett was protagonist in the movement for summer time, we are not saying that he was *pro* summer time; we are saying that he played a leading part in the movement. *Protagonist* should not be used in the sense merely of *advocate* or *champion*.

REDUNDANT

This is an imposing word and, no doubt for that reason, is used in senses that it will not bear. The idea of *too much* is inseparable from it; "superabundant, superfluous, excessive", is what the dictionary says. To treat it as meaning merely *inappropriate* is wrong.

The Authority are now reluctant to proceed with the provision of services for a 10,000 population in case their work becomes redundant due to the subsequent need for catering for a larger population.

It is nonsense to say that provision for a population of a certain size might become superabundant if it were subsequently necessary to cater for a larger population.

RESOURCE

There is much pardonable confusion between *resource, recourse* and *resort*. The most common mistake is to write "have resource to" instead of "have recourse to" or "have resort to". The correct usage can be illustrated thus:

> They had recourse (or had resort, or resorted) to their reserves; it was their last resource (or resort); they had no other resources.

TRANSPIRE

It is a common error to use transpire as if it meant *happen* or *occur*. It does not. It means *to become known*. An example of its wrong use is:

> Your letter arrived at my office while I was in Glasgow, attending what transpired to be a very successful series of meetings.

WASTAGE

There is a difference that ought to be preserved between *waste* and *wastage*; *wastage* should not be used as a more dignified alternative to *waste*. The ordinary meaning of *waste* is "useless expenditure or consumption, squandering (of money, time, etc.)". The ordinary meaning of *wastage* is "loss by use, decay, evaporation, leakage, or the like". You may, for instance, properly say that the daily wastage of a reservoir is so many gallons. But you must not say that a contributory factor is the wastage of water by householders if what you mean is that householders waste it.

A new duty seems to have been recently given to *waste* as a verb— that of signifying "convert into waste paper". This no doubt makes for brevity, but gives a surprising air to this instruction in a circular:

> Departments are asked to ensure that as many documents as possible are wasted at the earliest permissible date.

V

The Choice of Words (1)

INTRODUCTORY

> The craftsman is proud and careful of his tools: the surgeon does not operate with an old razor-blade: the sportsman fusses happily and long over the choice of rod, gun, club or racquet. But the man who is working in words, unless he is a professional writer (and not always then), is singularly neglectful of his instruments.
>
> IVOR BROWN

HERE we come to the most important part of our subject. Correctness is not enough. The words used may all be words approved by the dictionary and used in their right senses; the grammar may be faultless and the idiom above reproach. Yet what is written may still fail to convey a ready and precise meaning to the reader. That it does so fail is the charge brought against much of what is written nowadays, including much of what is written by officials. In the first chapter I quoted a saying of Matthew Arnold that the secret of style was to have something to say and to say it as clearly as you can. The basic fault of present-day writing is a tendency to say what one has to say in as complicated a way as possible. Instead of being simple, terse and direct, it is stilted, long-winded and circumlocutory; instead of choosing the simple word it prefers the unusual; instead of the plain phrase the cliché.

Ivor Brown, a connoisseur of words, has invented several names for this sort of writing. In one book he calls it "jargantuan", in another "barnacular" and in another "pudder".* The Americans have a word for it—"gobbledygook". Its nature can be studied not only in the original but also in translation. Ivor Brown has translated the Lord's Prayer, Sir Alan Herbert the Catechism, Mr. George Townsend Warner the Parable of the Good Samaritan and George Orwell the passage in Ecclesiastes about the race not being to the swift nor the battle to the strong, or, as it appears in his translation, about "success or failure in competitive activities exhibiting no tendency to be commensurate with innate capacity". It may be significant that all these critics of pudder have gone to the Bible or Prayer Book to find their greatest contrasts with it. English style must have

---

* *Jargantuan* and *barnacular* are self-explanatory; *pudder* is taken from Lear's prayer to " the gods who keep this dreadful pudder o'er our heads".

47

been immeasurably influenced by everyone's intimate knowledge of those two books whose cadences were heard every day at family prayers and every Sunday at matins and evensong. Now family prayers are said no longer, and few go to church.

The forms that pudder commonly takes in official writing will be examined in the following three chapters. In this one we are concerned (if I may borrow a bit of pudder from the doctors*) with the ætiology of the disease and with prescribing some general regimen for the writer that will help him to avoid catching it.

Why do so many writers prefer pudder to simplicity? Officials are far from being the only offenders. It seems to be a morbid condition contracted in early manhood. Children show no signs of it. Here, for example, is the response of a child of ten to an invitation to write an essay on a bird and a beast:

> The bird that I am going to write about is the owl. The owl cannot see at all by day and at night is as blind as a bat.
> I do not know much about the owl, so I will go on to the beast which I am going to choose. It is the cow. The cow is a mammal. It has six sides—right, left, an upper and below. At the back it has a tail on which hangs a brush. With this it sends the flies away so that they do not fall into the milk. The head is for the purpose of growing horns and so that the mouth can be somewhere. The horns are to butt with, and the mouth is to moo with. Under the cow hangs the milk. It is arranged for milking. When people milk, the milk comes and there is never an end to the supply. How the cow does it I have not yet realised, but it makes more and more. The cow has a fine sense of smell; one can smell it far away. This is the reason for the fresh air in the country.
> The man cow is called an ox. It is not a mammal. The cow does not eat much, but what it eats it eats twice, so that it gets enough. When it is hungry it moos, and when it says nothing it is because its inside is all full up with grass.

The writer had something to say and said it as clearly as he could, and so has unconsciously achieved style. But why do we write, when we are ten, "so that the mouth can be somewhere" and perhaps when we are thirty "in order to ensure that the mouth may be appropriately positioned environmentally"? What barnacular song do the puddering sirens sing to lure the writer into the land

---

*Puddery seems to be regrettably increasing in medicine. In my lifetime I have seen the *mad-doctor* pass through the chrysalis of *alienist* into the butterfly of *psychiatrist*. This is perhaps excusable, but why have *walking cases* suddenly become *ambulants*? Some seventy years ago a promising young neurologist made a discovery that necessitated the addition of a new word to the English vocabulary. He insisted that this should be *knee-jerk*, and *knee-jerk* it has remained, in spite of the efforts of *patellar reflex* to dislodge it. He was my father; so perhaps I have inherited a prejudice in favour of home-made words.

of jargantua? That, as we know, is the sort of question which though puzzling, is not beyond all conjecture. I will hazard one or two.

The first affects only the official. It is a temptation to cling too long to outworn words and phrases. The British Constitution, as everyone knows, has been shaped by retaining old forms and putting them to new uses. Among the old forms that we are reluctant to abandon are those of expressing ourselves in State documents. Every Bill begins with the words: "Be it enacted by the Queen's most Excellent Majesty by and with the advice and consent of the Lords Spiritual and Temporal and Commons in this present Parliament assembled and by the authority of the same as follows:" It ends its career as a Bill and becomes an Act when the Clerk of the Parliaments is authorised by the Queen to declare "La Reine le veult". That is all very well, because no one ever reads these traditional phrases; they are no longer intended to convey thought from one brain to another. But the official, living in this atmosphere, properly proud of the ancient traditions of his service, sometimes allows his style of letter-writing to be affected by it—*adverting* and *acquainting* and *causing to be informed*. There may even be produced in his mind a feeling that all common words lack the dignity that he is bound to maintain.

That, I think, is one song the sirens sing to the official. Another they certainly sing to all of us. Ivor Brown reminds us how Wells' Mr. Polly "revelled in 'sesquippledan verboojuice' ", and comments that he was behaving like William Shakespeare before him. There is something of Mr. Polly in most of us, especially when we are young. All young people of sensibility feel the lure of rippling or reverberating polysyllables. "Evacuated to alternative accommodation" can give a satisfaction that cannot be got from "taken to another house"; "ablution facilities" strikes a chord that does not vibrate to "wash-basins". Far-fetched words are by definition "recherché" words, and are thought to give distinction; thus such words as *implement*, *optimum* and *global* acquire their vogue. A newly-discovered metaphor shines like a jewel in a drab vocabulary; thus *blueprint*, *bottleneck*, *ceiling* and *target* are eagerly seized, and the dust settles on their discarded predecessors—*plan*, *hold-up*, *limit* and *objective*. But it will not do. Official writing is essentially of the sort of which Horace said: "Ornatum res ipsa vetat, contenta doceri"— the very subject matter rules out ornament; it asks only to be put across. "What style, sir", asked of an East India Director some youthful aspirant for literary renown, "is most to be preferred in the composition of official dispatches?" "My good fellow", responded the ruler of Hindustan, "the style *as* we like is the Humdrum".*

Another song I am sure the sirens have in their repertoire—a call to the instinct of self-preservation. It is sometimes dangerous to be precise. "Mistiness is the mother of safety", said Newman. "Your safe man in the Church of England is he who steers his course between the Scylla of 'Aye' and the Charybdis of 'No' along the channel of 'No meaning'." Ecclesiastics are not in this respect unique. Politicians have long known the dangers of precision of statement, especially at election time.

> "And now for our cry", said Mr. Taper.
> "It is not a Cabinet for a good cry", said Tadpole; " but then, on the other hand, it is a Cabinet that will sow dissension in the opposite ranks, and prevent them having a good cry."
> "Ancient institutions and modern improvements, I suppose, Mr. Tadpole."
> "Ameliorations is the better word; ameliorations. Nobody knows exactly what it means."†

That was written 100 years ago. But it does not seem to be out of date, as Mr. Stuart Chase testifies:

> A Senator, distinguished, powerful, an astute leader with surpassing skill in political management, told me that Americanism was to be this year's campaign issue. When I asked him what Americanism meant, he said he did not know, but that it was a damned good word with which to carry an election.‡

When the official does not know his Minister's mind, or his Minister does not know his own mind, or the Minister thinks it wiser not to speak his mind, the official must sometimes cover his utterance with a mist of vagueness. Civil Service methods are often contrasted unfavourably with those of business. But to do this is to forget that no Board of Directors of a business concern have to meet a committee of their shareholders every afternoon, to submit themselves daily to an hour's questioning on their conduct of the business, to get the consent of that committee by a laborious process to every important step they take, or to conduct their affairs with the constant knowledge that there is a shadow board eager for the shareholders' authority to take their place. The systems are quite different and are bound to produce different methods. Ministers are under daily attack, and their reputations are largely in the hands of their

---

*Bagehot, *Letters on the French Coup d'Etat*, Letter III.
†Disraeli's *Coningsby*.
‡Stuart Chase, *The Tyranny of Words*, Methuen, 7th ed., 1950.

staffs. Only if he has full and explicit authority from his Minister can a civil servant show in an important matter that prompt-ness and boldness which are said to be the attributes of men of business.

> The words which he writes will go on record, possibly for all time, certainly for a great many years. They may have to be published, and may have a wide circulation. They may even mean something in international relationships. So, even though mathematical accuracy may in the nature of things be unattainable, identifiable inaccuracy must at least be avoided. The hackneyed official phrase, the wide circumlocution, the vague promise, the implied qualification are comfortingly to hand. Only those who have been exposed to the temptation to use them know how hard it is to resist. But with all the sympathy that such understanding may mean, it is still possible to hold that something might be done to purge official style and caution, necessary and desirable in themselves, of their worst extravagances.

This is a quotation from a leading article in *The Times*. It arose out of a correspondent's ridicule of this extract from a letter written by a Government Department to its Advisory Council:

> In transmitting this matter to the Council the Minister feels that it may be of assistance to them to learn that, as at present advised, he is inclined to the view that, in existing circumstances, there is, *prima facie*, a case for. . . .

It is as easy to slip into this sort of thing without noticing it as to see the absurdity of it when pointed out. One may surmise that the writer felt himself to be in a dilemma: he wanted the Advisory Council to advise the Minister in a certain way, but did not want them to think that the Minister had made up his mind before getting their advice. But he might have done this without piling qualification on qualification and reservation on reservation; all that he needed to say was that the Minister thought so-and-so but wanted to know what the Advisory Committee thought before taking a decision.

This quotation illustrates another trap into which official writing is led when it has to leave itself a bolt-hole, as it so often has. Cautionary clichés are used automatically without thought of what they mean. There are two of them here: *inclined to think* and *as at present advised*. Being *inclined to think*, in the sense of inclining to an opinion not yet crystallised, is a reasonable enough expression, just as one may say colloquially *my mind is moving that way*. But excessive use of the phrase may provoke the captious critic to say that if being inclined to think is really something different from thinking, then the less said about it the better until it has ripened into something

that can be properly called thought.* We can hardly suppose that
the writer of the following sentence really needed time to ponder
whether his opinion might not be mistaken:

> We are inclined to think that people are more irritated by noise
> that they feel to be unnecessary than by noise that they cause them-
> selves.

As at present advised should be used only where an opinion has been
formed on expert (e.g. legal) advice, never, as it is too often, as the
equivalent of saying: "This is what the Minister thinks in the present
state of his mind but, as he is human, the state of his mind may
change". That may be taken for granted.

There is often a real need for caution, and it is a temptation to
hedging and obscurity. But it is no excuse for them. A frank admission
that an answer cannot be given is better than an answer that looks
as if it meant something but really means nothing. Such a reply
exasperates the reader and brings the Service into discredit.

Politeness plays its part too: pudder is less likely to give offence.
Politeness often shows itself in euphemism, a term defined by the
dictionary as "the substitution of a mild or vague expression for a
harsh or blunt one". It is prompted by the same impulse as led the
Greeks to call the Black Sea the Euxine (the hospitable one) in the
hope of averting its notorious inhospitableness, and the Furies the
Eumenides (the good-humoured ladies) in the hope that they might
be flattered into being less furious. For the Greeks it was the gods
and the forces of nature that had to be propitiated; for those who
govern us today it is the electorate. Hence the prevalence of what
the grammarians call *meiosis* (understatement) and the use of
qualifying adverbs such as *somewhat* and *rather* and the popularity of
the *not un-* device. This last is useful in its place. There are occasions
when a writer's meaning may be conveyed more exactly by (say)
not unkindly, not unnaturally or *not unjustifiably*, than by *kindly, naturally*
or *justifiably*. But the "not un-" habit is liable to take charge, with
disastrous effects, making the victim forget all straightforward
adjectives and adverbs. When an Inspector of Taxes writes "This is
a by no means uncomplicated case", we may be pretty sure that
he is employing meiosis. And "I think the officer's attitude was not

---

*A civil service correspondent takes me to task for having dealt too leniently
with this phrase. He calls the phrase " a monstrosity " which he says, " the cynic
regards as being typical of the civil servant, who is (in his eyes) incapable of
decisive thought ". Perhaps it is wise to avoid a phrase that can arouse feelings
of that sort in anyone. Sherlock Holmes reacted in the same way: "I am inclined
to think", . . . said I. "I should do so", remarked Holmes impatiently. (*The
Valley of Fear.*)

unduly unreasonable" seems a chicken-hearted defence of a subordinate. George Orwell recommended that we should all inoculate ourselves against the disease by memorising this sentence: "A not unblack dog was chasing a not unsmall rabbit across a not ungreen field".

Or a vague word may be preferred to a precise one because the vague is less alarming. As we shall see (p. 111), *emergency* does much service of this kind. A kindred device is to change names that have acquired unpleasant associations. Thus *distressed areas* were changed to *special areas* and schools for the backward and troublesome are now *special schools*. There are indeed no backward and troublesome children nowadays; as *The Times* has observed, those who used to be called the stupid, the unhappy and the queer are now the educationally subnormal, the maladjusted and the mentally abnormal. The poor have become the lower income brackets; criminal lunatics are now Broadmoor patients and rat-catchers rodent operators. This is no doubt a useful expedient in the art of democratic government, for the power of words is great. But it has its limitations. If the unpleasantness attaches to the thing itself, it will taint the new name; in course of time yet another will have to be found, and so *ad infinitum*. We do not seem to have done ourselves much good by assigning the blameless but unsuitable word *lavatory* to a place where there is nowhere to wash; we have merely blunted the language.

There remains one more siren-song to mention—that of laziness. As I observed in Chapter I, clear thinking is hard work. A great many people go through life without doing it to any noticeable extent. And, as George Orwell, from whom I then quoted, has pointed out, what we are now calling *pudder* "will construct your sentences for you and even think your thoughts for you to a certain extent". It is as though the builder of a house did not take the trouble to select with care the materials that he thought most suitable for his purpose, but collected chunks of masonry from ruined houses built by others and stuck them together anyhow. That is not a promising way to produce anything significant in meaning, attractive in form, or of any practical use.

So much for what I have termed the "aetiology" of pudder. Before turning to treatment it may be useful to illustrate the symptoms. To show that the British official is not the only (nor the worst) sufferer from the disease, I have gone for my examples to various sources, including writings by doctors and social workers, and drawing on the United States as well as our own country. I have added translations of the first three; the last two seem to me to defy translation.

Example	Translation
(From *The Economist*) " NATO has expressed its fundamental change of policy as ' evolving in place of the overriding medium-term defence hypothesis to which all economic planning was functionally subordinate, an antithesis of balancing *desiderata*, such as the politico-strategical necessity against the economico-social possibility and further these two components against the need for a maximum of flexibility ' ".	" What this really means (says *The Economist*) is that, whereas a national defence programme has been taken hitherto as something imposed from above which could not be altered, now the military requirements of NATO will be made to match the economic achievements of the individual countries."
The attitude of each, that he was not required to inform himself of, and his lack of interest in, the measures taken by the other to carry out the responsibility assigned to such other under the provision of plans then in effect, demonstrated on the part of each lack of appreciation of the responsibilities vested in them, and inherent in their positions.	Neither took any interest in the other's plans, or even found out what they were. This shows that they did not appreciate the responsibilities of their positions.
(Quoted in *The Lancet*, from which the translation also is taken). Experiments are described which demonstrate that in normal individuals the lowest concentration in which sucrose can be detected by means of gustation differs from the lowest concentration in which sucrose (in the amount employed) has to be ingested in order to produce a demonstrable decrease in olfactory acuity and a noteworthy conversion of sensations interpreted as a desire for food into sensations interpreted as a satiety associated with ingestion of food.	Experiments are described which demonstrate that a normal person can taste sugar in water in quantities not strong enough to interfere with his sense of smell or take away his appetite.

Diffusibilty of knowledge throughout the environment in which the families are to move is essential if the full expression of their potentiality is to become explicit in action. Facts pertain-

Example

ing to experience of every sort that the family is in course of digesting give the context and the full flavour of consciousness to their experience.

To reduce the risk of war and establish conditions of lasting peace requires the closer co-ordination in the employment of their joint resources to underpin these countries' economics in such a manner as to permit the full maintenance of their social and material standards as well as to adequate development of the necessary measures.

As a footnote to these examples I may add an extract from the periodical *Labour* lamenting the infectivity of this disease:

Managers do not look after their workers; they have functional responsibilities for works staffs. Workers do not ask to have a say in how a new design for a product is going to affect them; they claim equality in discovering the significance of that design in relation to themselves.

We can now turn to the question whether some general advice can be given to fortify the writer against infection. Two distinguished men tried their hands at this not very long ago—Fowler and Quiller-Couch. This is what Fowler says:

Anyone who wishes to become a good writer should endeavour, before he allows himself to be tempted by more showy qualities, to be direct, simple, brief, vigorous and lucid.
This general principle may be translated into general rules in the domain of vocabulary as follows:
Prefer the familiar word to the far-fetched.
Prefer the concrete word to the abstract.
Prefer the single word to the circumlocution.
Prefer the short word to the long.
Prefer the Saxon word to the Romance.

"These rules", he added, "are given in order of merit; the last is also the least."

He also pointed out that

all five rules will often be found to give the same answer about the same word or set of words. Scores of illustrations might be produced; let one suffice: *In the contemplated eventuality* (a phrase no worse than anyone can pick for himself out of his paper's leading article for the day) is at once the far-fetched, the abstract, the periphrastic, the long and the Romance, for *if so*. It does not very greatly matter by which of the five roads the natural is reached instead of the monstrosity, so long as it *is* reached. The five are indicated because (1) they differ in directness, and (2) in any given case only one of them may be possible.

Quiller-Couch, writing after Fowler, discussed these rules. He disagreed with the advice to prefer the short word to the long and the Saxon to the Romance. "These two precepts", he says, "you would have to modify by so long a string of exceptions that I do not commend them to you. In fact I think them false in theory and likely to be fatal in practice." He then gives his own rules, which are:

> Almost always prefer the concrete word to the abstract.
> Almost always prefer the direct word to the circumlocution.
> Generally use transitive verbs, that strike their object; and use them in the active voice, eschewing the stationary passive, with its little awaiting "is's" and "was's" and its participles getting in the light of your adjectives, which should be few. For, as a rough law, by his use of the straight verb and by his economy of adjectives you can tell a man's style, if it be masculine or neuter, writing or "composition".

I cannot set myself up as a judge between these high authorities, but as one who is now concerned only with a particular sort of prose, and who has made a close study of its common merits and faults, I respectfully agree with Quiller-Couch in refusing primary importance to the rule that the Saxon word must be preferred to the Romance, if only because it is not given to many of us always to be sure which is which. Any virtue that there may be in this rule, and in the rule to prefer the short word to the long is, I think, already implicit in the rule to prefer the familiar word to the far-fetched. Even Fowler said that "the Saxon oracle is not infallible", and before ever he had propounded the rule or Quiller-Couch criticised it, Bradley had said what most people are likely to think is all that need be said on the subject:

> The cry for "Saxon English" sometimes means nothing more than a demand for plain and unaffected diction, and a condemnation of idle taste for "words of learned length and thundering sound" which has prevailed at some periods of our literature. So far it is worthy of all respect; but the pedantry that would bid us reject the word fittest for our purpose because it is not of native origin ought to be strenuously resisted.

But the rule that Quiller-Couch adds to the two of Fowler's that he accepts, however sound its content, lacks the crispness that he preaches. What we are concerned with is not a quest for a literary style as an end in itself, but to study how best to convey our meaning without ambiguity and without giving unnecessary trouble to our readers. This being our aim, the essence of the advice of both these authorities may be expressed in the following three rules, and the rest of what I have to say in the domain of the vocabulary will be little more than an elaboration of them.

Use no more words than are necessary to express your meaning, for if you use more you are likely to obscure it and to tire your reader. In particular do not use superfluous adjectives and adverbs and do not use roundabout phrases where single words would serve.

Use familiar words rather than the far-fetched, if they express your meaning equally well; for the familiar are more likely to be readily understood.

Use words with a precise meaning rather than those that are vague, for they will obviously serve better to make your meaning clear; and in particular prefer concrete words to abstract, for they are more likely to have a precise meaning.

As Fowler pointed out, rules like these cannot be kept in separate compartments; they overlap. But in the next three chapters we will follow roughly the order in which the rules are set out and examine them under the headings "Avoiding the superfluous word", "Choosing the familiar word" and "Choosing the precise word".

VI

The Choice of Words (2)

AVOIDING THE SUPERFLUOUS WORD

> A reader of Milton must be always upon duty; he is surrounded with sense, it arises in every line, every word is to the purpose; there are no lazy intervals, all has been considered, and demands and merits observation. Even in the best writers you sometimes find words and sentences which hang on so loosely you may blow 'em off; Milton's are all substance and weight; fewer would not have serv'd the turn, and more would have been superfluous.
>
> JONATHAN RICHARDSON, quoted by F. E. HUTCHINSON
> in *Milton and the English Mind*, p. 137

THE fault of verbiage (which the O.E.D. defines as "abundance of words without necessity or without much meaning") is too multiform for analysis. But certain classifiable forms of it are specially common, and in this chapter we will examine some of these, ending with an indeterminate class which we will call "padding", to pick up what has been left outside the others.

VERBOSITY IN ADJECTIVES AND ADVERBS

Palmerston* wrote of one of Her Majesty's Ministers abroad who had neglected an admonition to go through all his despatches and strike out all words not necessary for fully conveying his meaning: "If Mr. Hamilton would let his substantives and adjectives go single instead of always sending them forth by twos and threes, his despatches would be clearer and easier to read".

It has been wisely said that the adjective is the enemy of the noun. If we make a habit of saying "The true facts are these", we shall come under suspicion when we profess to tell merely "the facts". If a *crisis* is always *acute* and an *emergency* always *grave*, what is left for those words to do by themselves? If *active* constantly accompanies *consideration*, we shall think we are being fobbed off when we are promised bare consideration. If a decision is always qualified by *definite*, a decision by itself becomes a poor filleted thing. If conditions are customarily described as *prerequisite* or *essential*, we shall doubt whether a *condition* without an adjective is really a

---

*Quoted by Sir C. K. Webster in *Politica*, August, 1934.

condition at all. If a part is always an *integral part* there is nothing left for a mere part except to be a spare part.

Cultivate the habit of reserving adjectives and adverbs to make your meaning more precise, and suspect those that you find yourself using to make it more emphatic. Use adjectives to denote kind rather than degree. By all means say an *economic crisis* or a *military disaster*, but think well before saying an *acute crisis* or a *terrible disaster*. Say if you like "The proposal met with noisy opposition and is in obvious danger of defeat". But do not say "The proposal met with considerable opposition and is in real danger of defeat". If that is all you want to say it is better to leave out the adjectives and say "The proposal met with opposition and is in danger of defeat".

Official writers seem to have a curious shrinking from certain adjectives unless they are adorned by adverbs. It is as though they were naked and must hastily have an adverbial dressing-gown thrown around them. The most indecent adjectives are, it seems, those of quantity or measure such as *short* and *long*, *many* and *few*, *heavy* and *light*. The adverbial dressing-gowns most favoured are *unduly*, *relatively* and *comparatively*. These adverbs can only properly be used when something has been mentioned or implied which gives a standard of comparison. But we have all seen them used on innumerable occasions when there is no standard of comparison. They are then meaningless. Their use is merely a shrinking from the nakedness of an unqualified statement. If the report of an accident says that about a hundred people were taken to hospital but comparatively few were detained, that is a proper use of the adverb. But when a circular says that "our diminishing stocks will be expended in a relatively short period", without mentioning any other period with which to compare it, the word signifies nothing.

Sometimes the use of a dressing-gown adverb actually makes the writer say the opposite of what he intended. The writer of the circular which said, "It is not necessary to be unduly meticulous in . . . " meant to say "you need not be meticulous", but what he actually said was "you must be meticulous but need not be unduly so", leaving the reader to guess when the limit of dueness in meticulousness has been reached.

Undue and *unduly* seem to be words that have the property of taking the reason prisoner. "There is no cause for undue alarm" is a phrase I have seen used in all sorts of circumstances by all sorts of people, from a Government spokesman about the plans of the enemy to a headmistress on the occurrence of a case of poliomyelitis. It is I suppose, legitimate to say "Don't be unduly alarmed", though I should not myself find much reassurance in it. But "there is no

E

cause for undue alarm" differs little, if at all, from "there is no
cause for alarm for which there is no cause", and that hardly seems
worth saying. Unduly has of course its own proper job to do, and
does it in such a sentence as "The speech was not unduly long for so
important an occasion".

As some adjectives seem to attract unnecessary adverbs, so do
some nouns unnecessary adjectives. I have mentioned *consideration*'s
fondness for the company of *active*, and I shall later refer to the
inseparable companionship of *alternative* and *accommodation*. *Danger*
is another word that is often given support it does not need, generally
real or *serious*.

> The special needs of children under 5 require as much considera-
> tion as those of the children aged 5-7, and there is a serious danger
> that they will be overlooked in these large schools. . . . There is a real
> danger . . . that the development of the children would be unduly
> forced. . . .

Here we have *serious*, *real* and *unduly* all used superfluously.
Serious is prompted by a feeling that *danger* always needs adjectival
support, and *real* is presumably what grammarians call "elegant
variation"* to avoid repeating the same word. *Unduly* is superfluous
because the word *forced* itself contains the idea of undue. *Real* danger
should be reserved for contrast with imaginary danger, as, for
instance, "Some people fear so-and-so but the real danger is so-and-
so". These things may seem trivial, but nothing is negligible that is
a symptom of loose thinking.

Vague adjectives of intensification like *considerable*, *appreciable* and
substantial are too popular. None of these three should be used
without three questions being asked. Do I need an adjective at
all? If so, would not a more specific adjective suit better? Or, failing
that, which of these three (with their different shades of meaning) is most apt? If those who write "This is a matter of considerable
urgency" were to ask themselves this question, they would realise
that "This is urgent" serves them better; and those who write "A
programme of this magnitude will necessarily take a considerable
period" will find it more effective to say "a long time". Strong words
like *urgent*, *danger*, *crisis*, *disaster*, *fatal*, *grave*, *paramount* and *essential*
lose their force if used too often. Reserve them for strong occasions,
and then let them stand on their own legs, without adjectival or
adverbial support.

It would be a fairly safe bet that the word *respectively* is used
unnecessarily or wrongly in legal and official writings more often

---

*See p. 145.

than any other word in the language. It has one simple straight-forward use, and that is to link up subjects and objects where more than one is used with a single verb. Thus, if I say "Men and women wear trousers and skirts" you are left in doubt which wears which— which indeed is no more than the truth nowadays. But if you add the word *respectively* you allot the trousers to the men and skirts to the women. It can also be used harmlessly in a distributive sense, as in the sentence "Local Authorities should survey the needs of their respective areas". But it contributes nothing to the sense; there is no risk of Local Authorities thinking that they are being told to survey one another's areas. Anyway it is neater to write "Each Local Authority should survey the needs of its area". *Respective* and *respectively* are used wrongly or unnecessarily far more often than they are used rightly, and I advise you to leave them alone. You can always get on without them. Even in the example I gave you just now you can say "Men wear trousers and women skirts", which has the advantage of being crisper and therefore better English. Here is a sentence in which the writer has fallen into one of the many traps set by this capricious word. He has tried to make it distribute two things among three, and so left the reader guessing.

> The Chief Billeting Officer of the Local Authority, the Regional Welfare Officer of the Ministry of Health, and the Local Officer of the Ministry of Labour and National Service will be able to supplement the knowledge of the Authority on the needs arising out of evacuation and the employment of women respectively.

It is as though one were to say "Men and women wear trousers and skirts and knickers respectively". Who has the knickers?

But any excessive fondness the official may have for *respective* and *respectively* is as nothing compared with the fascination they exercise on lawyers. These are the opening words of a coal-mining lease:

> This indenture witnesseth that in consideration of the rents reservations and covenants hereinafter respectively reserved and contained they the said A, B and C according to their several and respective shares estates rights and interests do hereby grant to the W. Company the several mines of coal called respectively X, Y and Z and also the liberty to lay down any tramroads railroads or other roads and to connect such roads trams and railroads respectively with any other roads of similar character respectively.

Six in this small compass, with none of them doing any good, and some positive harm! The draftsman seems to have used the word in much the same way as the psalmist uses *Selah*; he just puts it in light-heartedly when he feels that he has been long enough without one.

Here is a recent example, taken from a departmental circular, of the magnetism of this word:

> Owing to the special difficulty of an apportionment of expenditure between (1) dinners and (2) other meals and refreshments respectively. . . .

Having taken elaborate care so to arrange the sentence as to make *respectively* unnecessary, the writer found the lure of it irresistible after all.

Definite and *definitely* must be a good second to *respective* and *respectively* in any competition for the lead in adjectives and adverbs used unnecessarily. It can hardly be supposed that the adverb in the injunction—"Local Authorities should be definitely discouraged from committing themselves"—would make any difference to the official who has to carry it out; the distinction between discouraging a Local Authority definitely and merely discouraging it is too fine for most of us. Other examples are:

> This is definitely harmful to the workers' health.
> The recent action of the committee in approving the definite appointment of four home visitors.
> This has caused two definite spring breakages to loaded vehicles.

"Where is this to stop?" asks Sir Alan Herbert. "*Definite* and *definitely* can be slipped in almost anywhere. I offer a prize to the first Foreman of a jury to announce a verdict of *definitely guilty* and another to the judge who informs the prisoner that he will be 'definitely hanged by the neck until he is very definitely dead'."

It is wise to be sparing of *very*. If it is used too freely it ceases to have any meaning; it must be used with discrimination to be effective. Other adverbs of intensification, like *necessarily* and *inevitably*, are also apt to do more harm than good unless you want to lay stress on the element of necessity or inevitability. An automatic *inevitably*, contributing nothing to the sense, is common:

> The Committees will inevitably have a part to play in the development of the service.
> The ultimate power of control which flows inevitably from the agency relationship.

Irresistibly reminded is on the way to becoming a cliché, specially useful to after-dinner speakers who want to drag in an irrelevant story, but by no means confined to them.

Other intrusive words are *incidentally*, *specific* and *particular*. In conversation, *incidentally* (like *actually* and *definitely*) is often a noise without meaning; in writing it is an apology for irrelevance, sometimes unnecessary or even ambiguous:

> Dennis Brain will play horn concertos by Haydn and Mozart, both incidentally written to order.

Incidentally to the announcer's announcement or to the composer's career?

Particular intrudes (though perhaps more in a certain type of oratory than in writing) as an unnecessary reinforcement of a demonstrative pronoun:

> No arrangements have yet been made regarding moneys due to this particular country.
>
> We would point out that availabilities of this particular material are extremely limited.
>
> On the same day on which you advised the Custodian of the existence of this particular debt.

So much fun has been made of the common use of *literally* in the sense of "not literally but metaphorically" that it is perhaps hardly worth while to make more. But it would be a pity not to record some of the choicer blossoms from a recent flowering of this perennial in the correspondence columns of *The Times*.

> (In an account of a tennis match) Miss X literally wiped the floor with her opponent.
>
> (A comment by *Punch* on a statement in a newspaper that throughout a certain debate Mr. Gladstone had sat "literally glued to the Treasury Bench ") "That's torn it" said the Grand Old Man, as he literally wrenched himself away to dinner.
>
> (Of a certain horse) It literally ran away with the Two Thousand Guineas.
>
> (Of a rackets player) He literally blasted his opponent out of the court.
>
> M. Clemenceau literally exploded during the argument.
>
> He literally died in harness.

VERBOSITY IN PREPOSITIONS

In all utility writing today, official and commercial, the simple prepositions we have in such abundance tend to be forgotten and replaced by groups of words more imposing perhaps, but less precise. The commonest of these groups are:

> As regards
> As to
> In connexion with
> In regard to
> In relation to
> In respect of
> In the case of
> Relative to
> With reference to
> With regard to

They are useful in their proper places, but they are generally made to serve merely as clumsy devices to save a writer the labour of selecting the right preposition. In the collection that follows the right preposition is added in brackets:

A firm timetable *in relation to* the works to be undertaken should be drawn up (for).

It has been necessary to cause many dwellings to be disinfested of vermin, particularly *in respect of* the common bed-bug (of).

The Authority are fully conscious of their responsibilities *in regard to* the preservation of amenities (for).

It will be necessary to decide the priority which should be given to nursery provision *in relation to* other forms of education provision (over).

The rates vary *in relation to* the age of the child (with).

Coupons without restrictions *as to* how you should spend (on).

There may be difficulties *with regard to* the provision of suitable staff (in).

Similar considerations apply *with regard to* application for a certificate (to).

The best possible estimate will be made at the conference *as to* the total number of houses which can be completed in each district during the year (of).

As to deserves special mention because it leads writers astray in other ways besides making them forget the right preposition. It may tempt them into a more elaborate circumlocution:

The operation is a severe one as to the after-effects. (The after-effects of the operation are severe.)

It is no concern of the Ministry as to the source of the information. (The source of the information is no concern of the Ministry.)

As to also has a way of intruding itself where it is not wanted, especially before such words as *whether, who, what, how*. All the following examples are better without *as to*:

Doubt has been expressed as to whether these rewards are sufficient.

I have just received an enquiry as to whether you have applied for a supplement to your pension.

I am to ask for some explanation as to why so small a sum was realised on sale.

I will look into the question as to whether you are liable.

As to serves a useful purpose at the beginning of a sentence by way of introducing a fresh subject:

As to your liability for previous years, I will go into this and write further to you.

VERBOSITY IN ADVERBIAL AND OTHER PHRASES

Certain words beget verbosity. Among them are the following: *Case* and *instance*. The sins of *case* are well known; it has been said that there is perhaps no single word so freely resorted to as a trouble-saver and consequently responsible for so much flabby writing.

Here are some examples to show how what might be a simple and straightforward statement becomes enmeshed in the coils of phrases formed with *case*:

> The cost of maintenance of the building would be higher than was the case with a building of traditional construction. (The cost of maintenance of the building would be higher than that of a building of traditional construction.)
>
> That country is not now so short of sterling as was formerly the case. (As it used to be.)
>
> Since the officiating president in the case of each major institute takes up his office on widely differing dates. (Since the officiating presidents of the major institutes take up office on widely differing dates.)
>
> The National Coal Board is an unwieldy organisation, in many cases quite out of touch with the coalfields.

It is not easy to guess the meaning of this last example.

This trick use of *case* is even worse when the reader might be misled, if only momentarily, into thinking that a material case was meant:

> Cases have thus arisen in which goods have been exported without the knowledge of this Commission.
>
> Water for domestic use is carried by hand in many cases from road standpipes.

There are, of course, many legitimate uses of the word, and writers should not be frightened away from it altogether by Quiller-Couch's much-quoted and rather overdone onslaught. There are, for instance (to borrow from Fowler):

> A case of measles.
> You have no case.
> In case of need, or fire, or other emergency.
> A case of burglary or other crime.
> A law case of any sort.
> Circumstances alter cases.

But do not say "that is not the case" when you mean "that is not so", or "It is not the case that I wrote that letter", when you mean "It is not true that I wrote that letter", or merely "I did not write that letter".

Instance beguiles writers in the same way as *case* into roundabout ways of saying simple things:

> In the majority of instances the houses are three-bedroom. (Most of the houses are three-bedroom.)
> Most of the factories are modern, but in a few instances the plant is obsolete. (In a few of them.)

In the first instance can generally be replaced by *first*.

Another such word is *Concerned* in the phrase *as far as . . . is concerned*. A correspondent has written asking me to

> scarify the phrase "so far as . . . is concerned", e.g. "the war is over so far as Germany is concerned", an actual instance; or "so far as he was concerned interest in the game was over". After long and vigilant watch I have still to find a case in which a single preposition would not be clearer as well as shorter. I suspect that my fellow-journalists are more addicted to this use of the phrase than civil servants; but these are not guiltless.

It is perhaps putting the case too high to say that "so far as . . . is concerned" could always be replaced by a single preposition. I do not think that the phrase can be dispensed with by those who wish to emphasise that they have blinkers on, and are concerned only with one aspect of a question. "So far as I am concerned you may go home" implies that someone else has a say too. Or again:

> So far as the provisions of the Trading with the Enemy Act are concerned, the sum so released may . . . be utilised to reimburse you for expenses. . . .

There is no other equally convenient way of making clear that the writer is removing only the impediment created by the Act and is not concerned with any other impediment there may be.

Possibly, though less certainly, this sentence might claim the same indulgence:

> The effect of the suggested system, so far as the pharmaceutical industry is concerned, would be to ensure rewards for research and development work until the new preparations were absorbed into the B.P.

It might be argued that we should not get quite the same meaning from "on the pharmaceutical industry"; this destroys the suggestion that there may be other effects, but the writer is not concerning himself with them.

But these are exceptions. There is no doubt that the phrase is generally a symptom of muddled thinking:

> Some were opposed to hanging as a means of execution where women were concerned. (As a means of executing women.)

Wood pulp manufacture on a commercial scale is a very recent development so far as time is concerned. (Omit the last six words.)

The punishments at their disposal may not be of very serious effect so far as the persons punished are concerned. (on the persons punished.)

That is a matter which should be borne in mind because it does rule out a certain amount of consideration so far as the future is concerned.

I cannot translate this with any confidence. Perhaps it means "That is a matter which should be borne in mind because it circumscribes our recommendations for the future".

The fact that is an expression sometimes necessary and proper, but sometimes a clumsy way of saying what might be said more simply. When it is preceded by *in view of* or *owing to* or *in spite of* it may be merely an intricate way of saying *because* or *although*.

Owing to the fact that the exchange is working to full capacity. (Because the exchange . . .)

The delay in replying has been due to the fact that it was hoped to arrange for a representative to call upon you. (I delayed replying because I hoped to arrange for a representative to call on you.)

So too *until such time as* is usually merely a verbose way of saying *until*. It may be useful to convey a suggestion that the event contemplated is improbable or remote or has no direct connection with what is to last until it occurs. But it cannot do so in

You will be able to enjoy these facilities until such time that he terminates his agreement.

If the phrase is used, it should be *such time as*, not, as here, *such time that*.

There cannot, I think, ever be any justification for preferring the similar phrase *during such time as* to *while*.

As has other sins of superfluity imputed to it, besides the help it gives in building up verbose prepositions and conjunctions. (See pp. 63/4.) Dr. Ballard writes:

The word *as* has acquired a wide vogue in official circles. Wherever *as* can be put in, in it goes. A man in the public service used to draw his salary from a certain date; now he draws it as from a certain date. Time was when officials would refer to "the relationship between one department and another"; now they call it "the relationship as between one department and another". Agenda papers too often include as an item: "to consider as to the question of". If this sort of interpolation between the verb and its object were extended to ordinary speech, a man would no longer "eat his dinner" but "eat as to his dinner"; or, to make the parallel complete, "eat as to the diet of his dinner".

There is reason in saying, of a past date, "these allowances will be payable as from the 1st January last", but there is none in saying, of a future date, "these allowances will cease to be payable as from the 1st July next". "On the 1st July" is all that is needed. The phrase "as and from", not unknown, is gibberish.

As such is sometimes used in a way that seems to have no meaning:

> The statistics, as such, add little to our information.

If they do not do so as statistics, in what capacity do they? The writer probably meant "by themselves".

> There is no objection to the sale of houses as such.

Here the context shows the writer to have meant that there was no objection of principle to the sale of houses.

Certain pairs of words have a way of keeping company without being able to do any more together than either could have done separately. *Save and except* seems to have had its day, but we still have with us *as and when*, *if and when* and *unless and until*. *As and when* can be perhaps defended when used of something that will happen piecemeal ("Interim reports will be published as and when they are received"). Nothing can be said for the use of the pair in such a sentence as:

> As and when the Bill becomes an Act guidance will be given on the financial provisions of it as they affect hospital maintenance.

Bills cannot become Acts piecemeal.

If and when might plead that both are needed in such a sentence as "Further cases will be studied if and when the material is available", arguing that *if* alone will not do because the writer wants to emphasise that material becoming available will be studied immediately, and *when* alone will not do because it is uncertain whether the material ever will be available. But this is all rather subtle, and the wise course will almost always be to decide which conjunction suits you better, and to use it alone. I have not been able to find (or to imagine) the use of *unless and until* in any context in which one of the two would not have sufficed alone.

Point of view, *viewpoint*, *standpoint* and *angle*, useful and legitimate in their proper places, are sometimes no more than a refuge from the trouble of precise thought, and provide clumsy ways of saying something that could be said more simply and effectively. They are used, for instance, as a circumlocution for a simple adverb, such as "from a temporary point of view" for "temporarily". Here are a few examples:

He may lack the most essential qualities from the viewpoint of the Teaching Hospitals. (He may lack the most essential qualities for work in a Teaching Hospital.)

I can therefore see no reason why we need to see these applications, apart from an information point of view. (Except for information.)

This may be a source of embarrassment to the Regional Board from the viewpoint of overall planning and administration. (This is a particularly bad one. The plain way of putting it is: "This may embarrass the Regional Board in planning and administration".)

"Bare boards are unsatisfactory from every angle." (in every respect)

"From a cleaning point of view there are advantages in tables being of a uniform height." (for cleaning)

This development is attractive from the point of view of the public convenience. (This, I am told, provoked a marginal comment: "What is it like looking in the opposite direction?")

Aspect is the complement of *point of view*. As one changes one's point of view one sees a different aspect of what one is looking at. It is therefore natural that *aspect* should lead writers into the same traps as do *point of view*, *viewpoint* and *standpoint*. It induces writers, through its vagueness, to prefer it to more precise words, and it lends itself to woolly circumlocution. I cannot believe that there was any clear conception in the head of the official who wrote, "They must accept responsibility for the more fundamental aspects of the case". *Aspect* is one of the words that should not be used without deliberation, and it should be rejected if its only function is to make a clumsy paraphrase of an adverb.

VERBOSITY IN AUXILIARY VERBS

Various methods are in vogue for softening the curtness of *will not* or *cannot*. The commonest are *is not prepared to*, *is not in a position to*, *does not see his way to* and *cannot consider*. Such phrases as these are no doubt dictated by politeness, and therefore deserve respect. But they must be used with discretion. The recipient of a letter may feel better—though I doubt it—if he is told that the Minister "is not prepared to approve" than he would have done if the letter had said "the Minister does not approve". But there is not even this slender justification for the phrase if what he is told is that the Minister *is* prepared to approve.

The Board have examined your application and they are prepared to allocate 60 coupons for this production. I am accordingly to enclose this number of coupons. . . .

Prepared to allocate should be *have allocated*. Since the coupons are enclosed, the preparatory stage is clearly over.

But there is a legitimate use of *prepared to*, as in the following:

> In order to meet the present need, the Secretary of State is pre-
> pared to approve the temporary appointment of persons without
> formal qualifications.

Here the Secretary of State is awaiting candidates, prepared to
approve them if they turn out all right. But the phrase should never
be used in actually giving approval; it is silly, and if the habit takes
hold it will lead to such absurdities as

> I have to acknowledge your letter of the 16th June and in reply
> I am prepared to inform you that I am in communication with the
> solicitors concerned in this matter.

There are other dangers in these phrases. They may breed by
analogy verbiage that is mere verbiage and cannot call on politeness
to justify its existence. You may find yourself writing that the
Minister *will take steps to* when all you mean is he *will*, or that he will
cause investigation to be made with a view to ascertaining, when what you
mean is that he will *find out*. *Take steps to* is not always to be condemned. It is a reasonable way of expressing the beginning of a
gradual process, as in:

> Steps are now being taken to acquire this land.

But it is inapposite, because of its literal incongruity, in such a
sentence as:

> All necessary steps should be taken to maintain the present position.

There is a danger that some of these phrases may suggest un-
desirable ideas to the flippant. To be told that the Minister is
"not in a position to approve" may excite a desire to retort that he
might try putting his feet on the mantelpiece and see if that does any
good. The retort will not, of course, be made, but you should not
put ideas of that sort about your Minister into people's heads.
Pompous old phrases must be allowed to die if they collapse under
the prick of ridicule. Traditional expressions such as "I am to
request you to move your Minister to do so-and-so" and "The
Minister cannot conceal from himself" now run the risk of conjuring
up risible pictures—the one of physical pressure applied to a bulky
and inert object and the other of an honest man's prolonged and
painful struggle in unsuccessful self-deception.

VERBOSITY IN PHRASAL VERBS

The English language likes to tack a preposition to a simple verb
and so to create a verb with a different meaning. Verbs thus
formed have been called by Logan Pearsall Smith, following

Bradley, "phrasal verbs". This habit of inventing phrasal verbs has been the source of great enrichment of the language. Pearsall Smith says:

> From them we derive thousands of vivid colloquialisms and idiomatic phrases by means of which we describe the greatest variety of human actions and relations. We can take *to* people, take them *up*, take them *down*, take them *off* or take them *in*; keep *in* with them, keep them *down* or *off* or *on* or *under*; get *at* them or *round* them or *on with* them; do *for* them, do *with* them or *without* them, and do them *in*; make *up to* them; set them *up* or *down* or hit them *off*—indeed there is hardly any action or attitude of one human being to another which cannot be expressed by means of these phrasal verbs.

But there is today a tendency to form phrasal verbs to express a meaning no different from that of the verb without the particle. To do this is to debase the language, not to enrich it. Mr. Henry Strauss has protested in a letter to *The Times*:

> Must this government of illiterate exhortation continue to destroy the King's English? Must industries be fully "manned up" rather than "manned"? Must the strong, simple transitive verb, which is one of the main glories of our tongue, become as obsolete in England as it appears to be in America? There (or at least in Hollywood) you never meet a man, you "meet up with" him; you never visit friends, you "visit with" them; you never study a subject, you "study up on it".

Drown out, sound out, lose out, rest up, miss out on, are other examples of phrasal verbs which I am told are used in America in senses no different from that of the unadorned verb. These have so far found little favour in this country. On the other hand we seem to have welcomed the newcomer *measure up to* in the sense of to be adequate to an occasion: it conforms to our own practice of adding particles to give a verb a different meaning.

PADDING

All forms of verbosity might be described as padding, and the topic overlaps others we shall come to in the chapters on choosing the familiar word and choosing the precise word. I use *padding* here as a label for the type of verbosity Sir Winston Churchill referred to in a memorandum entitled "Brevity" that he issued as Prime Minister on the 9th August 1940. He wrote:

> Let us have an end of such phrases as these:
> "It is also of importance to bear in mind the following considerations . . ." or "consideration should be given to the possibility of carrying into effect. . . ." Most of these woolly phrases are mere padding, which can be left out altogether, or replaced by a single word. Let us not shrink from using the short expressive phrase even if it is conversational.

"Padding" then in the sense in which Sir Winston used the word consists of clumsy and obtrusive stitches on what ought to be a smooth fabric of consecutive thought. No doubt it comes partly from a feeling that wordiness is an ingredient of politeness, and blunt statement is crude, if not rude. There is an element of truth in this: an over-staccato style is as irritating as an over-sostenuto one. But it is a matter of degree; and official prose is of the sort that calls for plainness rather than elegance. Moreover the habit of "padding" springs partly from less meritorious notions—that the dignity of an official's calling demands a certain verbosity, and that naked truth is indecent and should be clothed in wrappings of woolly words.

Sir Winston gave two common examples based on *consideration*; he might equally well have chosen phrases based on *appreciate*. *It is appreciated that* (anticipating an objection that is to be met) and *it will be appreciated that* (introducing a reason for a decision that is to be given) are very prevalent. They can almost always be omitted without harm to the sense. (For more about *appreciate* see p. 109.)

I have already referred (p. 22) to one way in which padding shows itself in official letters. Each paragraph is thought to need introductory words—"I am to add"; "I am further to observe"; "I am moreover to remark"; "Finally I am to point out"; and so forth. Here is the same phenomenon in a circular sending a form for a statistical return:

(i) *It should be noted that* the particulars of expenditure . . . relate to gross costs.

(ii) *It is appreciated that* owing to staffing difficulties Local Authorities may not find it possible on this occasion to complete Tables. . . .

(iii) *It will be noted that* in Tables . . . the only overhead expenditure . . . which the Authorities are asked to isolate is. . . .

(iv) Table 4 . . . is intended to provide a broad picture.

The words italicised in the first three paragraphs are padding. They are no more needed there than in paragraph (iv), where the writer has wisely done without them. Perhaps he felt that he had run out of stock.

Other examples:

I am prepared to accept the discharge of this account by payment in instalments, but *it should be pointed out that* no further service can be allowed until the account is again in credit.

The opportunity is taken to mention that it is understood. . . . .

I regret that the wrong form was forwarded. *In the circumstances* I am forwarding a superseding one.

It should be noted that there is a possibility of a further sale.

This form of padding deserves special mention because the

temptation affects officials more than most people, and because it is comparatively easy to resist. It shows itself more plainly than other more subtle temptations to pad. For the rest, padding can be defined as the use of words, phrases and even sentences that contribute nothing to the reader's perception of the writer's meaning. Some seem to be specially tempting to writers. I have mentioned *consideration* and *appreciate;* among other seductive phrases are *in this connexion* and *for your information*. These have their proper uses, but are more often found as padding cliches. In none of the following examples do they serve any other purpose.

> I am directed to refer to the travelling and subsistence allowances applicable to your Department, and in this connexion I am to say . . .
> Mr. X is an applicant for appointment as a clerk in this Department and in this connexion I shall be glad if you will complete the attached form.
> The Minister's views in general in this connexion and the nature and scope of the information which he felt would assist him in this connexion was indicated at a meeting. . . .
> For your information this machine is required for the above-mentioned power station.
> For your information I should perhaps explain that there is still a shortage of materials.
> For your information I would inform you that it will be necessary for you to approach the local Agricultural Executive Committee.

This last example, taken from a letter I received myself, shows up the futility of this curious cliché. It was not even true that I was being told this "for information"; "for action" would have been more appropriate.

Of course is another adverbial phrase that needs watching lest it should creep in as padding. In journalism, especially of the gossip kind, *of course* is used to impress readers by showing the writer's familiarity with an out-of-the-way piece of information or with the families of great personages. The official, if he overworks the phrase, is more likely to do so from genuine humility. He puts it in so as not to seem didactic: "Don't think that I suppose you to be so stupid that you don't already know or infer what I am telling you, but I think I ought to mention it". Sometimes *of course* is wisely used for this purpose—if, for instance, the writer has good reason to say something so obvious as to make a touchy reader feel that he is being treated like a fool. It is better in such circumstances to say "of course" than its pompous variant "as you are doubtless aware". *Of course* might with advantage have been used in:

> It may be stated with some confidence that though it is possible for a blister-gas bomb to fall in a crater previously made by an H.E. bomb, the probability of such an occurrence is small.

In this example *It may be stated with some confidence that* is not only padding but also an absurdity. One might say with some confidence that this will not happen, or with complete confidence that it is improbable. But to feel only some confidence about its improbability is carrying intellectual timidity almost to imbecility.

The following extracts from two documents issued by the same Ministry about the same time are instructive.

The first is:

> I am to add that, doubtless, local authorities appreciate that it is a matter of prime importance that information about possible breaches of Defence Regulation . . . should reach the investigating officers of the Ministry . . . with the minimum of delay.

The second is:

> After six years of war almost every building in this country needs work doing to it. The whole of the building labour force could be employed on nothing else but repairs and maintenance. Yet there are hundreds of thousands of families who urgently need homes of their own and will keep on suffering great hardship until houses can be provided for them.

The first of these is bad. It is the sort of thing that those who say civil servants write badly point to in support of their case. The first 18 of its 38 words are padding, and the last five are a starchy paraphrase of "as soon as possible". The second is excellent. It has no padding, and says what it has to say in brisk businesslike English. Why this difference of style within the same Department? We can only guess, but I do not think the guess is difficult. The first was written for the guidance of Local Government officials only. It was a routine matter and no special care was taken over it; its language is the sort that Local Authorities expect and understand. But the second was intended to impress the man in the street, and the writer was at pains to put his point in a way that would be grasped at once and would carry conviction. That is, I have no doubt, the explanation, but it is not a sufficient one. Whatever the purpose, the first is bad and the second good.

The following introductory sentence to a circular is, I think, wholly padding, but I cannot be sure, for I can find no meaning in it.

> The proposals made in response to this request show differences of approach to the problem which relate to the differing recommendations of the Committee's Report, and include some modifications of those recommendations.

But padding is too multifarious for analysis. It can only be illustrated, and the only rule for avoiding it is to be self-critical.

VII

The Choice of Words (3)

CHOOSING THE FAMILIAR WORD

Literary men, and the young still more than the old of this class, have commonly a good deal to rescind in their style in order to adapt it to business. But the young, if they be men of sound abilities, will soon learn what is not apt and discard it; which the old will not. The leading rule is to be content to be commonplace—a rule which might be observed with advantage in other writings, but is distinctively applicable to these.

HENRY TAYLOR, *The Statesman*, 1836

BOSWELL tells of Johnson: "He seemed to take pleasure in speaking in his own style; for when he had carelessly missed it, he would repeat the thought translated into it. Talking of the comedy of 'The Rehearsal', he said, 'It has not wit enough to keep it sweet'. This was easy—he therefore caught himself, and pronounced a more round sentence; 'It has not vitality enough to preserve it from putrefaction'." The mind of another famous lover of the rotund phrase worked the opposite way. "'Under the impression', said Mr. Micawber, 'that your peregrinations in this metropolis have not as yet been extensive, and that you might have some difficulty in penetrating the arcana of the Modern Babylon . . . in short', said Mr. Micawber in a burst of confidence, 'that you might lose your way . . .'." The official should not hesitate which of these remarkable men to take as his model. He should cultivate Mr. Micawber's praiseworthy habit of instinctively translating the out-of-the-way into the everyday.* Thus we might find that, even though the Board of Trade could still not resist announcing that certain surplus Government factories are now "available for reallocation", they would not leave it at that. "In short", they would add in a burst of confidence, "they are to be relet".

The present inclination of the official is in the opposite direction. He is a Johnsonian rather than a Micawberite, and so handicaps himself in achieving what we have seen must be the writer's primary object, to affect the reader precisely as he wishes. The simple reader is puzzled; the sophisticated one is annoyed. Here is pent-up

---

*I was reminded of Mr. Micawber's praiseworthy habit by the footnote on p. 128 of Jespersen's *Growth and Structure of the English Language*.

annoyance blowing off a genial jet of steam in the leading columns of *The Times*:

It has always been the custom of the English to enrich their language with importations from abroad, and a similar policy has variegated their gardens, their forests and their fauna. Their taste in exotics has in the main been sound enough and where, here and there down the generations, a lapse has occurred its consequences have rarely been far-reaching. If the affection which some of our forefathers felt for the monkey-puzzle seems to us now misplaced, we are not greatly incommoded by its after-effects; no jungles of this spiderish growth have sprung up to hem us in. If we think that "boudoir" is a rather sickly, simpering word, or "portmanteau" not fit for use except in limericks about young men of Taranto, we can drop them without difficulty from our vocabulary.

But some foreign importations have shown a terrifying and uncontrollable vitality, so that the sins of their original sponsors are visited with dreadful rigour upon succeeding generations. The kindly nature-lover who first liberated a pair of grey squirrels has a great deal to answer for, including a large share of the salaries of numerous civil servants engaged on the task known to them, rather hopefully, as pest-elimination. In the etymological field a similar bad eminence is reserved in the minds of all right-thinking men, for the individual who first introduced into the English language the word "personnel". It is possible, just possible, that a more degrading, a more ill-favoured synonym for two or more members of the human race has at one time or another been coined; but, if it has, it has never gained the ubiquitous and tyrannical currency of this alien collective. Personnel, though in theory they are men and women, have only to be called personnel to lose their full status as human beings. They do not go, they proceed. They do not have, they are (or more often are not) in possession of. They do not ask, they make application for. Their minds, in so far as they may be deemed to have minds, are stocked not with the glories of knowledge but with irrelevant and unmemorable statistics, such as their father's nationality at birth and the date on which they were last inoculated against yellow fever. Once they either kept things or gave them up; now they must retain or surrender them. Want (it is true) they do not know, nor need; but deficiencies and requirements are just as inconvenient. They cannot eat, they can only consume; they perform ablutions; instead of homes they have place(s) of residence in which, instead of living, they are domiciled. They are not cattle, they are not ciphers, they certainly are not human beings; they are personnel.

It would be churlish to accuse an onslaught so disarming of not being quite fair. But may it not be argued that when we admitted women auxiliaries to our armed forces the expression "men and material" became unsuitable; we found a gap in our vocabulary and sensibly filled it, as we have so often done before, by borrowing from the French? Still, it cannot be denied that this word, like so many other high-sounding words of vague import, has exercised an unfortunate fascination over the official mind, or that the other examples given by the writer of the article strike home. The mischief of words of this sort is that they become such favourites that they seduce their users from clarity of thought; they mesmerise them and numb their discrimination.

The precept to choose the familiar word (which is also probably the short word) must of course be followed with discretion. Many wise men throughout the centuries, from Aristotle to Sir Winston Churchill, have emphasised the importance of using short and simple words. But no one knew better than these two authorities that sacrifice either of precision or of dignity is too high a price to pay for the familiar word. If the choice is between two words that convey a writer's meaning equally well, one short and familiar and the other long and unusual, of course the short and familiar should be preferred. But one that is long and unusual should not be rejected merely on that account if it is more apt in meaning. Sir Winston does not hesitate to prefer the uncommon word if there is something to be gained by it. If we were asked whether there was any difference in meaning between *woolly* and *flocculent* we should probably say no; one was commonplace and the other unusual, and that was all there was to it. But Sir Winston, in the first volume of his *Second World War*, uses *flocculent* instead of *woolly* to describe the mental processes of certain people, and so conveys to his readers just that extra ounce of contempt that we feel *flocculent* to contain, perhaps because the combination of *f* and *l* so often expresses an invertebrate state, as in *flop*, *flap*, *flaccid*, *flimsy*, *flabby* and *filleted*. Moreover there is an ugliness of shortness as well as an ugliness of length. On the same day in different daily papers I have seen the same official referred to as "Administrator of the Organisation for European Economic Co-operation" and as "Aid Boss". Neither title is euphonious, and few would unhesitatingly prefer the short one.

But there are no great signs at present of any urgent need of a warning not to overdo the use of simple diction. The commonest ways in which failure to choose the simple word in official writing leads to lack of precision are the use of jargon and legal language and an addiction to showy words.

JARGON AND LEGAL LANGUAGE

A dictionary definition of jargon is "a word applied contemptuously to the language of scholars, the terminology of a science or art, or the cant of a class, sect, trade or profession". When it was confined to that sense it was a useful word. But it has been handled so promiscuously of recent years that the edge has been taken off it, and now, as has been well said, it signifies little more than any speech that a person feels to be inferior to his own. I am here using the word in the dictionary sense. In that sense its growth of late has been alarming. Modern discoveries in the older sciences and the need of the newer ones (economics, psychology and sociology) to explain their ideas have led to an enormous increase in that part of our vocabulary that can be classed as jargon. No doubt this is to some extent inevitable. New concepts may demand new words: psychology can at least plead that if a new word is necessary for what my most recent dictionary defines as "the sum total of the instinctive forces of an individual", a less pretentious one could hardly have been found than *id*; never can so much meaning have been packed into so small a space since the sentence."Thy kingdom is divided and given to the Medes and Persians" was compressed into the word *Upharsin*. But I find Dr. Julian Huxley refreshing when he says:

> We need a term for the sum of these continuities through the whole of evolutionary time, and I prefer to take over a familiar word like *progress* instead of coining a special piece of esoteric jargon.

In the field of neurology Sir Francis Walshe has been provoked to a similar protest. Referring to the fondness of clinicians for inventing new words for newly-observed symptoms that may throw light on the mysteries of cerebral physiology, he says:

> Thus one phenomenon may have close on a dozen neologisms attached to it, and these are not always used with precision. All this has made for confusion, for it needs heroic virtues to plunge into the muddy waters of the relevant literature to pluck out truth from their depths.

"Really there are times", writes Mr. G. M. Young sadly, "when I feel that civilisation will come to an end because no one will understand what anybody else is saying."

Official writing plays a comparatively small part in building this new Tower of Babel. But it cannot escape all blame. When officials are accused of writing jargon, what is generally meant is that they affect a pompous and flabby verbosity. That is not what I mean. What I have in mind is that technical terms are used—especially conventional phrases invented by a Government department— which are understood inside the department but are unintelligible to outsiders. That is true jargon. A circular from the headquarters of a department to its regional officers begins:

> The physical progressing of building cases should be confined to ...

Nobody could say what meaning this was intended to convey unless he held the key. It is not English, except in the sense that the words are English words. They are a group of symbols used in conventional senses known only to the parties to the convention. It may be said that no harm is done, because the instruction is not meant to be read by anyone unfamiliar with the departmental jargon. But using jargon is a dangerous habit; it is easy to forget that the public do not understand it, and to slip into the use of it in explaining things to them. If that is done, those seeking enlightenment will find themselves plunged in even deeper obscurity. A member of the department has kindly given me this interpretation of the words quoted above, qualified by the words "as far as I can discover":

" 'The physical progressing of building cases' means going at intervals to the sites of factories, etc., whose building is sponsored by the department and otherwise approved to see how many bricks have been laid since the last visit. 'Physical' apparently here exemplifies a portmanteau usage (? syllepsis) and refers both to the flesh-and-blood presence of the inspector and to the material development of the edifice, neither of which is, however, mentioned. 'Progressing', I gather, should have the accent on the first syllable and should be distinguished from pro*gres*sing. It means recording or helping forward the progress rather than going forward. 'Cases' is the common term for units of work which consist of applying a given set of rules to a number of individual problems . . . 'should be confined to' means that only in the types of cases specified may an officer leave his desk to visit the site."

Let us take another example. "Distribution of industry policy" is an expression well understood in the Board of Trade and other departments concerned with the subject. But it is jargon. Intrinsically the phrase has no certain meaning. Not even its grammatical construction is clear. So far as the words go, it is at least as likely that it refers to distributing something called "industry-policy" as to a policy of distributing industry. Even when we know that "distribution-of-industry" is a compound noun-adjective qualifying *policy*, we still do not give to the words the full meaning that those who invented the phrase intended it to have. The esoteric meaning attached to it is the policy of exercising governmental control over the establishment of new factories in such a way as to minimise the risk of local mass unemployment. No doubt it is convenient to have a label for anything that can only be explained so cumbrously. But it must not be forgotten that what is written on the label consists of code symbols unintelligible to the outsider. Forgetfulness of this kind causes perplexity and irritation. A judge recently said that he could form no idea of what was meant by the sentence: "These prices are basis prices per ton for the representative-basis-pricing specification and size and quantity"; and the *Manchester Guardian* was once moved to expostulate:

> It is a pity that the Ministry of Supply's document "explaining" what is a genuine simplification should include passages of incomprehensible jargon like this:
>> The sub-authorisations required by its sub-contractors to re-authorise their orders as in (I) and (II) above. It should be borne in mind that sub-contractors may need re-authorisation not only of sub-authorisations already given for period II and beyond, but also for sub-authorisations for earlier periods, so as to revalidate orders or parts of orders as in (I).
> The sense of despair produced by this sort of thing does far more to defeat the intentions of planning than some of the departments concerned seem to realise.

Single words are sometimes given a special meaning for official purposes, especially words much used during the war. At a time when our lives were regulated at every turn by the distinction between what was and what was not "essential", that word sprouted curiously. Its development can be traced through these three quotations:

> I can only deal with applications of a highly essential nature.
> It is impossible to approve importations from the U.S.A. unless there is a compelling case of essentiality.
> It is confirmed that as a farmer you are granted high essentiality.

In the last at any rate, if not in the other two, the word has become jargon and given a meaning not known to the dictionaries. What the writer meant in the last one was, "you are high on our waiting list".

In its ordinary sense also, *essential* is frequently used unsuitably. Government departments have to issue so many instructions to all and sundry nowadays that the draftsmen of them get tired of saying that people must or should do things, and misguidedly seek to introduce the relief of variety by saying, for instance, that it is necessary or that it is important that things should be done, and from that it is only a step to work oneself up into saying that it is essential or vital or even of paramount importance. Here is an extract from a wartime departmental circular:

> In view of the national situation on the supply of textiles and buttons it is of paramount importance that these withdrawn garments shall be put to useful purposes. . . ."

To say that a thing is of paramount importance can only mean that it transcends in importance all other subjects. I cannot believe that anything to do with buttons can ever have been in that class.

Legal diction, as we have seen, is almost necessarily obscure, and explanations of the provisions of legal documents must be translated into familiar words simply arranged.

> With reference to your letter of the 12th August, I have to state in answer to question 1 thereof that where particulars of a partnership are disclosed to the Executive Council the remuneration of the individual partner for superannuation purposes will be deemed to be such proportion of the total remuneration of such practitioners as the proportion of his share in the partnership profits bears to the total proportion of the shares of such practitioner in those profits.

This is a good example of how not to explain. I think it means merely "Your income will be taken to be the same proportion of the firm's remuneration as you used to get of its profits". I may be wrong, but even so I cannot believe that language is unequal to any clearer explanation than the unfortunate correspondent received.

Here is another example of failure to shake off the shackles of legal language:

> Separate departments in the same premises are treated as separate premises for this purpose where separate branches of work which are commonly carried on as separate businesses in separate premises are carried on in separate departments in the same premises.

This sentence is constructed with that mathematical arrangement of words which lawyers adopt to make their meaning unambiguous. Worked out as one would work out an equation, the sentence serves its purpose; as literature, it is balderdash. The explanation could easily have been given in some such way as this:

> If branches of work commonly carried on as separate businesses are carried on in separate departments of the same premises, those departments will be treated as separate premises.

This shows how easily an unruly sentence like this can be reduced to order by turning part of it into an "if" clause.

Even without the corrupting influence of jargon or legal diction a careless explanation may leave the thing explained even more obscure than it was before. The *New Yorker* of the 17th August, 1948, quotes from a publication called *Systems Magazine*:

> Let us paraphrase and define work simplification as "that method of accomplishing a necessary purpose omitting nothing necessary to that purpose in the simplest fashion is best". This definition is important for it takes the mystery out of work simplification and leaves the essentials clearly outlined and succinctly stated.

The *New Yorker's* comment is: "It does indeed".

OVERWORKED METAPHORS

Those who like showy words are given to overworking metaphors. I have already (p. 49) referred to the usefulness and attractiveness of metaphors. They enable a writer to convey briefly and vividly ideas that might otherwise need tedious exposition. What should we have done, in our present economic difficulties, without our *targets*, *ceilings* and *bottlenecks*? But the very seductiveness of metaphors makes them dangerous, especially as we may be rather proud to have learned a new one and want to show off. Thus metaphors, especially new ones, tend to be used indiscriminately and soon get stale, but not before they have elbowed out words perhaps more commonplace but with meanings more precise. Sometimes metaphors are so absurdly overtaxed that they become a laughing-stock and die of ridicule. That has been the fate of "exploring every avenue" and of "leaving no stone unturned".

Another danger in the use of metaphors is of falling into incongruity. So long at least as they are "live"* metaphors, they must not be given a context that would be absurd if the words used metaphorically were being used literally. Nothing is easier to do; almost all writers fall occasionally into this trap. But it is worth while to take great pains to avoid doing so, because your reader, if he notices it, will deride you. So we should not refer to the biggest bottleneck when what we mean is the most troublesome one, for that will obviously be the narrowest. A "world-wide" bottleneck may sound alarming, but anything less constrictive can hardly be imagined. We should not speak of "extending" a ceiling when what we mean is raising it. The statesman who said that sections of the population were being squeezed flat by inflation was not then in his happiest vein, nor was the writer who claimed for American sociology the distinction of having always immersed itself in concrete situations, nor the enthusiastic scientist who announced the discovery of a virgin field pregnant with possibilities. The warning issued during a fuel shortage that gas rings might only be used by officers earmarked for the purpose suggests a curious method of identification, and the B.B.C. did not choose their words felicitously when they said that every facet of negro music would be heard that night; facets, like children, should

---

*A live metaphor is one that evokes in the reader a mental picture of the imagery of its origin; a dead one does not. If we write "the situation is in hand" and "he has taken the bit between his teeth", we are in both going to horsemanship for our metaphor. But to most readers the first would be a dead metaphor, and the sentence would have no different impact from "the situation is under control"; the second would be a live one, calling up, however faintly and momentarily, the picture of a runaway horse.

be seen not heard. We cannot but admit that there is no hope of checking the astonishing antics of *target* and of bringing that flighty word within reasonable bounds. But we do not want any more metaphors getting out of hand like that.

Among the metaphors specially popular at the present time the following deserve comment.

BACKGROUND

The O.E.D. recognises only two meanings for this word. One is "the ground or surface lying at the back of or beyond the chief objects of contemplation". The other is "a less prominent position, where an object is not readily noticed". The word has come into great favour, and is ranging a long way from the humble spheres assigned to it by the dictionary. Up to a point its extensions have been useful. To speak of examining the background of a proposal, in the sense of trying to find out what more there is in it than meets the eye, is a reasonable metaphor. So is what is called "background training" in the Civil Service to distinguish it from specialised training. And it is a reasonable extension of the metaphor to write:

> Men and women with widely divergent backgrounds, ranging from graduates and trained social workers to a coalminer, a railway clerk and a clerk in an ironmongery store, had in fact succeeded.

But, like all these new favourites, it is beginning to get out of hand, and to displace more precise words:

> From your particulars it would appear that your background is more suitable for posts in Government Departments employing quantity surveyors.

This does not seem to mean anything different from "you are better qualified".

> It is surprising to find more women than men, but local experience provides the background; during the war women left an area where there were no jobs for them.

Here it seems to be masquerading as *explanation*.

BACKLOG

The new use of *backlog* to mean an accumulation of arrears is common in the United States. For example, the list that our Telephone Department calls "List of waiting applicants" is called by the American Telephone Company "Backlog of held orders". This use is spreading here, and a Government department already finds it natural to write:

The most important step is to eliminate a very heavy backlog of orders on the manufacturers' books.

The metaphor seems to be from a log fire in which the backlog is the large log at the back that is never burned. Like *stockpile* the word is likely to establish itself here and to be regarded eventually as an enrichment of the language.

BLUEPRINT

This word has caught on as a picturesque substitute for *scheme* or *plan* and the shine is wearing off it. It is not reasonable to ask that metaphors should be anchored at their points of origin, but it would make for accuracy of language if writers who use this one remembeed that in the engineering industries, where it comes from, the blueprint marks the final stage of paper design.

BOTTLENECK

Bottleneck is a useful and picturesque metaphor to denote the point of constriction of something that ought to be flowing freely:

> Even if the manufacturers could obtain ample raw material, the shortage of skilled labour would constitute a bottleneck in production.

The metaphor is not new, but it has had a sharp rise in popularity, perhaps because our economy has been so full of bottlenecks. It needs to be handled carefully in order to avoid absurdity, as Mr. Henry Strauss pointed out in this letter to *The Times*:

> In order to illustrate the progress (or whatever it is) of our language I am compiling a brochure on bottlenecks. I shall accord ingly be grateful for any significant additions to these examples from recent journalism:
> (1) "The biggest bottleneck in housing", meaning the worst, most constricting and presumably narrowest bottleneck.
> (2) "Bottlenecks must be ironed out" (leading article in the daily press).
> (3) "Bottlenecks ahead" and "Bottleneck in bottles" (recent headlines).
> (4) "The economy of the Ruhr is bound to move within a vicious circle of interdependent bottlenecks."
> (5) "What is planned is actually a series of bottlenecks. The most drastic bottleneck is that of machine tools."
> (6) "One bottleneck . . . which is particularly far-reaching and decisive."

Mr. Strauss has recently made some additions to his collection:

> Finally, before leaving my Hon. Friend, I must thank him for adding his delightful "overriding bottleneck" to my celebrated collection of bottlenecks. Hitherto, my favourites were the "drastic

bottleneck", the "vicious circle of interdependent bottlenecks" and, perhaps the best of the whole collection, the "worldwide bottleneck".*

BRACKETS AND GROUPS

These words were put into currency by statisticians as synonyms for *class* or *category*, and they have been widely taken up. "These are likely in the main to be bought by the lower income groups." "Will the Chancellor of the Exchequer move to set up a Select Committee to consider the financial hardships of the small income groups?" *Income group* has indeed become an official cliché. Mr. Ivor Brown says of this innovation:

> The poor used to be called the poor; then they became, lest accuracy offend them, the under-privileged, or lower income groups. Recently they have been called, especially by economists aiming at style, the lower income brackets. I suppose the reference is to types and species bracketed together. But the usage is a stupid one. Somebody employed the term, I suppose, in an impressive article and so all the impressed readers decided to pay him the compliment of imitation.

Thus we are told of what used to be called naughty children but are now juvenile delinquents:

> It is some comfort to learn that the eight to thirteen bracket is the only one that involved more arrests.

BREAKDOWN

It is fashionable, though not always apt, to use *breakdown* in a pseudo-scientific sense vaguely connoting analysis, subdivision, or classification of statistical matter. It is certainly inept when used of things that can be physically broken down:

> The houses erected should be broken down into types. (classified according to type.)
> The breakdown of this number of houses into varying densities per acre. (division.)
> The Minister wishes to avoid fragmentation of the service by breaking down the two-tier system of administration provided for in the Act into a three-tier system.

Why *breaking down* in the last example? If the word *break* must be used at all *breaking up* would go better with *fragmentation*. But why not some ordinary word such as *changing, altering* or *converting*?

The fascination of this word may lead to quaint results.

> Care should be taken that the breakdown of patients by the department under whose care they were immediately before discharge is strictly followed.

---

*Hansard, 10th July 1953.

Unfortunately a complete breakdown of British trade is not possible.

Statistics have been issued of the population of the United States, broken down by age and sex.

CEILING

Ceiling is one of the bright young metaphors that are now so fashionable, and are displacing the old fogeys. *Ceiling*'s victims are *maximum* and *limit*. There is no great harm in that, so long as those who use the word remember to treat it as a metaphor.

The advisory Committee did not apply for a general increase in the ceilings.

Any ceiling imposed under this rule may be increased or waived if the contributor agrees.

Ceiling here means *maximum prices* in the first example and *maximum benefits* in the second. The writers forgot that if one wants more headroom one does not increase the ceiling, still less perform the curious operation of waiving it; one raises it. Similarly anyone who thinks that "the monetary licensing ceiling" is the most effective way of expressing his meaning (though I cannot believe it really is) ought at least to remember that our normal relationship to a ceiling is under it, not within it.

In determining the floor-space, a ceiling of 15,000 square feet should normally be the limit.

This is indeed a complicated way of saying that floor-space should not normally exceed 15,000 square feet. Why drag down the ceiling?

When this metaphor, not content with swallowing *maximum*, tries to absorb *minimum* too, we pass from the tolerable to the grotesque:

The effect of this announcement is that the total figure for 1950–51 of £410 million can be regarded as a floor as well as a ceiling.

LIQUIDATE and LIQUIDATION

Liquidation is the process of ascertaining a debtor's liabilities and apportioning his assets to meet them—winding up his affairs in fact. The meaning has lately been enlarged so as to signify other sorts of winding-up, especially, with a sinister twist, the removal of opposition in a totalitarian state by methods possibly undisclosed but certainly unpleasant. The reason for this extension is no doubt to be found in the extension of the practices for which it stands. There are some who deprecate this enlargement of the word's meaning, but I do not think there is any use in doing that; it is well established, and can justly claim to be expressive and vivid and to fill a need. Sir Winston Churchill uses it in *The Gathering Storm*:

> Many of the ordinary guarantees of civilised society had been already liquidated by the Communist pervasion of the decayed Parliamentary Government.

But *liquidate* is one of the words which, having once broken out, run wild. The far-fetched word *terminate*, having superseded the familiar *end*, is itself being superseded by the more far-fetched *liquidate*. It is now apparently regarded as suitable for denoting the ending of anything from massacring a nation to giving an employee notice. It should therefore be handled with care, and not put to such unsuitable duty as when the B.B.C. speaks of the liquidation of Britain's suzerainty over the Indian Native States, or a Local Authority writes:

> These still stand as examples of solid building construction, which will stand the test of many more years of wear and tear before their usefulness has been finally liquidated.

REPERCUSSION

The "vogue" use of this word is new, and unrecognised by any but the most recent dictionaries. One dictionary meaning is "repulse or recoil of a thing after impact" and another "the return or reverberation of a sound". Perhaps it is a combination of these two ideas that has led to the present common use of the word to signify those indirect consequences of a decision that bring unexpected embarrassment to the maker of it, especially when they multiply themselves. In this sense it is useful, and I have no quarrel with it. Many officials must have echoed in their own way the cry of Macbeth, who knew more about repercussions of this sort than most people,

> Bloody instructions which being taught return
> To plague th' inventor.

Besides, the word is indispensable to the Treasury in explaining their reasons for refusing sanction to a proposal in itself unexceptionable. But it must not be allowed to mesmerise writers into forgetting the existence of humdrum but useful words like *consequence, result* and *effect*.

SABOTAGE

Sabotage is defined as "deliberate and organised destruction of plant, machinery, etc., by dissatisfied workmen, hence, generally, any malicious or wanton destruction". It has come much into favour of late, especially to signify the wrecking of some project or agreement in an underhand way by one of the parties to it.

The right of sabotage to be a verb is disputed. "Let us by all means sabotage the verb", says Sir Alan Herbert, "for the robust verb *to wreck* will always do the same work better." When *wreck*, *destroy* or *damage* will serve as well, one of these words ought of course to be preferred. But will they always serve? They have not the same implication of disloyalty as *sabotage* has. The use of *sabotage* as a verb is recognised by the dictionaries and will take some sabotaging.

STERILISE

This word means to make unfruitful. It has come much into favour among officials to express the idea of a veto on the use of something for a profitable purpose, and shows signs of the usual usurping tendencies of such words; you may already find examples of *sterilised* used merely as a synonym for *wasted*. It also needs watching for another reason. To speak of sterilising coal needed for the support of buildings is to use an appropriate metaphor; the coal is being made unfruitful for the purposes for which we use coal. But to speak of sterilising land in the sense of preventing its being built on is to say exactly the opposite of what you mean: the land is being preserved in order that it may continue to be fruitful.

TARGET

Of all the metaphors that have been called on to help in the restoration of our balance of trade, *target* has been the most in demand.

At precisely what stage the word "target" infiltrated, under cover of more noticeably luxuriant verbiage, past the pickets of the purists to seize the commanding position in our vocabulary which it now holds none, probably, can say for certain. Students of jargon, a necessarily morbid class, may be able to explain how a word which originally meant "a light round shield or buckler" has come to signify the quantitative object of an industrial plan. The first stage of this transition—to "something aimed at or to be aimed at"—is easy enough to follow; most of us, at some stage in our careers, have discharged missiles or projectiles at "a shield-like structure marked with concentric circles". It is, as a matter of fact, our personal experience of targets which makes their sudden appearance on the plane of economic theory so puzzling in some of its aspects.

When, for instance, Mr. X speaks, as he is apparently obliged to, of the "coal target" we know roughly what he means, for a moment's thought convinces us that the relation between coal and the coal target cannot be the same as the relation between a rifle and a rifle target. But he gets us into deeper water when he talks about the "overall coal target", for, while the economist in us instantly visualises something very large indeed, the marksman can hardly refrain from recalling that the bigger a target was the easier it was to hit. Still more disconcerting and indeed alarming is the fact that neither

Mr. X nor anyone on his level seems to entertain the faintest hope of actually hitting their targets, even when these are overall or even global ones. In their most optimistic moods they speak of "reaching" or "attaining" the target, an achievement which, since the bow and arrow went out of use, has never been rated very high; nothing in our own experience of musketry suggests that shots which got as far as the mark did any good if they were also wide of it.

Since this article appeared in *The Times* there have been many new variants. We are urged not only to reach and attain our targets, but also to fight for them, to achieve them and to obtain them. We must not be lulled by a near target. It is discouraging to be a long way short of our target and (what seems to amount to the same thing) to be a long way behind it, but it is splendid to be a long way beyond it. The headline "Target in danger" means that it is in no danger of being hit, and "Target in sight" is intended to be exceptionally encouraging to those who are trying to hit it. In fact targets have got completely out of control. We must regard the life of this metaphor as having been as short as it certainly has been merry, and treat it as dead, driven into an early grave by overwork. Then we can all do anything we like to a target without giving offence to anyone. But readers ought not to be tried too hard. A lecturer has recorded that, when he read in a speech by one of our Ministers of a "global target" which, to the Minister's regret, could not be "broken down", the picture that came into his mind was of a drunken reveller attacking a Belisha beacon. Nor should journalists bring the metaphor to life again by saying that only so many tons of coal are needed to "top the year's bull's-eye", forgetting that bull's-eyes, like golf balls, give more satisfaction when hit in the middle than when topped. Nor can even the exigencies of headline language excuse the headline "Export Target Hit" to introduce the news that, owing to a dock strike, the export target is unlikely to be hit.

So much for the perils of some of our more fashionable metaphors. But it is not only in metaphors that a preference for the more showy word may lead a writer astray, and this chapter may fitly end with some common examples. All the words are good and useful words when properly used; my warning is only against the temptation to prefer them to other words which would convey better the meaning you want to express.

OTHER SEDUCTIVE WORDS

ACHIEVE

This word implies successful effort, and should not be treated as merely the equivalent of *getting* or *reaching*, as in the phrase, which I believe is not unknown, "Officers achieving redundancy". There is

an air of dignity about *achieve* which may lead writers to prefer misguidedly such sentences as "this was impossible of achievement" to
the simpler "this could not be done".

ANTICIPATE

The use of this word as a synonym for *expect* is now so common
that it may be a waste of time to fight longer. But it is a gross
example of the encroachment of a dignified word on the province
of a simple one, and I should like even now to put in a plea that the
official will set a good example by never using *anticipate* except in its
correct sense, that is to say, to convey the idea of forestalling an
event, as in the time-honoured reply of Chancellors of the Exchequer, "I cannot anticipate my budget statement". A safe rule
is to use it only with a substantive object, never with an infinitive
or a *that*-clause. I give two examples, the first of its right use and the
second of its wrong.

> Remember, in conducting, that your thought and gesture will
> almost certainly be too late rather than too early. Anticipate
> everything.
> It is anticipated that a circular on this and other matters will be
> issued at an early date.

As Sir Alan Herbert has pointed out, "John and Jane anticipated
marriage" is not likely to be interpreted as "John and Jane expected
to be married".

APPROXIMATE(LY)

This means very close(ly). An approximate estimate is one that
need not be exact, but should be as near as you can conveniently
make it. There is no need to use *approximately* when *about* or *roughly*
would do as well or even better, as in

> It is understood that Mr. X spent some time in America, approxi-
> mately from 1939 to 1946.

Moreover the habit of using *approximately* leads to the absurdity of
saying *very approximately* when what is meant is *very roughly*, that is to
say, *not* very approximately, as in

> An outline should be furnished to this Branch stating the relevant
> circumstances and a very approximate estimate of the expenditure
> involved.

CASUALTY

Casualty strictly means an accident, and not the person to whom
the accident happened, though its extension to cover that meaning

is now well established. But writers should not allow themselves to be mesmerised into encouraging it to drive out simple words like *killed, wounded, injured* or *hurt*; to say, for instance, that someone "became a casualty" when what they mean is that he was injured, or that the casualties, rather than the injured, were taken to hospital after an accident. The only merit in its extended sense is that it covers both killed and wounded, but that may be a demerit if it is proper to distinguish between the two.

COMPLEX

This word has been adopted by psychologists to express mental abnormality caused by suppressed tendencies. If the word is used in a psychological sense by lay writers, it should be given the meaning assigned to it by the profession. An *inferiority complex* is a state of mind that manifests itself in self-assertiveness; the term should not be applied, as it often is, to the shy and diffident. We already have some words (such as *unbending, cleave* and *oversight*) which can be used in precisely opposite senses; we do not want any more.

DEEM

This is an old-fashioned word which starches any letter in which it is used as a synonym for *think*. "This method is deemed to be contra-indicated" is an unpleasant and obscure way of saying "this method is thought unsuitable". But the word is still useful in its technical sense of signifying the constructive or inferential as opposed to the explicit or actual. "Everyone is deemed to have intended the natural and probable consequences of his actions": "Anyone who does not give notice of objection within three weeks will be deemed to have agreed": "Any expenditure incurred in the preparation of plans for any work . . . shall be deemed to be included in the expenditure incurred in carrying out that work."

DILEMMA

This word originally had a precise meaning which it would be a pity not to preserve. It should not therefore be treated as the equivalent of a difficulty, or, colloquially, of a fix or a jam. To be in a dilemma (or, if you want to show your learning, to be on the horns of a dilemma) is to be faced with two (and only two) alternative courses of action, each of which is likely to have awkward results.

ENVISAGE

There is a place for *envisage* to indicate a mental vision of something planned but not yet created, but not nearly such a big place

G

as is given to it. Like *anticipate*, it is used more suitably with a direct object than with a *that*-clause.

> Mr. X said that he envisaged that there would be no access to the school from the main road (thought).
>
> I would refer to your letter of the 26th February, 1948, in which you envisaged the repairs would be completed by the end of this month (said that you expected).
>
> Certain items will fall to be dealt with not by transfer to the Minister but in the way envisaged in Section 60 (described).

EVACUATE

This means to empty, and is a technical term of the military and medical sciences. As a military term it may be used (like *empty*) either of a place (*evacuate a fortress*) or of the people in it (*evacuate a garrison*). In the latter sense it was much used during the war to describe the process of moving people out of dangerous places, and they were given the convenient name of *evacuees*. Its inclination to encroach on the province of the simpler word *remove* needs watching. For the cliché *evacuate to alternative accommodation*, *see p.* 107.

GLOBAL

The meaning *spherical* is an archaism. The meaning *world-wide* is a novelty, but is gaining ground fast. The standard current meaning is "pertaining to or embracing the totality of a group of items, categories or the like". Thus the price paid by the State for the coal industry was arrived at by taking a "global" figure as the value of the industry as a whole, and not an "aggregate" figure of the values of the separate collieries. The word is enjoying a spell of popular favour; it is made too much of, and used in many senses which it will not bear. It has a curious affinity with *overall*, whose vagaries are discussed on p. 114.

IDEOLOGY

This word offends some purists, but I do not see why it should, provided that its mesmeric influence is kept in check; the old-fashioned *creed* or *faith* may sometimes serve. But now that people no longer care enough about religion to fight, massacre and enslave one another to secure the form of its observance, we need a word for what has taken its place as an excitant of those forms of human activity, and I know of none better.

IMPLEMENT

This verb, meaning to carry out or fulfil, used to be hardly known outside the "barbarous jargon of the Scottish Bar".* In 1926 Fowler

---

*David Irving, quoted by Fowler.

"could not acquit of the charge of pedantry" a writer who used the expression "implementing Labour's promises to the electorate". It is now too firmly established to be driven out, but the occasional use of *carry out* or *fulfil* for a change would be refreshing.

INTEGRATE

This is a useful word in its proper place, to describe the process of combining different elements into a whole. But it has become too popular. It seems now to be the inevitable word for saying that anything has been joined, mixed, combined or amalgamated with anything else.

LIMITED

It is pedantry to object to the use of *limited* in the sense of *restricted* on the ground that everything that is not unlimited must be limited. But the word should be used with discretion and should not be allowed to make a writer forget such words as *few* and *small*. Weseen, says:

> *Limited* is not in good use as a substitute for *small* or one of its synonyms. "A man of limited (meagre) education and limited (inadequate) capital is likely to be limited to a limited (scant) income."

MAJORITY

The major part, and *the majority* ought not to be used when a plain *most* would meet the case. They should be reserved for occasions when the difference between a majority and a minority is significant. Thus:

> Most of the members have been slack in their attendance.
> The majority of members are likely to be against the proposal.

MATERIALISE

Do not use this showy word, or the similar word *eventuate* when a simpler one would do as well or better, e.g. *happen, occur, come about, take place* or even the colloquial *come off.*

> It was thought at the time that the incoming tenant would take over the fixtures. This did not however materialise. (. . . But he did not.)

Materialise has its own work to do as a transitive verb in the sense of investing something non-material with material attributes, and as an intransitive verb in the sense of appearing in bodily form.

METICULOUS

Meticulous is derived from a Latin word meaning timid, and like its plebeian cousin *pernickety*, still retains a flavour of fussiness over trifles. It should only be used where the writer wants to suggest that carefulness is overdone; it should not be treated as a synonym for *scrupulous* or any other commendatory word.

OPTIMISTIC

Optimism is the quality of being disposed in all circumstances to hope for the best. The edge of the meaning of *optimistic* is being blunted by its being habitually used for *sanguine* or *hopeful*, when what is referred to is not a habit of mind, but an attitude towards particular circumstances.

An example of its unsuitable use is:

> The negotiations are making good progress, but it is too early to be either optimistic or pessimistic about them.

OPTIMUM

Do not treat *optimum* as a showy synonym for *best*. It should only be used of the product of conflicting forces. The optimum speed of a motor car is not the fastest it is capable of, but that which reconciles in the most satisfactory way the conflicting desires of its owner to move quickly, to economise petrol and to avoid needless wear and tear.

REHABILITATE

Ivor Brown says about this word:

> The present darling of the Departments . . . is rehabilitation, a word originally applied to the restoration of a degraded man's rank and privileges. By the middle of the nineteenth century it was occasionally used to mean restoration of other kinds. Suddenly it has become the administrator's pet. A year or two ago nothing was mended, renewed or restored. Everything had to be reconditioned. Now reconditioning has been supplanted by rehabilitation, which has the merit of being one syllable longer; the blessed word "goes" officially with everything from houses to invalids. I can see no reason why the Ministry of Health should not still seek to heal people instead of rehabilitating them. But heal—poor old Bible monosyllable! Will the next translation of the Bible be allowed to heal the sick? No, it will have to rehabilitate those who are suffering from psycho-physical maladjustment.

But it is only fair to remark that *rehabilitation*, thus used, means something more than *healing*. It means a course of treatment or instruction for the purpose of restoring people already healed of a disease or wound to a life of active usefulness. Because this extension of the healing art was a new conception, it was given a new name, reasonably enough, however ill-chosen the name may be thought to be. What is to be deplored is that "the blessed word goes officially with everything from houses to invalids".

RENDITION

The original meaning, now archaic, was *surrender*, and, like *surrender* and *give up*, it could be used of either a garrison or a fugitive. The word is now less common in England than in America, where it is freely used in the sense of translation or version, and of musical or dramatic performance. For these we in Britain still prefer *rendering*, though, with our usual disposition to imitate things American, we are giving *rendition* a run. There is no good authority in either country for using the word as an all-purposes noun for the act of rendering, but it seems to have a footing in the Services and in some civil departments.

> The Royal Navy have again requested some special action to introduce the special spanner; will you therefore expedite rendition of the necessary proforma for submission to the Arm. M.C.

UNILATERAL, MULTILATERAL, BILATERAL

These words are not for everyday use. They have long been part of the jargon of the diplomatist and the physiologist. And they have recently been admitted into that of the economist, where they are doing much hard work. But for ordinary purposes it is best to stick to *one-sided*, *many-sided* and *two-sided*. Under the influence of *unilateral* a sentiment that might have been plainly stated as "we will not be the only country to disarm" was recently expressed (by a politician) in the words "we will not adopt a policy of unilateral disarmament", and the repudiation of a debt was described (by a professor) as "unilateral refusal to pay".

> Dr. J. M. described the condition of a man in a Southwark court case as "bilateral periorbital haematoma and left subconjunctival haemorrhage". Asked what this meant he replied: "For we ordinary mortals, two lovely black eyes". (*Evening Standard*, 2nd March, 1949.)

It is a pity that the doctor marred the moral by saying "for we ordinary mortals".

USAGE and USER

These words are increasingly employed where *use* would be the right word. *Usage* does not mean *use*; it means either a manner of use (e.g. rough usage) or a habitual practice creating a standard (e.g. modern English usage). *User* (in its impersonal sense) is a legal term meaning the enjoyment of a right, and may be left to the lawyers. An example of *usage* wrongly employed for *use* is:

There is a serious world shortage of X-ray films due to increasing usage in all countries. In this country usage during the first six months of 1951 was 16 per cent greater than in the corresponding period of 1950.

UTILISE and UTILISATION

These words are rarely needed, for the simple word *use* will almost always serve. The official (not a Government official) who wrote "This document is forwarded herewith for the favour of your utilisation" might have written " please use this form". That says what needed to be said in four syllables instead of 21.

Nor is there any reason for preferring the longer word in:

> The sum so released may, upon receipt of same, be utilised to reimburse you for expenses.

Certainly *use* and *utilise* should not be employed merely by way of "elegant variation" as they apparently are in:

> It is expected that Boards will be able to utilise the accommodation now being used by the existing governing bodies.

The following is a list of some more words that are overworked in official documents, and beside them other words that might be used instead, if only, in some cases, as useful change-bowlers. I am not, of course, suggesting that they are necessarily synonyms of the words placed opposite to them or that those ought never to be used.

Acquaint	Inform or tell
Adumbrate	Sketch; outline; foreshadow
Advert	Refer
Ameliorate	Better; improve
Apprise	Inform
Assist	Help
Commence	Begin
Consider	Think
Desire	Wish
Donate	Give
Eventuate	Come about; happen; occur; result; turn out
Evince	Show; manifest; display
Factor	Fact; consideration; circumstance; feature; element; constituent; cause
Function (verb)	Work; operate; act
Inform	Tell
In isolation	By itself
Initiate	Begin; start
Locality	Place
Locate	Find
Major	Important; chief; main; principal
Minimise	Under-estimate; disparage; belittle; make light of

Practically	Virtually; almost; nearly; all but
Proceed	Go
Purport (noun)	Upshot, gist, tenor, substance
Question (noun)	Subject, topic, matter, problem
Purchase	Buy
Render	Make
Require	Want, need
Reside	Live
Residence	Home
State	Say
Sufficient	Enough
Terminate	End
Transmit	Send; forward
Visualise	Imagine; picture

VIII

The Choice of Words (4)

CHOOSING THE PRECISE WORD

> And even things without life giving sound, whether pipe or harp, except they give a distinction in the sounds, how shall it be known what is piped or harped? For if the trumpet give an uncertain sound, who shall prepare himself to the battle? So likewise ye, except ye utter by the tongue words easy to be understood, how shall it be known what is spoken?
>
> St. Paul

> How popular and how influential is the practice [of personifying abstract words] may be shown by such a list of words as the following: Virtue, Liberty, Democracy, Peace, Germany, Religion, Glory—all invaluable words, indispensable even, but able to confuse the clearest issues unless controlled.
>
> Ogden and Richard

THE LURE OF THE ABSTRACT WORD

THE reason for preferring the concrete to the abstract is clear. Your purpose must be to make your meaning plain. Now if, as we have seen, even such concrete words as *ship*, *gold* and *money* have a penumbra of uncertainty round them, an incomparably larger one surrounds all abstract words. If you use an abstract word when you might use a concrete one you are handicapping yourself in your task, difficult enough in any case, of making yourself understood.*

Unfortunately the very vagueness of abstract words is one of the reasons for their popularity. To express one's thoughts accurately is hard work, and to be precise is sometimes dangerous. We are tempted to prefer the safer obscurity of the abstract. It is the greatest vice of present-day writing. Writers seem to find it more natural to say "Was this the realisation of an anticipated liability?" than "Did

---

*This passage in *The Times* review of David Rynin's edition of Alexander Bryan Johnson's *Treatise on Language* (Lit. Supp., 19th July 1947) encourages me to think that I have not overstated the case against abstract words:

"In this *Treatise* it is assumed that since there is nothing objective corresponding to anything but a proper name, and no symbol can function as a proper name unless we are acquainted with what it means, all other words purporting to designate universals, abstractions or *insensibilia* are meaningless, or at best can only be attempts to refer to something associated, presumably by way of feeling, with *designata* for which concrete evidence is offered."

I did not know it was as bad as that.

you expect to have to do this?'; to say "Communities where anonymity in personal relationships prevails" than "Communities where people do not know one another". To resist this temptation, and to resolve to make your meaning plain to your reader even at the cost of some trouble to yourself, is more important than any other single thing if you would convert a flabby style into a crisp one. As Mr. G. M. Young has said, an excessive reliance on the noun at the expense of the verb will, in the end, detach the mind of the writer from the realities of here and now from when and how and in what mood the thing was done and insensibly induce a habit of abstraction generalisation and vagueness. To what lengths this can go may be illustrated by these two examples:

> The desirability of attaining unanimity so far as the general construction of the body is concerned is of considerable importance from the production aspect.
> The actualisation of the motivation of the forces must to a great extent be a matter of personal angularity.

The first 'which relates to the building of vehicles' means, I suppose, that in order to produce the vehicles quickly it is important to agree on a standard body. The meaning of the second is past conjecture. The perpetrator of it is an economist, not an official.

Here are some less extreme examples of the habit of using abstract words to say in a complicated way something that might be said simply and directly:

> There has been persistent instability in numbers of staff. (Staff has constantly varied in numbers.)
> The cessation of house-building operated over a period of five years. (No houses were built for five years.) Note the infelicity of "a cessation operated". *Operate* is just what cessations cannot do.
> A high degree of carelessness, pre-operative and post-operative, on the part of some of the hospital staff, took place. (Some of the hospital staff were very careless both before and after the operation.)
> The cessation of the present restrictions cannot be made. (The present restrictions cannot be ended.)

Sometimes abstract words are actually invented, so powerful is the lure of saying things this way.

> The reckonability of former temporary service for higher leave entitlement.

The following is not official writing, but as it appeared in a newspaper that never shrinks from showing up the faults of official writing, it deserves a place:

> Initiation of a temporary organisation to determine European economic requirements in relation to proposals by Mr. Marshall,

American Secretary of State, was announced in the House of Commons this evening.

This way of expressing oneself seems to be tainting official speech as well as writing. "We want you to deny indirect reception", said the goods clerk of my local railway station, telephoning to me about a missing case. "What does that mean?" I asked. "Why," he said, "we want to make sure that the case has not reached you through some other station".

Exponents of the newer sciences are fond of expressing themselves in abstractions. Perhaps this is unavoidable, but I cannot help thinking that they sometimes make things unnecessarily difficult for their readers. I have given an example on the last page of an economist's wrapping up his meaning in an impenetrable mist of abstractions. Here is one from psychology:

> Reserves that are occupied in continuous uni-directional adjust-ment of a disorder are no longer available for use in the ever-varying interplay of organism and environment in the spontaneity of mutual synthesis.

In official writing the words *availability*, *lack* and *dearth* contribute much to the same practice, though they do not produce the same obscurity. Perhaps the reason why those words are so popular is that we have suffered so much from what it is fashionable to call a lack of availability of so many useful things.

> We would point out that availabilities of this particular material are extremely limited. (. . . that this material is extremely scarce.)
> A despatch has been sent requesting information on the avail-ability of the facilities required. . . . (asking how far the required facilities are available.)
> The actual date of the completion of the purchase should coincide with the availability of the new facilities. (The purchase should not be completed until the new facilities are available.)

Lack is a useful word to denote a deficiency of something, and occasionally, though less commonly, the complete absence of some-thing. But this word is being pressed too much into service. For instance, "there is a complete lack of spare underground wire" is not the natural way of saying "we have no spare underground wire" or "There exists a considerable lack of knowledge about . . ." for "We do not know much about . . .", or "A dearth of information exists" for "We have very little information".

POSITION AND SITUATION

The words *position* and *situation* have a great fascination for those who are given to blurring the sharp outlines of what they have to say. A debate takes place in the House of Commons about an acute scarcity of coal during a hard winter. A speaker wants to say that he does not see how it would have been possible for the Government to make sure of there being enough coal. Does he say so? No; the miasma of abstract words envelops him and he says, "In view of all the circumstances I do not see how this situation could have been in any way warded off". Later the spokesman for the Government wants to strike a reassuring note, and express his confidence that we shall get through the winter without disaster. He too takes refuge in vague abstractions. "We shall", he says, "ease through this position without any deleterious effect on the situation." On an historic occasion it fell to a master of words to make an announcement at a time of even graver crisis. Sir Winston Churchill did not begin his broadcast on the 17th June, 1940: "The position in regard to France is extremely serious". He began: "The news from France is very bad". He did not end it: "We have absolute confidence that eventually the situation will be restored". He ended: "We are sure that in the end all will come right".

Position and *situation*, besides replacing more precise words, have a way of intruding into sentences that can do better without them. These words should be regarded as danger-signals, and the writer who finds himself using one should think whether he cannot say what he has to say more directly.

> It may be useful for Inspectors to be informed about the present situation on this matter. (to know how this matter now stands.)
> Unless these wagons can be moved the position will soon be reached where there will be no more wagons to be filled. (there will soon be no more. . . .)
> Should the position arise where a hostel contains a preponderance of public assistance cases. . . . (If a hostel gets too many public assistance cases. . . .)

All three sentences run more easily if we get rid of the *situation* and the *positions*.

It is common form for an Insurance Company, when asking for a renewal premium, to say:

> No-claim bonus is shown subject to the position in this respect remaining unprejudiced until expiry.

This wraps up in verbiage the simple statement that the right to the no-claim bonus is conditional on no claim being made before the expiry of the policy.

Position in regard to is an ugly expression, not always easy to avoid, but used more often than it need be. "The position in regard to the supply of labour and materials has deteriorated" seems to come more naturally to the pen than "labour and materials are more difficult to get". "No one has any doubt", writes the *Manchester Guardian*, "that deceased senior officials of the Civil Service have *in regard to* engraved on their hearts; and their successors to-day show no recovery from this kind of hereditary lockjaw". But it is not fair to put all the blame on officials. Even *The Times* is capable of saying, "The question of the British position in regard to the amount of authorisation" rather than "the question how much Britain is to get of the amount authorised".

THE ABSTRACT APPENDAGE

This brings us to what has been called the *abstract appendage*, for *position*, *situation* and *conditions* find themselves in that role more commonly than any other words. I take the term from a letter in *The Times* from Mr. John Buxton:

> SIR,—How long are we to suffer from "weather conditions"? There was a time when the Englishman's favourite topic of conversation was the weather. . . . Now it is no longer recognised as a substantial and elemental thing, but is reduced, by the addition of this abstract appendage, to the status of a symptom or an excuse, and no one knows what to do about it. Prime Minister, back bencher and Civil servant all irritate us with the phrase in print; it is left to the B.B.C. to go even further and, omitting the word "weather", to refer to "cold, wintry, snowy (etc.) conditions".
>
> > This is the weather the shepherd shuns
> > And so do I,
>
> wrote Thomas Hardy, not "The Present weather conditions are causing considerable inconvenience to the sheep-farmer". We cannot shun (or like) "weather conditions", and the sooner the sloppy phrase is destroyed the sooner our rulers will realise its powers for good or ill.

This may be thought over-critical. What exactly is the writer's objection to *weather conditions*? It cannot be the objection of a grammarian to using the word *weather* adjectivally; it is a common and useful English idiom to make nouns serve this purpose, and few words can claim a better right to be so employed than that which has given us *weather forecast, weather prophet, weather eye, weather quarter* and *weather tiles*. The objection must then be to the use of two words where one would do, a sound objection if it can be sustained. But can it here? *Weather conditions* imports a larger idea than *weather* does, at least in time of snow and frost. It embraces the conditions created by yesterday's weather and the likelihood of to-morrow's weather changing them. But the attack, even if badly aimed, was directed against a real fault in official English. If the writer had waited until the next day and attacked, as he might have done, the announcement that *blizzard conditions* had returned to the Midlands, he could not have been met with any such plea. It was not blizzard conditions that had returned; it was a blizzard. Similarly it is both unnecessary and quaint to say that temperatures will return to normal values instead of merely that they will return to normal. *Level* has also been greatly in demand of late as an abstract appendage. A correspondent has kindly presented me with a collection of hundreds of specimens, ranging from *pub-and-street-corner-level* to *world-level* through every conceivable intermediate level. This passion for picturing all our relations with one another as stratifications is an odd phenomenon at a time when we are supposed to be developing into a classless State.

THE HEADLINE PHRASE

More serious is the harm that is being done to the language by excessive use of nouns as adjectives. In the past, as I have said, the language has been greatly enriched by this free-and-easy habit. We are surrounded by innumerable examples—War Department, Highway Code, Nursery School, Coronation Service, Trades Union Congress and so on. But something has gone wrong recently with this useful practice; its abuse is corrupting English prose. It has become natural to say "World population is increasing faster than world food production" instead of "The population of the world is increasing faster than the food it produces". "The fats position will then be relieved" instead of "More fats will then be available", "The eggs position exceeds all expectation" instead of "Eggs are more plentiful than was expected". It is old-fashioned to speak of the "state of the world"; it must be the "world situation". The fact is, as Lord Dunsany has remarked, that "too many *of*s have dropped out of the language, and the dark of the floor is littered with this useful word". We meet daily, he adds, with things like "England side captain selection" instead of "Selection of captain of English eleven"; or even "England side captain selection difficulty". Nor would they stop nowadays at "England side captain selection difficulty rumour".

This sort of language is no doubt pardonable in headlines, where as many stimulating words as possible must be crowded into spaces so small that *treaties* have had to become *pacts*, *ambassadors envoys*, *investigations probes* and all forms of human enterprise *bids*. Headlines have become a language of their own, knowing no law and often quite incomprehensible until one has read the article that they profess to summarise. "Insanity Rules Critic" and "W. H. Smith Offer Success" have quite different meanings from their apparent ones. Who could know what is meant by "HANGING PROBE NAMES SOON" until he has read on and discovered that what it means is "The names of the members of the Royal Commission on Capital Punishment will shortly be announced"? Who could guess that the headline "UNOFFICIAL STRIKES CLAIM" introduces a report of a speech by a Member of Parliament who said that there was abundant evidence that unofficial strikes were organised and inspired by Communists as part of a general plan originating from abroad? I do not see how those three words by themselves can have any meaning at all; to me they convey a vague suggestion of the discovery of oil or gold by someone who ought not to have been looking for it. And if the announcement BULL GRANTS INCREASE is construed grammatically, it does not seem to deserve a headline at all: one would say that that was no more than was to be expected from any conscientious bull.

But what may be pardonable in headlines will not do in the text. *Nursery School* is a legitimate use of the noun-adjective, but *nursery school provision* is not at present regarded as a proper way of saying *the provision of nursery schools. Electricity crisis restrictions* and *world supply situation* may be all right as newspaper headlines but not in English prose. For instance:

> An extra million tons of steel would buy our whole sugar import requirements. (all the sugar we need to import.)
> Food consumption has been dominated by the world supply situation. (People have had to eat what they could get.)
> Rationing of meat must continue because of the world supply situation. (because there is not enough meat in the world.)

An exceptionally choice example is:

> The programme must be on the basis of the present head of labour ceiling allocation overall.

Here *Head of labour* means *number of building operatives. Ceiling* means *maximum. Overall*, as usual, means nothing (*see* p. 114). The whole sentence means "The programme must be on the assumption that we get the maximum number of building operatives at present alloted to us".

> Everything is being done to expedite plant installation within the limiting factors of steel availability and the preparation of sites.

The only thing that can be said for the writer of this is that his conscience pulled him up before the end, and he did not write "sites preparation". The sentence should have run, "So far as steel is available and sites can be prepared, everything is being done to expedite the installation of plant".

The use of a noun as an adjective should be avoided where the same word is already an adjective with a different meaning. Do not, for instance, say "material allocation" when you mean "allocation of material", but reserve that expression against the time when you may want to make clear that the allocation you are considering is not a spiritual one. For the same reason this phrase is not felicitous:

> In view of the restrictions recently imposed on our capital economic situation. . . .

By way of emphasising that the official is by no means the only offender, I will add two examples from elsewhere. The first is from a circular issued by a commercial firm:

> This compulsion is much regretted, but a large vehicle fleet operator restriction in mileage has now been made imperative in meeting the demand for petrol economy.

This translated into English presumably means:

> We much regret having to do this, but we have been obliged to restrict greatly the operation of our fleet of vehicles [or to restrict the operation of our fleet of large vehicles?] to meet the demand for economy in petrol.

The second is from an American sociological book:

> Examination of specific instances indicated that in most cases where retirement dissatisfaction existed advance activity programming by individuals had been insignificant or even lacking.

Here again I translate with diffidence, but the meaning seems to be:

> Examination of specific instances indicated that most of those who did not want to retire had given little or no thought to planning their future.

ABSTRACT ADJECTIVAL PHRASES

By this I mean using a phrase consisting of an abstract noun (e.g. *character, nature, basis, description, disposition*), with an adjective, where a simple adjective would do as well. This too offends against the rule that you should say what you have to say as simply and directly as possible in order that you may be readily understood.

Examples:

> These claims are of a very far-reaching character. (These claims are very far-reaching.)
> The weather will be of a showery character. (It will be showery.)
> The wages will be low owing to the unremunerative nature of the work.

The translation of the last example will present no difficulty to a student of Mr. Micawber who once said of the occupation of selling corn on commission: "It is not an avocation of a remunerative description—in other words, it does *not* pay".

Proposition is another abstract word used in the same way.

> Decentralisation on a regional basis is now a generally practical proposition. (It is now generally feasible.)
> Accommodation in a separate building is not usually a practical proposition. (Is not usually feasible.)
> The high cost of land in clearance areas makes it a completely uneconomic proposition to build cottages in those areas. (Makes it completely uneconomic to build cottages there.)

Proposition in the sense of *plan* or *project* has as yet hardly emerged from the slang stage.

Basis is specially likely to lead writers to express themselves in roundabout ways. When you find you have written "on a . . . basis" always examine it critically before letting it stand.

> Such officer shall remain on his existing salary on a mark-time basis. (shall mark time on his existing salary.)
> The organisation of such services might be warranted in particular localities and on a strictly limited basis. (scale.)
> The machines would need to be available both day and night on a 24-hour basis. (at any time of the day or night.)
> Please state whether this is to be a permanent installation or on a temporary line basis. (Or a temporary line.)

A legitimate use of *basis* is:

> The manufacturers are distributing their products as fairly as possible on the basis of past trading.

CLICHÉS

In the course of this book I have called numerous expressions clichés. A cliché may be defined as a phrase whose aptness in a particular context when it was first invented has won it such popularity that it has become hackneyed, and is used without thought in contexts where it is no longer apt. Clichés are notorious enemies of the precise word. To quote from the introduction to Eric Partridge's *Dictionary of Clichés*:

> They range from fly-blown phrases (explore every avenue) through sobriquets that have lost all point and freshness (the Iron Duke) to quotations that have become debased currency (cups that cheer but not inebriate), metaphors that are now pointless, and formulas that have become mere counters (far be it from me to . . .).

A cliché then is by definition a bad thing, not to be employed by self-respecting writers. Judged by this test, some expressions are unquestionably and in all circumstances clichés. This is true in particular of verbose and facetious ways of saying simple things (*conspicuous by its absence, tender mercies, durance vile*) and of phrases so threadbare that they cannot escape the suspicion of being used automatically (*leave no stone unturned, acid test, psychological moment, leave severely alone*). But a vast number of other expressions may or may not be clichés. It depends on whether they are used unthinkingly as reach-me-downs or deliberately chosen as the best means of saying what the writer wants to say. Eric Partridge's *Dictionary* contains some thousands of entries. But, as he says in his preface, what is a cliché is partly a matter of opinion. It is also a matter of occasion. Many of those in his dictionary may or may not be clichés; it depends on how they are used. Writers would be needlessly handicapped if they were never permitted such phrases as *cross the Rubicon, sui generis, swing of the pendulum, thin end of the wedge* and *white elephant*. These may be the fittest way of expressing a writer's meaning. If you choose one of them for that reason you need not be afraid of being called a cliché-monger. The trouble is that writers often use a cliché because they think it fine, or because it is the first thing that comes into their heads. It is always a danger-signal when one word suggests another and Siamese twins are born—*part and parcel, intents and purposes* and the like. There is no good reason why *inconvenience* should always be said to be *experienced* by the person who suffers it and *occasioned* by the person who causes it. Single words too may become clichés; they are used so often that their edges are blunted while more exact words are neglected. I have already said something in Chapter VII about those whose popularity comes from the allure of novelty or sparkle; here I will give some examples of a few more that have no such claim to preference; some indeed seem to attract by their very drabness.

ACCOMMODATION

"Accommodated", said Justice Shallow; "it comes of *accommodo*: very good, a good phrase. Good phrases are surely, and ever were, very commendable." Whitehall feels the same about the noun. They had a reverse not long ago when the phrase *accommodation unit* was most unkindly received by Sir Winston Churchill and finished off by Sir Hartley Shawcross, who said that it had lost the Labour Party (then in power) 50,000 votes, or if it had not it ought to have done. And so while we stay in the same place we can still call our house our house, or our flat our flat, or our lodgings our lodgings. But if Authority arranges to move us, it will not be to another house, or a different flat, or new lodgings. It will always be to alternative accommodation, and it is as likely as not that we shall be described as being evacuated there. This curious cliché, originally

H

coined by the legislature 20 years ago, has run wild, and its versatility is astonishing. Sometimes it means no more than *houses*:

> The real cause of bad relations between landlord and tenant is the shortage of alternative accommodation.

Or it may mean something less than houses:

> Experience has shown that many applications have been received for exemption certificates [*sc.* from the obligation to provide sanitary conveniences] on the ground that alternative accommodation is available. . . . Public sanitary conveniences should not be considered satisfactory alternative accommodation.

AFFECT

This word has won an undeserved popularity because it is colour-less—a word of broad meaning that saves a writer the trouble of thought. It is a useful word in its place, but not when used from laziness. It may be easier to say "The progress of the building has been *affected* by the weather", but it is better to use a more precise word—*hindered*, perhaps, or *delayed* or *stopped*. I used to think during the war, when I heard that gas-mains had been affected by a raid, that it would have been more sensible to say that they had been broken.

ALTERNATIVE

The use of *alternative* for such words as *other*, *new*, *revised* or *fresh* is rife. Perhaps this is due to infection spread by the cliché *alternative accommodation*. For instance, the Ministry of Health announced one spring that owing to the severe winter the house-building pro-gramme for the year had been abandoned, and added that no "alternative programme" would be issued. They might have said *other*, *new*, *fresh* or *revised*, but *alternative* must be wrong. There is nothing for it to be an alternative to; the old programme is torn up.

Innumerable examples could be given of this misuse. Here are two:

> The Ministry of Transport are arranging alternative transport for the passengers of the *Empire Windrush* [which is at the bottom of the Mediterranean].
> The Minister regrets that he will not be able to hold the Conference arranged for the 15th March. Members will be informed as soon as alternative arrangements have been made.

Alternative must imply a choice between two or more things, as in the following example:

> Authorities may order their requirements from one or more of the firms in Appendix II. An order addressed to Firm A may specify

Firms B and C as second and third choices. Where no alternative firm is given the order will, if necessary, be re-allocated.

Even in that popular phrase *alternative accommodation*, the adjective is generally incorrect, for the person to whom the accommodation is offered has usually no alternative to taking it.

Billeting Authorities are requested to report any such cases as they are unable to rebillet, in order that alternative arrangements may be made.

Other is the right word here.

It is generally regarded as pedantry to say that, because of its derivation, *alternative* must not be used where the choices are more than two.

Appreciate

The ordinary meaning of *appreciate*, as a transitive verb, is to form an estimate of the worth of anything, to set a value on it. It is therefore not surprising that it is useful to polite officials corresponding with members of the public who want more than they can get, as most of us do today. Refusals are softened by such phrases as "I appreciate how hard it is on you not to have it", and "you will appreciate the reasons why I cannot let you have it". Whatever the reason, there can be no doubt that *appreciate* is being used by the writers of official letters and circulars with a freedom that passes reason. An effective way of curbing it might be to resolve never to use the word with a *that* clause ("I appreciate that there has been delay"), but always give it a noun to govern ("I appreciate your difficulty").

Sometimes the word is used merely by way of polite padding (*see* p. 72), or where it would be more suitable to say *understand, realise, recognise, be grateful, be obliged*.

"It would be appreciated if" can usually be translated into "I shall be glad (or grateful, or obliged, or even pleased) if . . .". "You will appreciate" can often be better expressed by "you will realise", or even "of course".

Appropriate

This is an irreproachable word. But so also are *right, suitable, fitting* and *proper*, and I do not see why *appropriate* should have it all its own way. In particular, the Whitehall cliché *in appropriate cases* might be confined more closely than it is now to cases in which it is appropriate.

CLAIM

The proper meaning of *to claim* is to demand recognition of a right. But the fight to prevent it from usurping the place of *assert* has been lost in America and seems likely to be lost here also, especially as the B.B.C. have surrendered without a struggle. Here are some recent examples from this country:

> The police took statements from about forty people who claimed that they had seen the gunmen in different parts of the city.
> The State Department claims that discrimination is being shown against the American film industry.
> There are those who claim that the Atlantic Treaty has an aggressive purpose.
> I have a friend who claims to keep in his office a filing tray labelled "Too Difficult".

The enlargement of *claim* ought to be deplored by all those who like to treat words as tools of precision, and to keep their edges sharp. Why should *claim*, which has its own useful job to do, claim a job that is already being efficiently done by others? Perhaps the idea underlying this usage is that the writer claims credence for an improbable or unverified assertion.

DECIMATE

To *decimate* is to reduce *by* one-tenth, not *to* one-tenth. It meant originally to punish mutinous troops by executing one man in ten, chosen by lot. Hence by extension it means to destroy a large proportion; the suggestion it now conveys is usually of a loss much greater than 10 per cent. Because of the flavour of exactness that still hangs about it, an adverb or adverbial phrase should not be used with it. We may say "The attacking troops were decimated", meaning that they suffered heavy losses, but we must not say "The attacking troops were badly decimated", and still less "decimated to the extent of 50 per cent or more".

The following truly remarkable instance of the misuse of *decimate* was given in the course of correspondence in *The Times* about the misuse of *literally*. See p. 63.

> I submit the following, long and lovingly remembered from my "penny dreadful" days: "Dick, hotly pursued by the scalp-hunter, turned in his saddle, fired and literally decimated his opponent."

DEVELOP

The proper use of this word is to convey the idea of a gradual unfolding or building up. Do not use it as a synonym for *arise, occur, happen, take place, come.* A typical example of its misuse is "rising prices might develop" (for "prices might rise").

EMERGENCY

The Emergency Powers Act had to have a generic title because it was for use in all sorts of emergencies, whether due to war or civil commotion. But once the word got a footing it provided a splendid cloak for every kind of thing, from war downwards, that it was not quite nice to mention specifically. Look at these three extracts from a single memorandum about arrangements for evacuation in 1939:

> In the preceding paragraphs the action which would require to be taken in the event of an emergency has been sketched, because a picture of this action naturally follows on a discussion of the transport arrangements and will provide an indication of the manner in which the survey of accommodation now completed by the authority would be used in order to enable the plan to be put into operation at very short notice.

What the paragraph means as a whole is obscure, but it seems pretty clear that here *emergency* means bombing. The circular goes on to give this advice about expectant mothers:

> It will be necessary for each small group to be supervised and accompanied by at least one person qualified to guide them and to deal with any emergencies which may arise—preferably a midwife.

Here the word *emergencies* seems to be used in a quite different sense.

Finally, we have the following:

> An alternative method would be to ask every woman as a routine at booking (i.e. making arrangements for confinement) whether she would wish to be evacuated in an emergency.

Here we are left guessing which sort of an *emergency* is meant, and even wondering whether *evacuated* is used in the same sense as before.

I wrote this ten years ago, but the fascination of the word apparently persists. A correspondent in charge of the preparation of certain measures to be taken in the event of war writes:

> I have given instructions that the use of this word is to be avoided as far as possible. It is used in four different senses:
> (a) international tension such as may lead to war;
> (b) war;
> (c) a state of affairs during war when things get bad (e.g. May-September 1940);
> (d) a state of affairs in which supplies of some vital commodity run short, or a situation of some kind gets out of hand.
> There is a pernicious habit of inserting the phrase *in an emergency* without making clear which of the four meanings, if any, it has. Sometimes it should be replaced by "when war threatens", sometimes by "in war", sometimes by "when things become serious", sometimes by "in case of need" or "if the worst comes to the worst". Usually, however, it can be omitted altogether.

ENTAIL

This word is given too much work to do. Often some other word such as *need, cause, impose, necessitate, involve*, might be more appropriate, or at least make a refreshing change. Sometimes *entail* intrudes where no verb is needed, a common habit of *involve*.

> . . . a statement in writing that you are willing to bear the cost entailed of opening the case, withdrawing this amount and resealing.

If *entailed* must be used, the preposition should be *in*.

INVOLVE

The meaning of this popular word has been diluted to a point of extreme insipidity. Originally it meant *wrap up in something, enfold*. Then it acquired the figurative meaning *entangle a person in difficulties or embarrassment*, and especially *implicate in crime, or a charge*. Then it began to lose colour, and to be used as though it meant nothing more than *include, contain* or *imply*. It has thus developed a vagueness that makes it the delight of those who dislike the effort of searching for the right word. It is consequently much used, generally where some more specific word would be better and sometimes where it is merely superfluous.

This is no new phenomenon. More than forty years ago Sir Clifford Allbutt, writing about the English style of medical students at Cambridge, said:

> *To involve*, with its ugly and upstart noun *involvement*, has to do duty for to *attack*, to *invade*, to *injure*, to *affect*, to *pervert*, to *encroach upon*, to *influence*, to *enclose*, to *implicate*, to *permeate*, to *pervade*, to *penetrate*, to *dislocate*, to *contaminate* and so forth.

Here are a few recent examples from official writing:

> The additional rent involved will be £1. (Omit *involved*.)
> There are certain amounts of the material available without permit, but the quantities involved are getting less. (Omit *involved*.)
> It has been agreed that the capital cost involved in the installation of the works shall be included. (. . . that the capital cost of installing . . .)
> It has been inaccurately reported that anything from eight sheep to eight oxen were roasted at the affair. The facts are that six sheep only were involved. (*Involved* here seems to be an "elegant variation" for *roasted*.)
> Much labour has been involved in advertising. (Much labour has been expended on advertising.)

The following four examples all occur in one paragraph of a memorandum, covering less than half a page, and strikingly illustrate the ascendancy of this word over undiscriminating writers:

> The Ministry have indicated that they would not favour any proposal which would involve an increase in establishment at the present time. (*Involve* here is harmless, but in order to practise shaking off its yoke, let us substitute *mean* or *lead to*.)
>
> The Company would oppose this application unless compensation involving a substantial sum were paid. (This one cannot get off so lightly. The writer should have said "unless a substantial sum were paid in compensation".)
>
> We have been informed that the procedure involved would necessitate lengthy negotiation. . . . (Here *involved* is doing no work at all and should be omitted.)
>
> This would possibly involve the creation of a precedent that might embarrass the Government. (This illustrates the greatest of the sins into which *involve* seduces the writer—that of saying *involve the creation of* instead of the simple, direct and adequate *create*.)

Such are some of the sadly flabby uses to which this word of character is put. Reserve it for more virile purposes and especially for use where there is a suggestion of entanglement or complication, as we use *involved* when we say "this is a most involved subject". Here are two examples of its reasonable use:

> This experience has thrown into high relief the complications and delays involved in the existing machinery for obtaining approval.
>
> Mr. Menzies protested against the Australian Government's acceptance of the invitation to the conference at Delhi on the Indonesian dispute, holding that Australia ought not to be involved.

Issue (noun)

This word has a very wide range of proper meanings as a noun, and should not be made to do any more work—the work, for instance, of *subject, topic, consideration* and *dispute*.

Issue (verb)

To issue an article of equipment to a soldier is a well-established military phrase and an unexceptionable use of *issue*: the article is issued from store. But the practice has grown up of treating *issue* as though it meant *provide, supply* or *grant*, and this has spread into civilian life.

> You were issued with coupons to bring your wardrobe to the standard level.

Twenty-five years ago Fowler remarked gently, "This is not to be recommended". Fifteen years later Sir Alan Herbert said more firmly "This is black". But little notice seems to have been taken of them. Indeed the sentence "he was issued with a licence" is taken by Mr. Hugh Sykes Davies in his *Grammar Without Tears* as the text of a spirited defence of such constructions against the charge of being "bad grammar". But the true offence is not a matter of grammar: it is that there is no need for *issue with* to usurp the place of *grant*, and to allow it to do so is to contribute to the debasement of language by blurring the significance of words.

ITEM

This word is a great favourite, especially in business letters. It is made to mean almost anything. It is safe to say that any sentence in which this omnibus use occurs will be improved either by omitting the word or by substituting a word of more definite meaning. The following is a typical instance; it refers to the condition of a set of batteries:

> The accessory items, stands and other parts, are satisfactory, but the sediment approximates to 1-in. in depth and . . . this item can be removed conveniently when the renewals are effected.

Accessory items should be changed to *accessories* and *this item can be removed* to *this can be removed*.

The next example is from a notice of a meeting:

> *I shall be able to attend the meeting.
> *I shall not be able to attend the meeting.
> * Please delete item not required.

Here, what meant *sediment* in the first example appears to mean *words*.

MAJOR

This is a harmless word, but it is so much used that it is supplanting other more serviceable ones. Do not let *major* make you forget such words as *main, important, chief, principal*. For instance, *important* or *significant* might have been better than *major* in:

> We do not expect to see any major change in the near future.

OVERALL (adjective)

The favour that this word has won during the past few years is astonishing. It is an egregious example of the process I described as boring out a weapon of precision into a blunderbuss. Indeed the word seems to have a quality that impels people to use it in settings in which it has no meaning at all.

Examples of its meaningless use are:

The independence of the Teaching Hospitals and their freedom from the overall control of the Regional Boards. . . .

The overall growth of London should be restrained.

Radical changes will be necessary in the general scheme of Exchequer grants in aid of local authorities, therefore, to secure that overall the policy of the Government in concentrating those grants as far as possible where the need is greatest is further developed. (Here, it will be observed, *overall* is an adverb.)

When an individual leaves an establishment, and his departure results in a net reduction of one in the overall strength. . . .

It looks as if the yield for the first fortnight of 1949 will be fewer than forty fresh orders, representing an overall annual output of no more than a thousand.

The Controller should assume a general overall responsibility for the efficient planning of all measures.

When *overall* is not meaningless, it is commonly used as a synonym for some more familiar word, especially *average*, *total* and *aggregate*.

For *aggregate*:

Compared with the same week a year ago, overall production of coal showed an increase of more than 100,000 tons. [i.e. deep-mined plus opencast.]

For *in all* or *altogether*:

Overall the broadcasting of "Faust" will cover eight hours.

For *total*:

I have made a note of the overall demand of this company for the next year.

For *average*:

The houses here are built to an overall density of three to the acre.

For *supreme*:

Vice-Admiral Duncan, of the United States Navy, was in overall command.

For *on the whole*:

The Secretary of State for the Colonies stated that the overall position in Malaya had greatly improved, although in some places it was still difficult.

For *generally*:

Small vital schemes of repair and adaptation which continually arise and must be dealt with irrespective of any attempt to improve overall hospital standards.

For *overriding*:

They came forward as witnesses because of the overall fear of being involved in a capital charge.

For *comprehensive*:

> An overall plan for North Atlantic Defence measures was approved yesterday by the Defence Minister at the Hague.

For *whole*:

> Mr. C. said he could quite understand that the Conservative Party were unwilling to look at the overall picture.

For *bird's-eye*:

> Our observer will be in the control tower, where he will have an overall view of the aerodrome.

For *complete*:

> One volume was published, but the overall plan was never finished

For *absolute*:

> The Conservatives will have an overall majority in the new Parliament.

For *on balance*:

> The purpose of the plan is to enable a larger initial payment to be made and correspondingly lower payments subsequently, entailing an overall saving to the customer.

Overall, according to the dictionaries, means "including everything between the extreme points", as one speaks of the overall length of a ship. For this purpose it is useful, but it is high time that its excursions into the fields of other words were checked. So pervasive has the word become that it is a pleasant surprise to come across an old-fashioned *general* in such sentences as:

> These reports may be used for obtaining a general picture of the efficiency of a given industry.
> Although Europe's general deficit with the outside world fell by over $2 billion during 1949, its deficit with the United States fell hardly at all.

Most writers today would say "overall picture" and "overall deficit" almost automatically.

Percentage, Proportion, Fraction

Do not use the expression *a percentage* or *a proportion* when what you mean is *some*, as in:

> This drug has proved of much value in a percentage of cases.
> The London Branch of the National Association of Fire Officers, which includes a proportion of station officers. . . .

Here *percentage* and *proportion* pretend to mean something more than *some*, but do not really do so. They do not give the reader any idea of the number or proportion of the successful cases or station officers. One per cent is just as much "a percentage" as 99 per cent. So, for that matter, is 200 per cent.

Do not forget the simple words *many*, *few* and *some*; and use *percentage* or *proportion* only if you want to express not an absolute number but the relation of one number to another, and can give at least an approximate degree of exactitude; so that, though you may not be able to put an actual figure on the percentage or proportion, you can at any rate say "a high percentage", "a large proportion", "a low percentage", "a small proportion".

But *fraction* is different. It has become so common to use "only a fraction" in the sense of "only a small fraction" that it would be pedantry to object that $\frac{999}{1000}$ is as much a fraction as $\frac{1}{1000}$ just as it would certainly be pedantry to point out to anyone who says "He has got a temperature" that 98 degrees is just as much "a temperature" as 104.

REACTION

Reaction has had a meteoric career, almost rivalling that of *overall* and *target*. It now seems to come naturally to an official writer, answering an enquiry where certain equipment can be bought, to end his letter:

> Would you therefore communicate with the XY Co. Ltd., and let me have your reaction.

Reaction may be properly used as a technical term of chemistry (the response of a substance to a reagent), of biology (the response of an organ of the body to an external stimulus), or of mechanics ("to every action there is an equal and opposite reaction"). One would think that was as much work as a word could reasonably be asked to do. Its present vogue means that a word which connotes essentially an automatic rather than an intellectual response is being used habitually to replace such words as *opinion*, *views* or *impression*. Never say "What is your reaction to this proposal?" instead of "what do you think of this proposal?" unless you wish to imply that the person you are questioning must answer instantly without reflection. *Reaction's* extension of its meaning was harmless at first, and even useful. One cannot quarrel with:

> I suggest that Mr. X communicates with some of the firms named with a view to testing market reactions to his products.

But the further encroachments of the word should be discouraged because they blunt exactitude of meaning.

The preposition after *reaction* must be *to*, not *on*. It is permissible to say "His reaction to your letter was unfavourable". But it is not permissible to say "Your letter had an unfavourable reaction on him". To say that is to imply a belief that one of the meanings of *reaction* is *effect*.

REALISTIC

This word is becoming dangerously popular, perhaps because it has a question-begging flavour. What is realistic is what the writer thinks sensible. A leading article in a certain journal recently said of a certain minister:

> He made great play, as he has done before, with the word "realistic", which he is in danger of associating with anything he thinks.

Realistic is ousting words like *sensible, practical, feasible, workmanlike.* Everything nowadays seems to be either academic or realistic.

IX

The Handling of Words

Proper words in proper places make the true definition of style.

SWIFT

If language is not correct, then what is said is not what is meant;
if what is said is not what is meant, then what ought to be done
remains undone.

CONFUCIUS

WE must now return to what I called in Chapter IV "correctness",
and consider what it means not in the choice of words but in handling them when chosen. That takes us into the realm of grammar,
syntax and idiom—three words that overlap and are often used
loosely, with grammar as a generic term covering them all.

Grammar has fallen from the high esteem that it used to enjoy.
A hundred and fifty years ago William Cobbett said that "grammar
perfectly understood enables us not only to express our meaning
fully and clearly but so to express it as to defy the ingenuity of man
to give our words any other meaning than that which we intended
to express". The very name of grammar school serves to remind us
that grammar was long regarded as the only path to culture and
learning. But that was Latin grammar. When our mother-tongue
encroached on the paramountcy of the dead languages, questions
began to be asked. Even at the time when Cobbett was writing his
grammar, Sydney Smith was fulminating about the unfortunate
boy who was "suffocated by the nonsense of grammarians, over-
whelmed with every species of difficulty disproportionate to his age,
and driven by despair to pegtop and marbles". Very slowly over
the past hundred years the idea seems to have gained ground that
the grammar of a living language, which is changing all the time,
cannot be fitted into the rigid framework of a dead one; nor can the
grammar of a language such as Latin, which changes the forms of
its words to express different grammatical relations, be profitably
applied to a language such as English, which has got rid of most of
its inflexions, and expresses grammatical relations by devices like
prepositions and auxiliary verbs and by the order of its words. It is
nearly fifty years since the Board of Education itself declared:
"There is no such thing as English grammar in the sense which
used to be attached to the term". George Saintsbury denounced the

futility of trying to "draw up rules and conventions for a language that is almost wholly exception and idiom". Jespersen preached that the grammar of a language must be deduced from a study of how good writers of it in fact write, not how grammarians say it ought to be written. George Orwell went so far as to say that "correct grammar and syntax are of no importance so long as one makes one's meaning clear". And quite recently a teacher of English has written a book* in which, after surveying the development of our language from the clumsy and tortuous synthetic beginnings of its Gothic origins to the grace and flexibility of its present analytical structure, he shows how in this great and beneficent reform the hero is what he calls the "lowly man" and the villain the grammarian, who constantly tried to hamper the freedom of the lowly man to go his own way; and he advocates a "grammatical moratorium" in which we may all be free to disregard the rules of grammar and continue the good work.

The old-fashioned grammarian certainly has much to answer for. He created a false sense of values that still lingers. I have ample evidence in my own correspondence that too much importance is still attached to grammarians' fetishes and too little to choosing the right words. But we cannot have grammar jettisoned altogether; that would mean chaos. There are certain grammatical conventions that are, so to speak, a code of good manners. They change, but those current at the time must be observed by writers who wish to express themselves clearly and without offence to their readers. Mr. Sykes Davies himself says that his grammatical moratorium must be preceded by some instruction in the principles of language "which will not shy from the inescapable necessity of starting from nowhere else than the position we stand in at the moment, conditioned by the past". In this chapter, then, I shall concern myself with some points of current usage on which I have noticed guidance to be needed.

Strictly, idiom is different from grammar: the two are often in conflict. Idiom is defined by the O.E.D. as "a peculiarity of phraseology approved by usage and often having a meaning other than its logical or grammatical one". When anything in this book is called "good English idiom" or "idiomatic", what is meant is that usage has established it as correct. Idiom does not conflict with grammar or logic as a matter of course; it is usually grammatically and logically neutral. Idiom requires us to say *aim at getting*, not *aim to get*, and *try to get*, not *try at getting*. Logic and grammar do not object to this, but they would be equally content with *aim to get* and *try at*

Grammar without Tears, by Hugh Sykes Davies, The Bodley Head, 1951.

getting. At the same time idiom is, in Jespersen's phrase, "a tyran-nical, capricious, utterly incalculable thing", and if logic and gram-mar get in its way, so much the worse for logic and grammar. It is idiomatic—at least in speech—to say "I won't be longer than I can help" and "it's me". That the first is logically nonsense and the second a grammatical howler is neither here nor there; idiom makes light of such things. Yet during the reign of pedantry attempts were constantly made to force idiom into the mould of logic. We were not to speak of a *criminal being executed,* for "a sentence can be executed but not a person"; we were not to say *vexed question* for "though many a question vexes none is vexed"; nor *most thoughtless* for "if a person is without thought there cannot be degrees of his lack of that quality"; nor *light the fire,* for "nothing has less need of lighting"; nor *round the fireside,* for "that would mean that some of us were behind the chim-ney". So argued Landor,* a stout and undiscriminating defender of his language against the intrusion of the illogical. In spite of Fowler and Jespersen, some trace still lingers of the idea that what is illogical or ungrammatical "must" be wrong, such as condemnation of *under the circumstances* and of the use of a plural verb with *none.* The truth is, as Logan Pearsall Smith says:

> Plainly a language which was all idiom and unreason would be impossible as an instrument of thought; but all languages permit the existence of a certain number of illogical expressions: and the fact that, in spite of their vulgar origin and illiterate appearance, they have succeeded in elbowing their way into our prose and poetry, and even learned lexicons and grammars, is proof that they perform a necessary function in the domestic economy of speech.†

In this chapter advice will be given about common troubles in the handling of words. After an opening section on the arrangement of words, these troubles will be classified under those with Conjunctions (p. 127): Negatives (p. 132): Number (p. 135): Prepositions (p. 139): Pronouns (p. 143): Verbs (p. 155). The chapter will end with sec-tions on Some Points of Idiom (p. 164): Some Common Causes of Confused Expression (p. 171): and A Few Points of Spelling (p. 174).

TROUBLES IN ARRANGEMENT

Of these three—grammar, syntax and idiom—it is syntax, in its strict sense of "orderly arrangement", that is of the greatest practical importance. The quotation that heads this chapter says that proper words in proper places make the true definition of style. But some-thing more than "style" depends on putting words in their proper

---

*Imaginary Conversations between Horne Tooke and Dr. Johnson and the Author and Archdeacon Hare.

†*Words and Idioms,* Constable & Co., 5th ed., 1943.

places. In a language like ours, which, except in some of its pronouns, has got rid of its different forms for the subjective and objective cases, your very meaning may depend on your arrangement of words. In Latin, the subject of the verb will have a form that shows it is "in the nominative", and the object one that shows it is "in the accusative"; you may arrange them as you like, and the meaning will remain the same. But English is different. In the two sentences "Cain killed Abel" and "Abel killed Cain" the words are the same, but when they are reversed the meaning is reversed too.

If all you want to say is a simple thing like that, there is no difficulty. But that is rarely so. You probably want to write a more complicated sentence telling not only the central event but also its how, why and where. The Americans have a useful word, *modifier*, by which they mean "words or groups of words that restrict, limit or make more exact the meaning of other words". The "modifiers" bring the trouble.

The rule is easy enough to state. It is, in the words of an old grammarian, "that the words or members most nearly related should be placed in the sentence as near to each other as possible, so as to make their mutual relation clearly appear". But it is not so easy to keep. We do not always remember that what is clear to us may be far from clear to our readers. Sometimes it is not clear even to us which "words or members" are "most nearly related", and if there are many "modifiers" we may be confronted with difficulties of the jig-saw type.

The simplest type of faulty arrangement, and the easiest to fall into, is illustrated by the following examples. Their offence is that they obscure the writer's meaning, if only momentarily, and usually make him appear to be guilty of an absurdity.

> There was a discussion yesterday on the worrying of sheep by dogs in the Minister's room.
> The official statement on the marriage of German prisoners with girls made in the House of Commons. . . .
> It is doubtful whether this small gas company would wish to accept responsibility for supplying this large area with all its difficulties.
> Whatever her thoughts, they were interrupted as the hotel lobby door opened and a young woman carrying a baby and her husband entered. (Quoted by *The New Yorker* from a novel.)

Faulty arrangement of this sort is not unknown even in model regulations issued by Government departments to show local authorities how things ought to be done:

> No child shall be employed on any weekday when the school is not open for a longer period than four hours.

"For a longer period than four hours" qualifies *employed*, not *open*, and should come immediately after *employed*.

And in departmental regulations themselves:

> Every woman by whom . . . a claim for maternity benefit is made shall furnish evidence that she has been, or that it is to be expected that she will be, confined by means of a certificate given in accordance with the rules. . . .

It is not surprising that a Department which sets this example should receive letters like this:

> In accordance with your instructions I have given birth to twins in the enclosed envelope.

I shall have something more to say on this subject (pp. 181/2) in pointing out the danger of supposing that disorderly sentences can be set right by vagrant commas. But one cause of the separation of "words or members most nearly related" is so common that, although I have already touched on it (p. 23), an examination of some more examples may be useful. That is the separation of the subject from the verb by intervening clauses, usually defining the subject.

> (1) Officers appointed to permanent commissions who do not possess the qualifications for voluntary insurance explained in the preceding paragraphs and officers appointed to emergency commissions direct from civil life who were not already insured at the date of appointment (and who, as explained in para. 3, are therefore not required to be insured during service) may be eligible. . . ."
>
> (2) The cases where a change in the circumstances affecting the fire prevention arrangements at the premises is such that, if the number of hours stated in the certificate were recalculated, there would be a reduction (or an increase) in the number of hours of fireguard duty which the members concerned would be liable to perform for the local authority in whose area they reside, stand, however, in an entirely different position.

In these examples the reader is kept waiting an unconscionable time for the verb. The simplest way of correcting this will generally be to change the order of the words or to convert relative clauses into conditional, or both. For instance:

> (1) Officers appointed to permanent commissions may be eligible though they do not possess the qualifications for voluntary insurance explained in the preceding paragraph. So may officers appointed to emergency commissions direct from civil life who . . . etc.
>
> (2) The circumstances affecting the fire prevention arrangements at the premises may, however, so change that, if the number of hours stated in the certificate were recalculated, there would be a reduction, or an increase, in the number of hours of fireguard duty which the members concerned would be liable to perform for the local authority in whose area they reside. These cases stand in an entirely different position.

I

Sometimes the object allows itself to be driven a confusing distance from the verb. A poet can plead the exigencies of rhyme for separating his object from his verb and say, as Calverley did,

> O be careful that thou changest
> On returning home thy boots.

But the official has no such excuse. He must invert the order and say "It is of paramount importance"—for that may be the expression he will be tempted to use—"that young ladies after standing in wet grass should change their boots on returning home".

In the following example the writer has lumbered ponderously along without looking where he was going and arrived at the object (*officers*) of the verb *are employing* with a disconcerting bump:

> One or two of the largest Local Authorities are at present employing on their staff as certifying officers and as advisers to the Mental Deficiency Act Committees officers having special qualification or experience in mental deficiency.

He would have given himself little more trouble, and would have saved his reader some, if he had turned the sentence round and written:

> Officers having special qualification or experience in mental deficiency are at present being employed on the staff of one or two of the largest Local Authorities as certifying officers and as advisers to the Mental Deficiency Act Committees.

Other common errors of arrangement likely to give the reader unnecessary trouble, if they do not actually bewilder him, are letting the relative get a long way from its antecedent and the auxiliary a long way from the main verb. Examples:

(Of relative separated from antecedent.)

> Enquiries are received from time to time in connection with requests for the grant of leave of absence to school children during term time for various reasons, which give rise to questions as to the power to grant such leave.

What is the antecedent of *which*? *Enquiries, requests* or *reasons*? Probably *enquiries*, but it is a long way off. In this sentence it matters little, but in other sentences similarly constructed it might be important for the antecedent to be unmistakable. The surest way of avoiding ambiguity, when you have started a sentence like this, is to put a full stop after *reasons*, and begin the next sentence *These enquiries*, or *these requests* or *these reasons*, whichever is meant.

(Of verb separated from auxiliary.)

> The Executive Council should, in the case of approved institutions employing one doctor, get into touch with the committee.

The Council should accordingly, after considering whether they wish to suggest any modifications in the model scheme, consult with the committee. . . .

It is a bad habit to put all sorts of things between the auxiliary and the verb in this way; it leads to unwieldy sentences and irritated readers.

Adverbs sometimes get awkwardly separated from the words they qualify. "They should be so placed in a sentence as to make it impossible to doubt which word or words they are intended to affect." If they affect an adjective or past participle or another adverb their place is immediately in front of it (*accurately placed, perfectly clear*). If they affect another part of a verb, or a phrase, they may be in front or behind. It is usually a matter of emphasis: *he came soon* emphasises his promptitude; *he soon came* emphasises his coming.

The commonest causes of adverbs going wrong are the fear, real or imaginary, of splitting an infinitive (*see* p. 162) and the wayward-ness of the adverbs *only* and *even*. *Only* is a capricious word. It is much given to deserting its post and taking its place next the verb, regardless of what it qualifies. It is more natural to say "he only spoke for ten minutes" than "he spoke for only ten minutes". The sport of pillorying misplaced *onlys* has a great fascination for some people, and *only*-snooping seems to have become as popular a sport with some purists as split-infinitive-snooping was a generation ago. A recent book, devoted to the exposing of errors of diction in con-temporary writers, contained several examples such as:

> He had only been in England for six weeks since the beginning of the war.
> This only makes a war lawful: that it is a struggle for law against force.
> We can only analyse the facts we all have before us.

These incur the author's censure. By the same reasoning he would condemn Sir Winston Churchill for writing in *The Gathering Storm*:

> Statesmen are not called upon only to settle easy questions.

Fowler took a different view. Of a critic who protested against "he only died a week ago" instead of "he died only a week ago," Fowler wrote:

> There speaks one of those friends from whom the English language may well pray to be saved, one of the modern precisians who have more zeal than discretion. . . .

But it cannot be denied that the irresponsible behaviour of *only* does sometimes create real ambiguity. Take such a sentence as:

> His disease can only be alleviated by a surgical operation.

We cannot tell what this means, and must rewrite it either:

> Only a surgical operation can alleviate his disease (it cannot be alleviated in any other way),

or:

> A surgical operation can only alleviate his disease (it cannot cure it).

Again:

> In your second paragraph you point out that carpet-yarn only can be obtained from India, and this is quite correct.

The writer must have meant "can be obtained only from India", and ought to have so written, or, at the least, "can only be obtained from India". What he did write, if not actually ambiguous (for it can hardly be supposed that carpet-yarn is India's only product), is unnatural, and sets the reader puzzling for a moment.

So do not take the *only*-snoopers too seriously. But be on the alert. It will generally be safe to put *only* in what the plain man feels to be its natural place. Sometimes that will be its logical position, sometimes not. When the qualification is more important than the positive statement, to bring in the *only* as soon as possible is an aid to being understood; it prevents the reader from being put on a wrong scent. In the sentence "The temperature will rise above 35 degrees only in the south-west of England", *only* is carefully put in its right logical place. But the listener would have grasped more quickly the picture of an almost universally cold England if the announcer had said, "the temperature will only rise above 35 degrees in the south-west of England".

A purist might condemn:

> I am to express regret that it has only been possible to issue a licence for part of the quantity for which application was made,

but the ordinary reader will think that this conveys the writer's meaning more readily and naturally than:

> I am to express regret that it has been possible to issue a licence for only part of the quantity for which application was made.

Even has a similar habit of getting the wrong place. The

importance of putting it in the right place is aptly illustrated in the *A.B.C. of English Usage* thus:

> Sentence: "I am not disturbed by your threats".
>> (i) Even I am not disturbed by your threats (let alone anybody else).
>> (ii) I am not even disturbed by your threats (let alone hurt, annoyed, injured, alarmed).
>> (iii) I am not disturbed even by your threats (*even* modifies the phrase, the emphasis being on the threats).

It is also possible, though perhaps rather awkward, to put *even* immediately before *your*, and so give *your* the emphasis (your threats, let alone anybody else's).

TROUBLES WITH CONJUNCTIONS*

(i) *And.* There used to be an idea that it was inelegant to begin a sentence with *and.* The idea is now as good as dead. And to use *and* in this position may be a useful way of indicating that what you are about to say will reinforce what you have just said.

(ii) *And which.* There is a grammarians' rule that it is wrong to write *and which* (and similar expressions such as *and who, and where, but which, or which,* etc.) except by way of introducing a second relative clause with the same antecedent as one that has just preceded it. It is an arbitrary and pointless rule (unknown in French) which will probably be destroyed eventually by usage, but for the present its observance is expected from those who would write correctly. According to this rule, Nelson was wrong grammatically, as well as in other more important ways, when he wrote to Lady Nelson after his first introduction to Lady Hamilton:

> She is a young woman of amiable manners and who does honour to the station to which he has raised her.

To justify the *and who* grammatically a relative is needed in the first part of the sentence, for example:

> She is a young woman whose manners are amiable and who, etc.

Conversely, the writer of the following sentence has got into trouble by being shy of *and which*:

> Things which we ourselves could not produce and yet are essential to our recovery.

Here *which* cannot double the parts of object of *produce* and subject of *are.* To set the grammar right the relative has to be repeated:

> Things which we ourselves could not produce and which are, etc.

---

*This is an elastic heading. It may for instance be said that neither *both* nor *like* is strictly a conjunction. But their caprices make it convenient to include them in this section.

The wisest course is to avoid the inevitable clumsiness of *and which*, even when used in a way that does not offend the purists. Thus these two sentences might be written:

> She is a young woman of amiable manners who does honour to the station to which he has raised her.
>
> Things essential to our recovery which we ourselves could not produce.

(iii) *As* must not be used as a preposition, on the analogy of *but*. (*See* next page.) You may say "no one knows the full truth but me", but you must not say "no one knows the truth as fully as me". It must be "as fully as I". The first *as* is an adverb and the second a conjunction.

We say "as good *as* ever" and "better *than* ever". But should we use *as* or *than*, or both, if we say "as good or better"? The natural thing to say is "as good or better than ever", ignoring the *as* that *as good* logically needs, and you commit no great crime if that is what you do. But if you want both to run no risk of offending the purists and to avoid the prosy "as good as or better than", you can write "as good as ever or better". Thus you could change:

> Pamphlets have circulated as widely, and been not less influential, than those published in this volume,

into

> Pamphlets have circulated as widely as those published in this volume, and have been not less influential.

(For the superfluous *as* see p. 67.)

(iv) *Both*. When using *both . . . and*, be careful that these words are in their right positions and that each carries equal weight. Nothing that comes between the *both* and the *and* can be regarded as carried on after the *and*. If words are to be carried on after the *and* they must precede the *both*; if they do not precede the *both* they must be repeated after the *and*. For instance:

> He was both deaf to argument and entreaty.

Since *deaf to* comes after *both* it cannot be "understood" again after *and*. We must adjust the balance in one of the following ways:

> He was both deaf to argument and unmoved by entreaty.
>
> He was deaf both to argument and to entreaty.
>
> He was deaf to both argument and entreaty.

An extreme example of the unbalanced *both* is:

> The proposed sale must be both sanctioned by the Minister and the price must be approved by the District Valuer.

Do not use *both* where it is not necessary because the meaning of the sentence is no less plain if you leave it out:

> Both of them are equally to blame. (They are equally to blame.)
> Please ensure that both documents are fastened together. (. . . that the documents are fastened together.)

(v) *But*, in the sense of *except*, is sometimes treated as a preposition, but more commonly as a conjunction. Mrs. Hemans would not have been guilty of "bad grammar" if she had written "whence all but him had fled", but in preferring *he* she conformed to the usual practice. That is the worst of personal pronouns: by retaining the case-inflexions that nouns have so sensibly rid themselves of they pose these tiresome and trivial questions. (*See also I and Me* p. 147 and *Who and Whom* p. 153.) If the sentence could have been "whence all but the boy had fled" no one could have known whether *but* was being used as a conjunction or a preposition, and no one need have cared.

In using *but* as a conjunction an easy slip is to put it where there should be an *and*, forgetting that the conjunction that you want is one that does not go contrary to the clause immediately preceding but continues in the same sense.

> It is agreed that the primary condition of the scheme is satisfied, but it is also necessary to establish that your war service interrupted an organised course of study for a professional qualification comparable to that for which application is made, *but* as explained in previous letters, you are unable to fulfil this condition.

The italicised *but* should be *and*. The line of thought has already been turned by the first *but*; it is now going straight on.

A similar slip is made in:

> The Forestry Commission will probably only be able to offer you a post as a forest labourer, or possibly in leading a gang of forest workers, but there are at the moment no vacancies for Forest Officers.

Either *only* must be omitted or the *but* must be changed to *since*.

(vi) *If*. The use of *if* for *though* or *but* may give rise to ambiguity or absurdity. It is ambiguous in such a sentence as

> There is evidence, if not proof, that he was responsible.

Its absurdity is demonstrated in Sir Alan Herbert's imaginary example:

> Milk is nourishing, if tuberculous.

Care is also needed in the use of *if* in the sense of *whether*, for this too may cause ambiguity.

> Please inform me if there is any change in your circumstances.

Does this mean "Please inform me now whether there is any change" or "if any change should occur please inform me then"? The reader cannot tell. If *whether* and *if* become interchangeable, unintentional offence may be given by the lover who sings:

> What do I care,
> If you are there?

(vii) *Inasmuch as.* This is sometimes used in the sense of *so far as* and sometimes as a clumsy way of saying *since.* It is therefore ambiguous, and might well be dispensed with altogether.

(viii) *Like.* Colloquial English admits *like* as a conjunction, and would not be shocked at such a sentence as "Nothing succeeds like success does". In America they go even further, and say "It looks like he was going to succeed". But in English prose neither of these will do. *Like* must not be treated as a conjunction. So we may say "nothing succeeds like success"; but it must be "nothing succeeds *as* success does" and "it looks *as if* he were going to succeed".

(ix) *Provided that.* This form of introduction of a stipulation is better than *provided* without the *that* and much better than *providing.* The phrase should be reserved for a true stipulation, as in:

> He said he would go to the meeting provided that I went with him.

and not used loosely for *if* as in:

> I expect he will come tomorrow, provided that he comes at all.

Sometimes this misuse of *provided that* creates difficulties for a reader:

> Such emoluments can only count as qualifying for pension provided that they cannot be converted into cash.

The use of *provided that* obscures the meaning of a sentence that would have been clear with *if.*

(x) *Than* tempts writers to use it as a preposition, like *but* (*see* preceding page) in such a sentence as "he is older than me". Examples can be found in good writers, including a craftsman as scrupulous as Mr. Somerset Maugham. But the compilers of the Oxford English Dictionary will not have it. According to them we must say "he is older than I" (i.e. than I am). We may say "I know more about her than him" if what we mean is that my knowledge of her is greater than my knowledge of him, but if we mean that my knowledge of her is greater than his knowledge of her, we must say "I know more about her than he (does)".

But one exception is recognised—whom. We must say "than

whom", and not "than who", even though the only way of making grammatical sense of it is to regard *than* as a preposition. But that is rather a stilted way of writing, and can best be left to poetry:

> Beelzebub . . . than whom, Satan except, none higher sat.

Be careful not to slip into using *than* with words that take a different construction. *Other* and *else* are the only words besides comparatives that take *than*. *Than* is sometimes mistakenly used with such words as *preferable* and *different*, and sometimes in place of *as*:

> Nearly twice as many people die under 20 in France than in Great Britain, chiefly of tuberculosis.

(xi) *That*. For *that* (conjunction) *see* p. 152.

(xii) *When*. It is sometimes confusing to use *when* as the equivalent of *and then*.

> Let me have full particulars when I will be able to advise you. (Please let me have full particulars. I shall then be able to advise you.)
> Alternatively the Minister may make the order himself when it has the same effect as if it has been made by the Local Authority. (. . . the Minister may make the order himself, and it then has the same effect, etc. . . .)

(xiii) *While*. It is safest to use this conjunction only in its temporal sense ("Your letter came while I was away on leave"). That does not mean that it is wrong to use it also as a conjunction without any temporal sense, equivalent to *although* ("while I do not agree with you, I accept your ruling"). But it should not be used in these two different senses in the same sentence, as in:

> While appreciating your difficulties while your mother is seriously ill. . . .

Moreover, once we leave the shelter of the temporal sense, we are on the road to treating *while* as a synonym for *and*:

> Nothing will be available for some time for the desired improvement, while the general supply of linoleum to new offices may have to cease when existing stocks have run out.

There is no point in saying *while* when you mean *and*. If you are too free with *while* you are sure sooner or later to land yourself in the absurdity of seeming to say that two events occurred simultaneously which could not possibly have done so.

> The first part of the concert was conducted by Sir August Manns . . . while Sir Arthur Sullivan conducted his then recently composed *Absent Minded Beggar*.

TROUBLES WITH NEGATIVES

(i) *Double Negatives*. It has long been settled doctrine among English grammarians that two negatives cancel each other and produce an affirmative. As in mathematics —(— *x*) equals + *x*, so in language "he did not say nothing" must be regarded as equivalent to "he said something".

It is going too far to say, as is sometimes said, that this proposition is self-evident. The Greeks did not think that two negatives made an affirmative. On the contrary, the more negatives they put into a sentence the more emphatically negative the sentence became. Nor did Chaucer think so, for, in a much-quoted passage, he wrote:

> He never yit no vileineye ne sayde
> In al his lyf, unto no maner wight
> He was a verray parfit gentil knyght.

Nor did Shakespeare, who made King Claudius say:

> Nor what he said, though it lacked form a little,
> Was not like madness.

Nor do the many thousands of people who find it natural today to deny knowledge by saying "I don't know nothing at all about it". And the comedian who sings 'I ain't going to give nobody none of mine" is not misunderstood.

> Such repeated negatives, says Jespersen, are usual in a great many languages in which the negative element is comparatively small in phonetic bulk, and is easily attracted to various words. If the negation were expressed once only, it might easily be overlooked; hence the speaker, who wants the negative sense to be fully appreciated, attaches it not only to the verb, but also to other parts of the sentence: he spreads, as it were, a thin layer of negative colouring over the whole of the sentence instead of confining it to one single place. This may be called pleonastic, but is certainly not really illogical.

Still, the grammarians' rule should be observed in English today. Breaches of it are commonest with verbs of surprise or speculation ("I shouldn't wonder if there wasn't a storm." "I shouldn't be surprised if he didn't come today"). Indeed this is so common that it is classed by Fowler among his "sturdy indefensibles". A recent speech in the House of Lords affords a typical instance of the confusion of thought bred by double negatives:

> Let it not be supposed because we are building for the future rather than the present that the Bill's proposals are not devoid of significance.

What the speaker meant, of course, was "Let it not be supposed that the bill's proposals *are* devoid of significance".

Another example is:

> There is no reason to doubt that what he says in his statement . . .
> is not true.

Here the speaker meant, "There is no reason to doubt that his statement *is* true".

And another:

> It must not be assumed that there are no circumstances in which
> a profit might not be made.

Avoid multiple negatives when you can. Even if you dodge the traps they set and succeed in saying what you mean, you give your reader a puzzle to solve in sorting the negatives out. Indeed it is wise never to make a statement negatively if it could be made positively. A correspondent sends me

> The elementary ideas of the calculus are not beyond the capacity
> of more than 40 per cent of our certificate students,

and comments "I am quite unable to say whether this assertion is that two-fifths or three-fifths of the class could make something of the ideas". If the writer had said that the ideas were within the capacity of at least sixty per cent, all would have been clear. Here are two more examples of sentences that have to be unravelled before they yield any meaning:

> Few would now contend that too many checks cannot be at least
> as harmful to democracy as too few.
> The Opposition refused leave for the withdrawal of a motion to
> annul an Order revoking the embargo on the importation of cut glass.

(ii) *Neither . . . Nor.* Some books tell you that *neither . . . nor* should not be used where the alternatives are more than two. But if you decide to ignore this advice as pedantry you will find on your side not only the translators of the Bible,

> Neither death, nor life, nor angels, nor principalities, nor powers,
> nor things present, nor things to come, nor height, nor depth, nor
> any other creature, shall be able to separate us from the love of God,

but also, though not quite so profusely, Sir Harold Nicolson,

> Neither Lord Davidson nor Sir Bernard Paget nor Mr. Arthur
> Bryant will suffer permanently from the spectacle which they have
> provided.

(iii) *Nor* and *Or.* When should *nor* be used and when *or*? If a *neither* or an *either* comes first there is no difficulty; *neither* is always followed by *nor* and *either* by *or*. There can be no doubt that it is wrong to write "The existing position satisfies neither the psychologist, the judge, or the public". It should have been "neither the psychologist, nor the judge, nor the public". But when the initial negative is a simple *not* or *no*, it is often a puzzling question whether *nor* or *or* should follow. Logically it depends on whether the sentence is so framed that the initial negative runs on into the second part of it or is exhausted in the first; practically it may be of little importance which answer you give, for the meaning will be clear.

> He did not think that the Bill would be introduced this month, nor indeed before the recess.

"He did not think" affects everything that follows *that*. Logically therefore *nor* produces a double negative, as though one were to say "he didn't think it wouldn't be introduced before the recess".

> The blame for this disorder does not rest with Parliament, or with the bishops, or with the parish priests. Our real weakness is the failure of the ordinary man.

Here the negative phrase "does not rest" is carried right through the sentence, and applies to the bishops and the parish priests as much as to Parliament. There is no need to repeat the negative, and *or* is logically right. But *nor* is so often used in such a construction that it would be pedantic to condemn it: if logical defence is needed one might say that "did he think it would be introduced" in the first example, and "does it rest" in the second were understood as repeated after *nor*. But if the framework of the sentence is changed to:

> The blame for this disorder rests not with Parliament nor with the bishops, nor with the parish priests, but with the ordinary man,

it is a positive verb (*rests*) that runs through the sentence; the original negative (*not*) is attached not to the verb but to *Parliament*, and exhausts itself in exonerating Parliament. The negative must be repeated, and *nor* is rightly used.

(iv) *Not*.

(*a*) "Not all".

It is idiomatic English, to which no exception can be taken, to write "all officials are not good draftsmen" when you mean that only some of them are. Compare "All that glitters is not gold". But it is clearer, and therefore better, to write "Not all officials are good draftsmen".

(*b*) "Not . . . but."

It is also idiomatic English to write "I did not go to speak but to listen". It is pedantry to insist that, because logic demands it, this ought to be "I went not to speak but to listen". But if the latter way of arranging a "not . . . but" sentence runs as easily and makes your meaning clearer, as it often may, it should be preferred.

(*c*) "Not . . . because."

Not followed by *because* sometimes leads to ambiguity. "I did not write that letter because of what you told me" may mean either "I refrained from writing that letter because of what you told me" or "It was not because of what you told me that I wrote that letter." Avoid this ambiguity by rewriting the sentence.

TROUBLES WITH NUMBER

The rule that a singular subject requires a singular verb, and a plural subject a plural verb, is an easy one to remember and generally to observe. But it has its difficulties.

(i) Collective words.

In using collective words or nouns of multitude (*Department, Parliament, Government, Committee* and the like), ought we to say "the Government have decided" or "the Government has decided"; "the Committee are meeting" or "the Committee is meeting"? There is no rule; either a singular or plural verb may be used. The plural is more suitable when the emphasis is on the individual members, and the singular when it is on the body as a whole. "A committee *was* appointed to consider this subject"; "the committee *were* unable to agree". Sometimes the need to use a pronoun settles the question. We cannot say "The committee differed among itself", nor, without risk of misunderstanding, "the committee on whom I sat". But the number ought not to be varied in the same document without good cause. Accidentally changing it is a common form of carelessness:

> The firm *has* given an undertaking that in the event of *their* having to restrict production. . . .
> The industry *is* capable of supplying all home requirements and *have* in fact been exporting.
> It will be for each committee to determine in the light of *its* responsibilities how far it is necessary to make all these appointments, and no appointment should be made unless the committee *are* fully satisfied of the need.

Conversely a subject plural in form may be given a singular verb if it signifies a single entity such as a country (the United States has agreed) or an organisation (the United Nations has resolved) or a measure (six miles is not too far; twelve months is a long time to wait).

(ii) Words linked by *and*.

To the elementary rule that two singular nouns linked by *and* should be given a plural verb justifiable exceptions can be found where the linked words form a single idea. The stock example is

Kipling's "The tumult and the shouting dies"; "the tumult and the shouting", it is explained, are equivalent to "the tumultuous shouting". But *die* would not have rhymed with *sacrifice*. Rhyming poets must be allowed some licence.

Perhaps these official examples might be justified in the same way:

> Duration and charge was advised at the conclusion of the call.
> Your desire and need for a telephone service is fully appreciated.

It might be argued that "duration and charge" was equivalent to "the appropriate charge for that duration", and that "your desire and need" was equivalent to "the desire arising from your need". But it is safer to observe the rule, and to leave these questionable experiments to the poets.

Other instances of singular verbs with subjects linked by *and* cannot be so easily explained away. They are frequent when the verb comes first. Shakespeare has them ("Is Bushy, Green and the Earl of Wiltshire dead?") and so have the translators of the Bible ("Thine is the kingdom, the power and the glory"). If we may never attribute mere carelessness to great writers, we must explain these by saying that the singular verb is more vivid, and should be understood as repeated with each noun—"Is Bushy, (is) Green and (is) the Earl of Wiltshire dead?" Those who like to have everything tidy may get some satisfaction from this, but the writer of official English should forget about these refinements. He should stick to the simple rule.

(iii) Words linked by *with*.

If the subject is singular the verb should be singular. "The Secretary of State together with the Under-Secretary is coming".

(iv) Alternative subjects.

Either and *neither* must always have a singular verb unless one of the alternative subjects is a plural word. It is a very common error to write such sentences as:

> I am unable to trace that either of the items have been paid.
> Neither knowledge nor skill are needed.

(v) When *each* is the subject of a sentence the verb is singular and so is any pronoun:

> Each has a room to himself.

When a plural noun or pronoun is the subject, with *each* in apposition, the verb is plural:

> They have a room each.

(vi) Attraction.

The verb must agree with the subject, and not allow itself to be attracted into the number of the complement. Modern grammarians will not pass "the wages of sin is death". The safe rule for the ordinary writer in sentences such as this is to regard what precedes the verb as the subject and what follows it as the complement, and so to write "the wages of sin are death" and "death is the wages of sin".

A verb some way from its subject is sometimes lured away from its proper number by a noun closer to it, as in:

> We regret that assurances given us twelve months ago that a sufficient supply of suitable local labour would be available to meet our requirements has not been fulfilled.
> So far as the heating of buildings in permanent Government occupation are concerned. . . .

Sometimes the weight of a plural pushes the verb into the wrong number, even though they are not next to one another:

> Thousands of pounds' worth of damage have been done to the apple crop.

In these sentences *has*, *are* and *have* are blunders. So is the common attraction of the verb into the plural when the subject is *either* or *neither* in such sentences as "Neither of the questions have been answered" or "Either of the questions were embarrassing". But in one or two exceptional instances the force of this attraction has conquered the grammarians. With the phrase *more than one* the pull of *one* is so strong that the singular is always used (e.g. "more than one question was asked"), and owing to the pull of the plural in such a sentence as "none of the questions were answered" *none* has come to be used indifferently with a singular or a plural verb. Conversely, owing to the pull of the singular *a* in the expression *many a*, it always takes a singular verb. "There's many a slip twixt cup and lip" is idiomatic English.

(vii) It is a common slip to write *there is* or *there was* where a plural subject requires *there are* or *there were*.

> There was available one large room and three small ones.

Was should be *were*.

It is true that Ophelia said "there is pansies". But she was not herself at the time. (

(viii) Certain nouns are sometimes puzzling.

Agenda, though in form plural, has been admitted to the language as a singular word. Nobody would say "the agenda for Monday's meeting *have* not yet reached me". If a word is needed for one of the components of the agenda, say "item No. so-and-so of the agenda", not "agendum No. so-and-so", which would be the extreme of pedantry. If one is wanted for the plural of the word itself it must be *agendas* or *agenda papers*.

Data, unlike *agenda*, remains the plural word that it is in Latin.

> Unless firm data is available at an early date. . . .

This is wrong. *Is* should be *are*.

If a singular is wanted, it is usually *one of the data*, not *datum*. The ordinary meaning of *datum* is:

> Any position or element in relation to which others are determined: chiefly in the phrases: *datum point*, a point assumed or used as a basis of reckoning, adjustment or the like—*datum line* a horizontal line from which heights and depths of points are reckoned, as in a railroad plan. . . . (Webster.)

Means in the sense of "means to an end" is a curious word; it may be treated either as singular or as plural. Supposing, for instance, that you wanted to say that means had been sought to do something, you may if you choose treat the word as singular and say "a means was sought" or "every means was sought". Or you may treat it as plural and say "all means were sought". Or again, if you use just the word *means* without any word such as *a* or *every* or *all* to show its number, you may give it a singular or plural verb as you wish: you may say either "means was sought" or "means were sought"; both are idiomatic. Perhaps on the whole it is best to say "a method (or way) was sought" if there was only one, and "means were sought" if there was more than one.

Means in the sense of monetary resources is always plural.

Number. Like other collective nouns *number* may take either a singular or a plural verb. Unlike most of them, it admits of a simple and logical rule. When all that it is doing is forming part of a composite plural subject, it should have a plural verb, as in:

> A large number of people are coming today.

But when it is standing on its own legs as the subject it should have a singular verb, as in:

> The number of people coming today is large.

The following are accordingly unidiomatic:

> There is a number of applications, some of which were made before yours.
> There is a large number of outstanding orders.

The true subjects are not "a number" and "a large number" but "a number-of-applications" and "a-large-number-of-outstanding-orders".

Of the following examples the first has a singular verb that should be plural and the second a plural verb that should be singular.

> There was also a number of conferences calling themselves peace conferences which had no real interest in peace.
>
> The number of casualties in H.M.S. *Amethyst* are thought to be about fifteen.

Those kind of things. The use of the plural *these* or *those* with the singular *kind* or *sort* is common in conversation, and instances of it could be found in good authors. But public opinion generally condemns it. As I have said (p. 35), the phrase *those kind of things*, like *different to*, *very pleased*, *drive slow*, and the split infinitive used to be among the shibboleths by which it was supposed to be possible to distinguish those who were instructed in their mother-tongue from those who were not. Years ago *Punch* published a poem containing this verse:

> Did you say those sort of things
> Never seem to you to matter?
> Gloomily the poet sings
> *Did* you say those sort of things?
> Frightened love would soon take wings
> All his fondest hopes you'd shatter
> Did you say "those sort of things
> Never seem to you to matter"?

We have a better sense of values today. But even now it is as well to humour the purists by writing *things of that kind*.

TROUBLES WITH PREPOSITIONS

(i) Ending sentences with prepositions.

Do not hesitate to end a sentence with a preposition if your ear tells you that that is where the preposition goes best. There used to be a rather half-hearted grammarian's rule against doing this, but no good writer ever heeded it, except Dryden, who seems to have invented it. The translators of the Authorised Version did not know it ("but I have a baptism to be baptised with"). The very rule itself, if phrased "do not use a preposition to end a sentence with", has a smoother flow and a more idiomatic ring than "do not use a preposition with which to end a sentence". Sometimes, when the final word is really a verbal particle, and the verb's meaning depends on it, they form together a phrasal verb (*see* pp. 70/1)—*put up with* for instance—and to separate them makes nonsense. It is said that Sir Winston Churchill once made this marginal comment against a sentence that clumsily avoided a prepositional ending: "This is the sort of English up with which I will not put". The ear is a pretty safe guide. Nearly a hundred years ago Dean Alford protested against this so-called rule. "I know", he said, "that I am at variance with the rules taught at very respectable institutions for enabling young ladies to talk unlike their elders. But that I cannot help." The story is well known of the nurse who performed the remarkable feat of getting four* prepositions at the end of a sentence by asking her charge: "What did you choose that book to be read to out of for?" She said what she wanted to say perfectly clearly, in words of one syllable, and what more can one ask?

But the championship of the sport of preposition-piling seems now to have been wrested from the English nurse by an American poet:

> I lately lost a preposition;
>   It hid, I thought, beneath my chair
> And angrily I cried, "Perdition!
>   Up from out of in under there."

> Correctness is my vade mecum,
>   And straggling phrases I abhor,
> And yet I wondered, "What should he come
>   Up from out of in under for?"†

(ii) Cannibalism by prepositions.

Cannibalism is the name given by Fowler to a vice that prepositions are specially prone to, though it may infect any part of speech. One of a pair of words swallows the other:

> Any articles for which export licences are held or for which licences have been applied.

The writer meant "or for which export licences have been applied for", but the first *for* has swallowed the second.

For circumlocutory prepositions (*in regard to* and the like) (*see* pp. 63/4).

(iii) Some particular prepositions

(*a*) *Between* and *among*. The O.E.D. tells us not to heed those who tell us that *between* must only be used of two things and that when there are more the preposition must be *among*. It says:

> *Between* is still the only word available to express the relation of a thing to many surrounding things severally and individually, *among* expressing a relationship to them collectively and vaguely: we should not say "the space lying among the three points", or "a treaty among three powers" or "the choice lies among the three candidates in the select list" or "to insert a needle among the closed petals of a flower".

---

*It has been pointed out to me by a correspondent that there are really only three. *Out* is an adverb, forming, with *of*, a composite preposition.

†Morris Bishop in the *New Yorker*, 27th September, 1947.

(*b*) *Between each.* Grammarians generally condemn the common use of *between* with *each* or *every*, as in "there will be a week's interval between each sitting". It is arguable that this can be justified as a convenient way of saying "between each sitting and the next", and that, considering how common it is, only pedantry can object. But those who want to be on the safe side can say either "weekly intervals between the sittings" or "a week's interval after each sitting".

(*c*) *Between . . . or and between . . . and between.* If *between* is followed by a conjunction, this must always be a simple *and*. It is wrong to say: "the choice lies between Smith or Jones", or to say "we had to choose between taking these offices and making the best of them and between perhaps finding ourselves with no offices at all". If a sentence has become so involved that *and* is not felt to be enough it should be recast. This mistake is not unknown in high places:

> It is thought that the choice lies between Mr. Trygve Lie continuing for another year or the election of Mr. Lester Pearson.

(*d*) For *between you and I* see *I and me* (p. 147).

(*e*) *Due to.* *Owing to* long ago established itself as a prepositional phrase. But the orthodox still keep up the fight against the attempt of *due to* to do the same: they maintain that *due* is an adjective and should not be used otherwise. That means that it must always have a noun to agree with. You may say: "Floods due to a breach in the river bank covered a thousand acres of land". But you must not say: "Due to a breach in the river bank a thousand acres of land were flooded". In the first *due to* agrees properly with floods, which were in fact due to the breach. In the second it can only agree with a thousand acres of land, which were not due to the breach, or to anything else except the Creation.

Due to is rightly used in:

> The closing of the telephone exchange was due to lack of equipment. (*Due to* agrees with closing.)
> The delay in replying has been due to the fact that it was hoped to call upon you. (*Due to* agrees with delay.)

Due to is wrongly used in:

> We must apologise to listeners who missed the introduction to the talk due to a technical fault.
> As listeners probably know, there was no play at Trent Bridge to-day due to the rain.

It must be admitted that the prepositional use is very common and it may have come to stay. I have already quoted Fowler's remark about it: "perhaps idiom will beat the illiterates, perhaps the

illiterates will beat idiom; our grandsons will know". Now that the
B.B.C. has taken the side of the illiterates they will probably win.
Perhaps the battle is already lost. An American writer, Professor
Kenyon, has said regretfully:

> Strong as is my own prejudice against the prepositional use of
> *due to*, I greatly fear it has staked its claim and squatted in our midst
> alongside of and in exact imitation of *owing to*, its aristocratic neigh-
> bour and respected fellow-citizen.*

(*f*) *Following.* Grammarians do not admit *following* as a preposition, though its use as one is becoming so common that they may
soon have to give it *de facto* recognition. The orthodox view is that
it is the participle of the verb *follow*, and must have a noun to agree
with, as it has in:

> Such rapid promotion, following his exceptional services, was not
> unexpected.

But as a preposition it is unnecessary when it usurps the place of
in consequence of, *in accordance with*, or *as a result of*, as in:

> Following judgments of the High Court, Ministers of Religion
> are not regarded as employed under a contract of service.
> It has been brought to my notice following a recent visit of an
> Inspector of this Ministry to the premises of . . . that you are an
> insured person under the Act.
> Following heavy rain last night the wicket is very wet.

Still less can there by any justification for it with a merely temporal significance. It might perhaps put in a plea for a useful
function as meaning something between the two—between the
propter hoc of those prepositional phrases and the *post hoc* of *after*.
This announcement might claim that justification:

> A man will appear at Bow Street this morning following the
> destruction of Mr. Reg Butler's statue of the Political Prisoner.

But the word shows little sign of being content with that rather
subtle duty. More and more, under the strong lead of B.B.C.
announcers, it is becoming merely a pretentious substitute for *after*.

> Following the orchestral concert, we come to a talk by Mr. X.
> Following that old English tune, we go to Latin-America for the
> next one.

(*g*) *Prior to.* There is no good reason to use *prior to* as a preposition
instead of *before*. *Before* is simpler, better known and more natural,
and therefore preferable. It is moreover at least questionable whether
prior to has established itself as a preposition. By all means use the

*Quoted in Perrin, *Writer's Guide and Index to English.*

phrase a *prior engagement*, where *prior* is doing its proper job as an adjective. But do not say that you made an engagement *prior to* receiving the second invitation.

> Mr. X has requested that you should submit to him, immediately prior to placing orders, lists of components. . . .
>
> Sir Adrian Boult is resting prior to the forthcoming tour of the B.B.C. Symphony Orchestra.

In sentences such as these *prior to* cannot have any advantage over the straightforward *before*.

TROUBLES WITH PRONOUNS

"The use of pronouns", said Cobbett, "is to prevent the repetition of nouns, and to make speaking and writing more rapid and less encumbered with words". In more than one respect they are difficult parts of speech to handle.

(i) It is an easy slip to use a pronoun without a true antecedent.

> He offered to resign but it was refused.

Here *it* has not a true antecedent, as it would have had if the sentence had begun "he offered his resignation". This is a purely grammatical point, but unless care is taken over it a verbal absurdity may result. Cobbett gives this example from Addison:

> There are indeed but very few who know how to be idle and innocent, or have a relish of any pleasures that are not criminal; every diversion they take is at the expense of some one virtue or other, and their very first step out of business is into vice or folly.

As Cobbett points out, the only possible antecedent to *they* and *their* is the "very few who know how to be idle and innocent", and that is the opposite of what Addison means.

(ii) Be sure that there is no real ambiguity about the antecedent. This is more than a grammatical point; it affects the intelligibility of what you write. Special care is needed when the pronouns are *he* and *him*, and more than one male person has been mentioned. Latin is sensible enough to have two pronouns for *he* and *him*, one of which is used only when referring to the subject of the sentence; but English affords no such aids.

Stevenson lamented this and said:

> When I invent a language there shall be a direct and an indirect pronoun differently declined—then writing would be some fun.

DIRECT	INDIRECT
He	Tu
Him	Tum
His	Tus

> Example: He seized tum by tus throat; but tu at the same time

caught him by his hair. A fellow could write hurricanes with an inflection like that. Yet there would be difficulties too.*

Handicapped as we are by the lack of this useful artifice, we must be careful to leave no doubt about the antecedents of our pronouns, and must not make our readers guess, even though it may not be difficult to guess right. As Jespersen points out, a sentence like "John told Robert's son that he must help him" is theoretically capable of six different meanings. It is true that Jespersen would not have us trouble overmuch when there can be no real doubt about the antecedent, and he points out that there is little danger of misunderstanding the theoretically ambiguous sentence:

> If the baby does not thrive on raw milk, boil it.

Nevertheless, he adds, it is well to be very careful about one's pronouns.

Here are one or two examples, to show how difficult it is to avoid ambiguity:

> Mr. S. told Mr. H. he was prepared to transfer part of his allocation to his purposes provided that he received £10,000.

The *his* before *purposes* refers, it would seem, to Mr. H. and the other three pronouns to Mr. S.

> Mr. H. F. saw a man throw something from his pockets to the hens on his farm, and then twist the neck of one of them when they ran to him.

Here the change of antecedent from "the man" to Mr. H. F. and back again to "the man" is puzzling at first.

There are several possible ways of removing ambiguities such as these. Let us take by way of illustration the sentence, "Sir Henry Ponsonby informed Mr. Gladstone that the Queen had been much upset by what he had told her" and let us assume that the ambiguous *he* refers to Mr. Gladstone. We can make the antecedent plain by

1. Not using a pronoun at all, and writing "by what Mr. Gladstone had told her".
2. Parenthetic explanation—"by what he (Mr. Gladstone) had told her".
3. The *former-latter* device—"by what the latter had told her".
4. By rewriting the sentence—"The Queen was much upset by what Mr. Gladstone told her, and Sir Henry Ponsonby so informed him".

---

*Letter to E. L. Burlingame, March 1892.

5. The device that Henry Sidgwick called "the polite alias" and Fowler "elegant variation", and writing (say) "by what the Prime Minister had told her", or the "G.O.M." or "the veteran statesman".

It may safely be said that the fifth device should seldom if ever be adopted,* and the third only when the antecedent is very close.

(iii) Do not be shy of pronouns.

So far we have been concerned in this section with the dangers that beset the user of pronouns. But for the official no less a danger is that of not using them when he ought. Legal language, which must aim above all things at removing every possible ambiguity, is more sparing of pronouns than ordinary prose, because of an ever-present fear that the antecedent may be uncertain. For instance, opening at random an Act of Parliament, I read:

> The Secretary of State may by any such regulations allow the required notice of any occurrence to which the regulations relate, instead of being sent forthwith, to be sent within the time limited by the regulations.

Anyone not writing legal language would have avoided repeating *regulations* twice; he would have put *they* in the first place and *them* in the second.

Officials have so much to read and explain that is written in legal English that they become infected with pronoun-avoidance. The result is that what they write is often, in Cobbett's phrase, "more encumbered with words" than it need be.

> The examiner's search would in all cases be carried up to the date of the filing of the complete specification, and the examiner (he) need not trouble his head with the subject of disconformity.

> The Ministry of Agriculture and Fisheries are anxious that the Rural Land Utilisation Officer should not in any way hinder the acquisition or earmarking of land for educational purposes, but it is the duty of the Rural Land Utilisation Officer (his duty) to ensure. . . .

> Arrangements are being made to continue the production of these houses for a further period, and increased numbers of these houses them) will, therefore, be available.

---

journalistic trick is out of favour now. But it used to be an accepted of fine writing. There is a remarkable example in the extract from *The* 6th December, 1848, printed in the issue of 6th December, 1948. The is to a forthcoming demonstration of M. Molk's newly invented "electric ht":

this period of the evening the moon will be in its zenith, but M. Molk not apprehend any sensible diminution of the lustre of his light from the sence of that beautiful luminary."

Often the repeated word is embroidered by *such*:

> . . . the admission of specially selected Public Assistance cases, provided that no suitable accommodation is available for such cases (them) in a home. . . .

This also is no doubt due to infection by legal English, where this use of *such* is an indispensable device for securing economy of words. The draftsman, whose concern is to make his meaning certain beyond the possibility of error, avoids pronouns lest there should be an ambiguity about their antecedents, but escapes the need for repeating words of limitation by the use of *such* or *such . . . as aforesaid*. The official need not usually be so punctilious.

But using *such* in the way the lawyers use it is not always out of place in ordinary writing. Sometimes it is proper and useful.

> One month's notice in writing must be given to terminate this agreement. As no such notice has been received from you. . . .

Here it is important for the writer to show that in the second sentence he is referring to the same sort of notice as in the first and the *such* device is the neatest way of doing it.

(iv) It is usually better not to allow a pronoun to precede its principal. If the pronoun comes first the reader may not know what it refers to until he arrives at the principal.

> I regret that it is not practicable, in view of its size, to provide a list of the agents.

Here, it is true, the reader is only momentarily left guessing what *its* refers to. But he would have been spared even that if the sentence had been written:

> I regret that it is not practicable to provide a list of the agents; there are too many of them.

(v) *Each other*. Grammarians used to say that *each other* is the right expression when only two persons or things are referred to and *one another* when there are more than two. But Fowler, quoted with approval by Jespersen, says of this so-called rule, "This differentiation is neither of present utility nor based on historical usage".

(vi) *Former* and *latter*. Do not hesitate to repeat words rather than use *former* or *latter* to avoid doing so. The reader probably has to look back to see which is which, and so you annoy him and waste his time. And there is no excuse at all for using *latter* merely to serve as a pronoun, as in:

> In these employments we would rest our case for the exclusion of young persons directly on the grounds of the latter's moral welfare. (Their moral welfare.)

Remember that *former* and *latter* can refer to only two things and if you use them of more than two you may puzzle your reader. If you want to refer otherwise than specifically to the last of more than two things, say *last* or *last-mentioned*, not *latter*.

(vii) *I* and *me*. About the age-long conflict between *it is I* and *it is me*, no more need be said than that, in the present stage of the battle, most people would think "it is I" pedantic in talk and "it is me" improper in writing.

What calls more for examination is the practice of using *I* for *me* in combination with some noun or other pronoun, e.g. "between you and I", "let you and I go". Why this has become so prevalent is not easy to say. Perhaps it comes partly from an excess of zeal in correcting the opposite error. When Mrs. Elton said "Neither Mr. Suckling nor me had ever any patience with them", and Lydia Bennet "Mrs. Forster and me are such friends", they were guilty of a vulgarism that was, no doubt, common in Jane Austen's day, and is not unknown to-day. One might suppose that this mistake was corrected by teachers of English in our schools with such ferocity that their pupils are left with the conviction that such combinations as *you and me* are in all circumstances ungrammatical. But that will not quite do. It might explain a popular broadcaster's saying "that's four to Margaret and I", but it cannot explain why Shakespeare wrote: "All debts are cleared between you and I".*

It is the combination of oneself with someone else that proves fatal. The official who wrote: "I trust that it will be convenient to you for my colleague and I to call upon you next Tuesday" would never, if he had been proposing to come alone, have written "I trust that it will be convenient to you for I to call upon you . . .". A sure and easy way of avoiding this blunder is to ask oneself what case the personal pronoun would have been in—would it have been *I* or *me*—if it had stood alone. It should remain the same in partnership as it would have been by itself.

The association of someone else with oneself sometimes prompts the use of *myself* where a simple *I* or *me* is all that is needed, e.g. "The inspection will be made by Mr. Jones and myself". *Myself* should be used only for emphasis ("I saw it myself") or as the reflexive form of the personal pronoun ("I have hurt myself").

(viii) *It*. This pronoun is specially troublesome because the convenient English idiom of using *it* to anticipate the subject of a

---

*Shakespeare is notoriously the grammarians' despair. Even Hamlet, a young man of scholarship standard if ever there was one, said "between who?" when Polonius asked him, "What is the matter, my Lord?"

sentence tends to produce a plethora of *its*. A correspondent sends me this example:

> It is to be expected that it will be difficult to apply A unless it is accompanied by B, for which reason it is generally preferable to use C in spite of its other disadvantages.

This, he justly says, could be put more effectively and tersely by writing:

> C is generally preferable, in spite of its disadvantages, because application of A without B is difficult.

"Never put an *it* on paper", said Cobbett, "without thinking well what you are about. When I see many *its* on a paper I always tremble for the writer."

(ix) *One.*

(*a*) *One* has a way of intruding in such a sentence as "The problem is not an easy one". "The problem is not easy" may be a neater way of saying what you mean.

(*b*) What pronoun should be used with *one*? *His* or *one's*, for example? That depends on what sort of a *one* it is, whether "numeral" or "impersonal", to use Fowler's labels. Fowler illustrates the difference thus:

> One hates *his* enemies and another forgives them (numeral).
> One hates *one's* enemies and loves *one's* friends (impersonal).

But any sentence that needs to repeat the impersonal *one* is bound to be inelegant, and you will do better to rewrite it.

(*c*) "One of those who. . . ." A common error in sentences of this sort is to use a singular verb instead of a plural, as though the antecedent of *who* were *one* and not *those*—to write, for instance, "It is one of the exceptional cases that calls for (instead of call for) exceptional treatment".

(x) *Same.* Four hundred years ago, when the Thirty-nine Articles were drawn up, it was good English idiom to use *the same* as a pronoun where we should now say *he* or *she*, *him* or *her*, *they* or *them*, or *it*.

> The riches and goods of Christians are not common, as touching the right title and possession of the same, as certain Anabaptists do falsely boast.

This is no good reason for the present pronominal use of *the same* and *same*, which survives robustly in commercialese. It is to be found to some extent in official writing also, especially in letters on business subjects. This use of *same* is now by general consent reprehensible because it gives an air of artificiality and pretentiousness.

EXAMPLE	ALTERNATIVE VERSION
As you have omitted to insert your full Christian names, I shall be glad if you will advise me of same.	As you have omitted to insert your full Christian names, I shall be glad if you will let me know what they are.
With reference to the above matter, and my representative's interview of the 12th October, relative to same. . . .	With reference to this matter and my representative's interview of the 12th October about it. . . .
I enclose the necessary form for agreement and shall be glad if you will kindly complete and return same at your early convenience.	(For *same* substitute *it*.)

In the following sentence,

> I am informed that it may be decided by X Section that this extra will not be required. I await therefore their decision before taking further action in an attempt to provide,

I like to think that the writer stopped abruptly after *provide*, leaving it objectless, in order to check himself on the brink of writing *same*. But he might harmlessly have written *it*.

(xi) *They* for *he or she*. It is common in speech, and not unknown in serious writing, to use *they* or *them* as the equivalent of a singular pronoun of a common sex, as in: "Each insisted on their own point of view, and hence the marriage came to an end". This is stigmatised by grammarians as a usage grammatically indefensible. The Judge ought, they would say, to have said "He insisted on his own point of view and she on hers". Jespersen says about this:

> third person it would have been very convenient to have a
> x pronoun, but as a matter of fact English has none and
> ore use one of the three makeshift expedients shown in
> ng sentences:
> er's heart—if he or she have any. (Fielding.)
> hath ears to hear let him hear. (A.V.)
> prevents you, do they? (Thackeray.)

l writer will be wise for the present to use the first or
not to be tempted by the greater convenience of the
necessity may eventually force it into the category of
m. The Ministry of Labour and National Service have
her device, but it is an ugly one, suitable only for

> Each worker must acknowledge receipt by entering the serial number of the supplementary coupon sheet issued to him/her in column 4 and signing his/her name in column 5.

Whatever justification there may be for using *themselves* as a singular common-sex pronoun, there can be no excuse for it when only one sex is referred to.

> The female manipulative jobs are of a type to which by no means everyone can adapt themselves with ease.

There is no reason why *herself* should not have been written instead of *themselves*

(xii) *What.* *What*, in the sense of *that which*, or *those which*, is an antecedent and relative combined. Because it may be either singular or plural in number, and either subjective or objective in case, it needs careful handling.

Fowler says that its difficulties of number can be solved by asking the question "what does it stand for?"

> What is needed is more rooms.

Here Fowler would say that *what* means *the thing that*, and the singular verb is right: On the other hand, in the sentence "He no doubt acted with what are in his opinion excellent reasons", *are* is right because *what* is equivalent to *reasons that*. But this is perhaps over subtle, and there is no great harm in treating *what* as plural in such a construction whenever the complement is plural. It sounds more natural.

Because *what* may be subjective or objective, writers may find themselves making the same word do duty in both cases, a practice condemned by grammarians. For instance:

> This was what came into his head and he said without thinking.

What is here being made to do duty both as the subject of *came* and as the object of *said*. If we want to be punctiliously grammatical we must write either:

> This is what (subjective) came into his head and what (objective) he said without thinking.

or, preferably,

> This is what came into his head, and he said it without thinking.

(xiii) *Which.* The *New Yorker* of the 4th December, 1948, quoted a question asked of the *Philadelphia Bulletin* by a correspondent:

> My class would appreciate a discussion of the wrong use of *which* in sentences like "He wrecked the car which was due to his carelessness",

answer given by that newspaper:

e fault lies in using *which* to refer to the statement "*He wrecked
ar*". When *which* follows a noun it refers to that noun as its
cedent. Therefore in the foregoing sentence it is stated that the
was due to his carelessness, which is nonsense.

at is? Carelessness? is the *New Yorker's* query.
ich shows how dangerous it is to dogmatise about the use of
with an antecedent consisting not of a single word but of a
e. *Punch* has also provided an illustration of the same danger
n a novel"):

Mrs. Brandon took the heavy piece of silk from the table, unfolded
and displayed an altar cloth of her own exquisite embroidery . . .
pon which everyone began to blow their nose. . . .

ne fact is that this is a common and convenient usage, but needs
e handled discreetly to avoid ambiguity or awkwardness.

The required statement is in course of preparation and will be
forwarded as soon as official records are complete, which will be in
about a week's time.

Here it is unnecessary; the sentence can be improved by omitting
the words "which will be", and so getting rid of the relative
altogether.

The long delay may make it inevitable for the authorities to
consider placing the order elsewhere which can only be in the United
States which is a step we should be anxious to avoid.

Here the writer has used *which* in this way twice in a single
sentence, and shown how awkward its effect can be. He might have
put a full-stop after *elsewhere* and continued, "That can only be in
the United States and is a step we should be anxious to avoid".

(xiv) *Which* and *that*. On the whole it makes for smoothness of
writing not to use the relative *which* where *that* would do as well,
and not to use either if a sentence makes sense and runs pleasantly
without. But that is a very broad general statement, subject to many
exceptions.

That cannot be used in a "commenting"* clause; the relative
must be *which*. With a "defining"* clause either *which* or *that* is permissible, but *that* is to be preferred. When in a "defining" clause
the relative is in the objective case, it can often be left out altogether.
Thus we have the three variants:

This case ought to go to the Home Office, *which* deals with police
establishments. (Commenting relative clause.)

---

*These terms are explained on p. 180.

> The Department *that* deals with police establishments is the Home Office. (Defining relative clause.)
> This is the case you said we ought to send to the Home Office. (Defining relative clause in which the relative pronoun, if it were expressed, would be in the objective case.)

That is an awkward word because it may be one of three parts of speech—a conjunction, a relative pronoun and a demonstrative pronoun. "I think that the paper that he wants is that one" illustrates the three in the order given. More than one modern writer has tried the experiment of spelling the word differently (*that* and *thatt*) according to its function; but not all readers are likely to find this expedient helpful, and any official who used it would be likely to get into trouble.

It is a sound rule that *that* should be dispensed with whenever this can be done without loss of clarity or dignity. For instance, the sentence just given might be written with only one *that* instead of three: "I think the paper he wants is that one". Some verbs seem to need a conjunctive *that* after them more than others do. *Say* and *think* can generally do without. The more formal words like *state* and *assert* cannot.

The conjunctive *that* often leads writers into error, especially in long sentences. This is not so much a matter of rule as of being careful.

> It was agreed that, since suitable accommodation was now available in a convenient position, and that a move to larger offices was therefore feasible, Treasury sanction should be sought for acquiring them.

Here a superfluous *that* has slipped into the middle of the sentence. The first *that* was capable of doing all the work.

> All removing residential subscribers are required to sign the special condition, that if called upon to share your line that you will do so.

That is another case of careless duplication.

> As stated by the Minister of Fuel and Power on the 8th April, a standard ration will be available for use from 1st June, 1948, in every private car and motor cycle currently licensed and that an amount equivalent to the standard ration will be deducted. . . .

The draftsman of this forgot how he had begun his sentence. He continued it as though he had begun "The Minister of Fuel and Power stated . . ." instead of "As stated by the Minister of Fuel and Power". The consequence was that he put in a *that* which defies both sense and grammar.

> The Ministry of Food allow such demonstrations only if the materials used are provided by the staff and that no food is sold to the public.

In this sentence the use of *that* for *if* is less excusable because the writer had less time to forget how he had begun.

> Their intention was probably to remove from the mind of the native that he was in any way bound to work, and that the Government would protect him from bad employers.

This example shows the need of care in sentences in which *that* has to be repeated. If you do not remember what words introduced the first *that*, you may easily find yourself, as here, saying the opposite of what you mean. What this writer meant to say was that the intention was to remove the first idea from the native's mind and to put the second into it, not, as he has accidentally said, to remove both.

(xv) *Who* and *whom*. *Who* is the subjective case and *whom* the objective. The proper use of the two words should present no difficulty. But we are so unaccustomed to different case-formations in English that when we are confronted with them we are liable to lose our heads. In the matter of *who* and *whom* good writers have for centuries been perverse in refusing to do what the grammarians tell them. They will insist on writing sentences like "Who should I see there?" (Addison), "Ferdinand whom they suppose is drowned" (Shakespeare), "Whom say men that I am?" (translators of the Bible). Now any schoolboy can see that, by the rules, *who* in the first quotation, being the object of *see*, ought to be *whom*, and that *whom* in the second and third quotations, being in the one the subject of *is*, and in the other the complement of *am*, ought to be *who*. What then is the ordinary man to believe? There are some who would have us do away with *whom* altogether, as nothing but a mischief-maker. That might be a useful way out. But then, as was asked in the correspondence columns of the *Spectator* by one who signed himself "A. Woodowl" (31st December, 1948):

> Regarding the suggested disuse of *whom*, may I ask by who a lead can be given? To who, to wit, of the "cultured" authorities can we appeal to boo *whom* and to boom *who*?

Whom will take some killing, too. Shakespeare and the translators of the Bible have their distinguished followers to-day, such as Sir Winston Churchill ("The slaves of the lamp . . . render faithful service to whomsoever holds the talisman"), Mr. E. M. Forster ("A creature whom we pretend is here already"), Lord David Cecil ("West, whom he knew would never be seduced away from him"), *The Times* ("He was not the man whom the police think may be able to help them") and even Mr. Somerset Maugham ("Bateman could not imagine whom it was that he passed off as his nephew"). This usage is moreover defended by Jespersen.

Sometimes, though more rarely, the opposite mistake is made:

> A Chancellor who, grudging as was the acknowledgment he received for it, everyone knew to have saved his party.

But it has not yet become pedantic—at any rate in writing—to use *who* and *whom* in what grammarians would call the correct way, and the ordinary writer should so use them, ignoring these vagaries of the great. He should be specially careful about such sentences as:

> The manager should select those officers *who* he desires should sign on his behalf.
> The manager should select those officers *whom* he authorises to sign on his behalf.
> There has been some argument about *who* should be authorised to sign on the manager's behalf.

(xvi) *Whose*. There is a grammarians' rule that *whose* must not be used of inanimate objects: we may say "authors whose books are famous", but we must not say "books whose authors are famous"; we must fall back on an ugly roundabout way of putting it, and say, "books the authors of which are famous". This rule, even more than that which forbids the split infinitive, is a cramping one, productive of ugly sentences and a temptation to misplaced commas.

> There are now a large number of direct controls, the purpose of which is to allocate scarce resources of all kinds between the various applicants for their use.

Here the writer, having duly respected the prejudice against the inanimate *whose*, finds that *controls the purpose* is an awkward juxtaposition, with its momentary flicker of a suggestion that *controls* is a verb governing *purpose*.* So he separates them by a comma, although the relative clause is a "defining" one (*see* pp. 180/1), and the comma therefore misleading. In his effort to avoid one ambiguity he has created another.

> Sir Alexander Cadogan added that legislatures were not unaccustomed to ratifying decisions the entry into force of which was contingent on circumstances beyond their control.

Here the writer has properly resisted the temptation to lessen the inevitable ugliness of the construction by putting a comma after *decisions*. How much more smoothly each sentence would run if the

---

*Care should be taken to avoid the "false scent" that comes from grouping words in a way that suggests a different construction from the one intended, however fleeting the suggestion may be. In the sentence:

"Behind each part of the story I shall tell lies an untold and often unsuspected story of hard work . . ."

the words "I shall tell lies" irresistibly group themselves together until the eye has passed on. Never try to correct this sort of thing with a comma; always reconstruct.

writer had felt at liberty to say *controls whose purpose* and *decisions whose entry*.

The rule is so cramping and so pointless that even the grammarians are in revolt against it. Onions regards it as permissible to use *whose* in such circumstances in order to avoid the "somewhat awkward collocation of *of which* with the definite article". Fowler said:

> Let us in the name of common sense prohibit the prohibition of *whose inanimate*; good writing is surely difficult enough without the forbidding of things that have historical grammar and present intelligibility and obvious convenience on their side, and lack only—starch.

There are welcome signs that Fowler's advice is now being followed in official publications:

> The hospital whose characteristics and associations link it with a particular religious denomination.
> That revolution the full force of whose effects we are beginning to feel.
> There has been built up a single centrally organised blood-transfusion service whose object is. . . .

TROUBLES WITH VERBS

(i) *ing endings*

Words ending in *ing* are mostly verbal participles or gerunds, and, as we shall see, it is not always easy to say which is which. By way of introduction it will be enough to observe that when they are of the nature of participles they may be true verbs (*I was working*) or adjectives (*a working agreement*) or in rare cases prepositions (*concerning this question*) or conjunctions (*supposing this happened*); if they are of the nature of gerunds they are always nouns (*I am pleased at his coming*)—or rather a hybrid between a noun and a verb, for you may use the gerund with the construction either of a noun (*after the careful reading of these papers*) or of a mixture between a verb and a noun (*after carefully reading these papers*). It is most confusing, but fortunately we are seldom called on to put a label on these words, and so I have preferred to give this section an indeterminate title.

Numerous pitfalls beset the use of *ing*-words. Here are some of them.

(*a*) Absolute construction.

This is, in itself, straightforward enough. The absolute construction, in the words of the O.E.D., is a name given to a phrase "standing out of grammatical relation or syntactical construction with other words". In the sentence "The chairman having restored

L

order, the committee resumed", the phrase "the chairman having restored order" forms an absolute construction.

But there is no absolute construction in the sentence "The chairman, having restored order, called on the last speaker to continue". Here *the chairman* is the subject of the sentence.

Because of a confusion with that type of sentence, it is a curiously common error to put a comma in the absolute construction. *See* COMMA (iv) p. 181.

(*b*) Unattached (or unrelated) participle.

This blunder is rather like the last. A writer begins a sentence with a participle (which, since it is a sort of adjective, must be given a noun to support it) and then forgets to give it its noun, thus leaving it "unattached".

> Arising out of a collision between a removal van and a fully loaded bus in a fog, E. C. F., removal van driver, appeared on a charge of manslaughter.

Grammatically in this sentence it was the van-driver, not the charge against him, that arose out of the collision. He probably did; but that was not what the writer meant.

> Whilst requesting you to furnish the return now outstanding you are advised that in future it would greatly facilitate. . . .

Requesting is unattached. If the structure of this rather clumsy sentence is to be retained it must run "Whilst requesting you . . . I advise you that . . .".

As I have said, some *ing*-words have won the right to be treated as prepositions. Among them are *regarding, considering, owing to, concerning* and *failing*. When any of these is used as a preposition, there can be no question of its being misused as an unattached participle:

> Considering the attack that had been made on him, his speech was moderate in tone.

If, however, *considering* were used not as a preposition-participle but as an adjective-participle, it could be unattached. It is so in:

> Considering the attack on him beneath his notice, his speech was moderate in tone.

Past participles, as well as present, may become unattached:

> Administered at first by the National Gallery, it was not until 1917 that the appointment of a separate board and director enabled a fully independent policy to be pursued.

The writer must have started with the intention of making the Tate Gallery (about which he was writing) the subject of the sentence but changed his mind, and so *administered* is left unattached.

> Formal application is now being made for the necessary way-leave consent, and as soon as received the work will proceed.

Grammatically *received* can only be attached to work; and that is nonsense. The writer should have said "as soon as this is received".

(*c*) Unattached gerund.

A gerund can become unattached in much the same way as a participle:

> Indeed we know little of Stalin's personality at all: a few works of Bolshevik theory, arid and heavy, and speeches still more impersonal, without literary grace, repeating a few simple formulas with crushing weight—after reading these Stalin appears more a myth than a man.

Grammatically "after reading these" means after Stalin has read them, not after we have.

The use of unattached participles and gerunds is becoming so common that grammarians may soon have to throw in their hand and recognise it as idiomatic. But they have not done so yet; so it should be avoided.

(*d*) Gerund versus infinitive.

In what seems to be a completely arbitrary way, some nouns, adjectives and verbs like to take an infinitive, and some a gerund with a preposition.

For instance:

Aim at doing	Try to do
Dislike of doing	Reluctance to do
Capable of doing	Able to do
Demur to doing	Hesitate to do
Prohibit from doing	Forbid to do

Instances could be multiplied indefinitely. There is no rule; it can only be a matter of observation and consulting a dictionary when in doubt.

(*e*) The "fused participle".

All authorities agree that it is idiomatic English to write "the *Bill's* getting a second reading surprised everyone": that is to say it is correct to treat *getting* as a gerund requiring *Bill's* to be in the possessive. What they are not agreed about is whether it is also correct to treat *getting* as a participle, and write "the *Bill* getting a second reading surprised everyone". If that is a legitimate grammatical construction, the subject of the sentence, which cannot be *Bill* by itself, or *getting* by itself, must be a fusion of the two. Hence the name "fused participle".

This is not in itself a matter of any great interest or importance. But it is notable as having been the occasion of a battle of the giants, Fowler and Jespersen.* Fowler condemned the "fused participle" as a construction "grammatically indefensible" that is "rapidly corrupting modern English style". Jespersen defended it against both these charges. Those best competent to judge seem to have awarded Jespersen a win on points.

What is certain is that sometimes we feel one construction to be the more idiomatic, and sometimes the other, and, in particular, that proper names and personal pronouns seem to demand the gerund. Nobody would prefer "He coming (or Smith coming) surprised me" to "His coming (or Smith's coming) surprised me". That is sure ground.

For the rest, it is always possible, and generally wise, to be on the safe side by turning the sentence round, and writing neither "the Bill getting, etc." (which offends some purists) nor "the Bill's getting, etc." (which sounds odd to some ears) but "everyone was surprised that the Bill got a second reading".

(ii) *Subjunctive*

The subjunctive is the mood of imagination or command. Apart from the verb *to be*, it has no form separate from the indicative, except in the third person singular of the present tense, where the subjunctive form is the same as the indicative plural (*he have*, not *he has*; *he go*, not *he goes*). Generally therefore, in sentences in which the subjunctive might be fitting, neither the writer nor the reader need know or care whether the subjunctive is being used or not.

But the verb *to be* spoils this simple picture. The whole of the present tense is different, for the subjunctive mood is *be* throughout —*I be, he be, we be, you be* and *they be*. The singular (but not the plural) of the past tense is also different—*I were* and *he were* instead of *I was* and *he was*. In the subjunctive mood what looks like the past tense does not denote pastness; it denotes a greater call on the imagination. Thus:

"If he is here" implies that it is as likely as not that he is.
"If he be here" is an archaic way of saying "if he is here".
"If he were here" implies that he is not.

The subjunctive is dying; the indicative is superseding it more and more. Its only remaining regular uses are:

(*a*) In certain stock phrases: "Be it so", "God bless you", "come what may", "if need be" and others.

Society for Pure English, Tracts XXII *et seq.*

(*b*) In legal or formal language: "I move that Mr. Smith be appointed Secretary".

In America this last usage is not confined to formal language, but is usual in such sentences as "I ask that he be sent for", "It is important that he be there", and even in the negative form "he insisted that the statement not be placed on record", in which the custom in this country is to insert a *should*. With our present propensity to imitate American ways, we may follow suit. A correspondent of *The Times* has recently written:

> There have been many suggestions . . . that the river be made the basis of a large-scale irrigation scheme.

(*c*) In conditional sentences where the hypothesis is not a fact:

> Were this true, it would be a serious matter.
> If he were here I would tell him what I think of him.

(*d*) With *as if* and *as though*, if the hypothesis is not accepted as true, thus:

> He spoke of his proposal as if it were a complete solution of the difficulty.

Other correct uses of the subjunctive may be found in contemporary writings, but it is probably true of all of them that the indicative would have been equally correct, and certainly true of many of them that the subjunctive has a formal, even pedantic, air. The notice "Please do not ring unless an answer be required", though still, I believe, to be found on some academic front doors, strikes us to-day as an archaism.

(iii) *Misuse of the passive*

Grammarians condemn such constructions as the following, which indeed condemn themselves by their contorted ugliness:

> The report that is proposed to be made.
> Several amendments were endeavoured to be inserted.
> A question was threatened to be put on the paper.
> A sensational atmosphere is attempted to be created.

Anyone who finds that he has written a sentence like this should recast it, e.g. "the proposed report", "attempts were made to insert several amendments", "a threat was made to put a question on the paper", "an attempt is being made to create a sensational atmosphere".

Hope should not be used in the passive except in the impersonal phrase *it is hoped*. We may say "It is hoped that payment will be made next week", or "payment is expected to be made next week", but not "payment is hoped to be made next week". The phrasal verb *hope for*, being transitive, can of course be used in the passive.

(iv) *Omission of verb*

Where a verb is used with more than one auxiliary (e.g. "he must and shall go") make sure that the main verb is repeated unless, as in this example, its form is the same. It is easy to slip into such a sentence as:

> The steps which those responsible can and are at present taking to remedy this state of affairs.

Can taking makes no sense. The proper construction is shown in:

> The board must take, and are in fact taking, all possible steps to maintain production.

(v) *Shall* and *will*

Twenty pages devoted to this subject in *The King's English* begin with the following introduction:

> It is unfortunate that the idiomatic use, while it comes by nature to southern Englishmen (who will find most of this section superfluous), is so complicated that those who are not to the manner born can hardly acquire it; and for them the section is in danger of being useless. In apology for the length of these remarks it must be said that the short and simple directions often given are worse than useless. The observant reader soon loses faith in them from their constant failure to take him right; and the unobservant is the victim of false security.

Fowler's view in short amounts to this: that if anyone has been brought up among those who use the right idiom, he has no need of instruction; if he has not, he is incapable of being instructed, because any guidance that is short and clear will mislead him and any that is full and accurate will be incomprehensible to him.

Every English text-book will be found to begin by stating the rule that to express the "plain" future *shall* is used in the first person and *will* in the second and third:

> I shall go
> You will go
> He will go

and that if it is a matter not of plain future but of volition, permission or obligation it is the other way round:

> I will go (I am determined to go or I intend to go)
> You shall go (You must go, or you are permitted to go)
> He shall go (He must go, or he is permitted to go)

But the idiom of the Celts is different. They have never recognised "I shall go". For them "I will go" is the plain future. The story is a very old one of the drowning Scot who was misunderstood by

English onlookers and left to his fate because he cried, "I will drown and nobody shall save me".

American practice follows the Celtic, and in this matter, as in so many others, the English have taken to imitating the American. If we go by practice rather than by precept, we can no longer say dogmatically that "I will go" for the plain future is wrong, or smugly with Dean Alford:

> I never knew an Englishman who misplaced *shall* and *will*; I hardly ever have known an Irishman or Scotsman who did not misplace them sometimes.

The Irish and the Scots are having their revenge for our bland assumption that English usage must be "right" and theirs "wrong".

Nevertheless the rule for the official must be to be orthodox on doubtful points of doctrine, and text-book orthodoxy in England still prescribes *shall* with the first person to express the plain future.

(vi) *Would* and *should*

The various shades of meaning of *would* and *should* derive in the main from the primary ideas of resolve in *will* and of obligation in *shall*: ideas illustrated in their simplest form by "he would go" (he was determined to go, or he made a habit of going) and "he should go" (he ought to go).

As colourless auxiliaries, merely indicating the subjunctive mood, the text-book rule is that *should* is used in the first person and *would* in the second and third. *Should*, which is colourless in the first person, resumes its tinge of *ought* in the others: in "If you tried you should succeed" it has a nuance not present in "If I tried I should succeed". But the rule requiring *should* in the first person is now largely ignored (compare *Shall* and *will*); *would* and *should* are used indifferently. Even a Professor of Poetry can now use them merely by way of elegant variation:

> If we could plot each individual poet's development, we would get a different pattern with each and we would see the pattern changing. . . . We should notice Mr. Auden, for example, breaking suddenly away from the influence of Thomas Hardy. . . .

In such a phrase as "In reply to your letter of . . . I would inform you . . ." *would* is not a mere auxiliary expressing the conditional mood; it retains the now archaic meaning of "I should like to". On another page (19) I have deprecated the use of this expression on the ground that, since it is archaic, it cannot help being stiff.

Because *would* has this meaning, grammarians condemn such phrases as "I would like to", "I would be glad if", "I would be obliged if" and so on. *Should*, they say, ought always to be used: to say *would* is tantamount to saying "I should like to like to", "I should like to be glad if", "I should like to be obliged if" and so on.

"It would appear" and "I should think" are less dogmatic, and therefore more polite, ways of saying "it appears" and "I think".

(vii) *Split infinitive*

The well-known grammarians' rule against splitting an infinitive means that nothing must come between *to* and the verb. It is a bad name, as was pointed out by Jespersen, a grammarian as broad-minded as he was erudite.

> This name is bad because we have many infinitives without *to*, as "I made him go". *To* therefore is no more an essential part of the infinitive than the definite article is an essential part of a nominative, and no one would think of calling *the good man* a split nominative.

It is a bad rule too; it increases the difficulty of writing clearly and makes for ambiguity by inducing writers to place adverbs in unnatural and even misleading positions.

> A recent visit to Greece has convinced me that the modern Englishman fails completely to recognise that. . . .
> Some of the stones . . . must have been of such a size that they failed completely to melt before they reached the ground.

Does the modern Englishman completely fail to recognise, or does he fail to completely recognise? Did the hailstones completely fail to melt, or did they fail to completely melt? The reader has to guess and he ought never to have to guess. In these two examples the context shows that the right guess for one will be the wrong guess for the other.

Nor is this all. The split infinitive taboo, leading as it does to the putting of adverbs in awkward places, is so potent that it produces an impulse to put them there even though there is not really any question of avoiding a split infinitive. I have myself been taken to task by a correspondent for splitting an infinitive because I wrote "I gratefully record". He was, no doubt, under the influence of the taboo to an exceptional extent. But sufferers from the same malady in a milder form can be found on every hand. We cannot doubt that the writer of the sentence "they appeared completely to have adjusted themselves to it" put the adverb in that uncomfortable position because he thought that to write "to have completely adjusted" would be to split an infinitive. The same fear, probably subconscious, may also be presumed to account for the unnatural placing of the adverb in "so tangled is the web that I cannot pretend for a moment that we have succeeded entirely in unweaving it". In this there is no possibility of splitting an infinitive because there is no infinitive. But the split infinitive bogy is having such a devastating effect that people are beginning to feel that it must be wrong to put an adverb between any auxiliary and any part of a verb, or between any preposition and any part of a verb.

The infinitive can be split only by inserting a word or words between *to* and the word which, with *to*, forms the infinitive of the verb. "To fully understand" is a split infinitive. So is "to fully have understood". But "to have fully understood" is not.

In the first edition of *Plain Words* I wrote of the rule against the split infinitive:

> Still, there is no doubt that the rule at present holds sway, and on my principle the official has no choice but to conform; for his readers will almost certainly attribute departures from it to ignorance of it, and so, being moved to disdain of the writer, will not be "affected precisely as he wishes".

A friend whose opinion I value has reproached me for this, making no secret of his view that I am little better than a coward. I ought, he tells me, to have the courage of my convictions. I ought to say about the split infinitive, as I said about the "inanimate whose", that it is right for the official to give a lead in freeing writers from this fetish. The farthest I ought to allow myself to go along the road of safety-first is, according to him, to say that it is judicious for an official to avoid splitting whenever he can do so without sacrificing clarity, ease and naturalness of expression. But rather than make that sacrifice he should resolutely split.

My friend may be right. Rebels will find themselves in good company. Here is an example of a good literary craftsman goaded into apologetic rebellion against this tyranny:

> As for Spotted Fat, that prudent animal (whom the Go-go now proceeded to condignly beat till ordered to desist) had swum straight ashore without the slightest effort.

Having written this sentence in his book *On the Eaves of the World*, Reginald Farrer appended the footnote:

> I have never yet, I believe, split an infinitive in my life; here, for the first time in my experience, I fancy the exigencies of rhythm and meaning do really compel me.

George Bernard Shaw was emphatically on the side of the rebels. In 1892 he wrote to the *Chronicle*:

> If you do not immediately suppress the person who takes it upon himself to lay down the law almost every day in your columns on the subject of literary composition, I will give up the *Chronicle*. The man is a pedant, an ignoramus, an idiot and a self-advertising duffer. . . .

Your fatuous specialist . . . is now beginning to rebuke "second-rate" newspapers for using such phrases as "to suddenly go" and "to boldly say". I ask you, Sir, to put this man out . . .without interfering with his perfect freedom of choice between "to suddenly go", "to go suddenly" and "suddenly to go". . . . Set him adrift and try an intelligent Newfoundland dog in his place.*

But the most vigorous rebel could hardly condone splitting so resolute as the crescendo of this lease.

The tenant hereby agrees:
    (i) to pay the said rent;
    (ii) to properly clean all the windows;
    (iii) to at all times properly empty all closets;
    (iv) to immediately any litter or disorder shall have been made by him or for his purpose on the staircase or landings or any other part of the said building or garden remove the same.

SOME POINTS OF IDIOM

AGREE

Following the example set by *approve*, *agree* is showing a disposition to shake off its attendant prepositions *to*, *on* and *with*, and to pose as a transitive verb. "I agree your figures", "We must agree the arrangements for this", "I agree your draft". Some correspondents would have me castigate this, but I do not think there is any great harm in it. It is true that established idiom requires "I agree with your figures", "We must agree on the arrangements" and "I agree with" or (if from a superior) "I agree to your draft". But the change has probably come to stay, and will be absorbed into English idiom.

AVAIL

The proper construction is to avail oneself of something. Avoid the ugly passive construction such as "this opportunity should be availed of". "Taken" or "seized" or "made use of" will do instead.

AVERSE and ADVERSE

It is usual to say *averse from*, though there is good authority for *averse to*. (What cat's averse to fish?) But *adverse* is always *to*.

CIRCUMSTANCES

It used to be widely held by purists that to say "under the circumstances" must be wrong because what is around us cannot be over us. "In the circumstances" was the only correct expression. This argument is characterised by Fowler as puerile. Its major premiss is not

---

*Quoted in Grant Richards' *Author Hunting*, Hamish Hamilton, 1938.

true ("a threatening sky is a circumstance no less than a threatening bulldog") and even if it were true it would be irrelevant, because, as cannot be too often repeated, English idiom has a contempt for logic. There is good authority for *under the circumstances*, and if some of us prefer *in the circumstances* (as I do), that is a matter of taste, not of rule.

COMPARE

There is a difference between *compare to* and *compare with*; the first is to liken one thing to another; the second is to note the resemblances and differences between two things. Thus:

> Shall I compare thee to a summer's day?
> If we compare the speaker's notes with the report of his speech in *The Times*. . . .

CONSIST

There is a difference between *consist of* and *consist in*. *Consist of* denotes the substance of which the subject is made; *consist in* defines the subject.

> The writing desks consist of planks on trestles.
> The work of the branch consists in interviewing the public.

DEPEND

It is wrong in writing, though common in speech, to omit the *on* or *upon* after depends, as in:

> It depends whether we have received another consignment by then.

DIFFER

In the sense of to be different, the idiom is to differ *from*.

In the sense of to disagree, it is either to differ *from* or to differ *with*, which you please.

DIFFERENT

There is good authority for *different to*, but *different from* is today the established usage. *Different than* is not unknown even in *The Times*:

> The air of the suburb has quite a different smell and feel at eleven o'clock in the morning or three o'clock in the afternoon than it has at the hours when the daily toiler is accustomed to take a few hurried sniffs of it.

But this is condemned by the grammarians, who would say that *than* in this example should have been *from what*.

Direct and Directly

Direct, although an adjective, is also no less an adverb than *directly*. To avoid ambiguity, it is well to confine *directly* to its meaning of *immediately* in time, and so avoid the possibility of confusion between "he is going to Edinburgh direct" and "he is going to Edinburgh directly". Here are two examples from recent departmental circulars, the first of the right use of *direct* and the second of the wrong use of *directly*:

> Committees should notify departments direct of the names and addresses of the banks.
> He will arrange directly with the authority concerned for the recruitment and training of technicians.

Doubt

Idiom requires *whether* after a positive statement and *that* after a negative.

> I doubt whether he will come today.
> I have no doubt that he will come today.

Either

Either means one or other of two. Its use in the sense of each of two, as in:

> On either side the river lie
> Long fields of barley and of rye,

or in:

> The concert will be broadcast on either side of the nine o'clock news,

is common, and there does not seem to be any good ground for Fowler's dictum that it "is archaic and should be avoided except in verse or special contexts".

Equally

Do not let *as* intrude between *equally* and the word it qualifies. Not *equally as good*, but *equally good*.

First and Firstly

There used to be a grammarians' rule that you must not write *firstly*; your enumeration must be: *first, secondly, thirdly*. It was one of those arbitrary rules whose observance was supposed by a certain class of purist to be a hallmark of correct writing. This rule, unlike many of the sort, had not even logic on its side. Of late years there has been a rebellion against these rules, and I do not think that any contemporary grammarian will mind much whether you say *first* or *firstly*.

FIRST TWO

For more than a hundred years pretty arguments have been carried on from time to time round the question whether one should say *the first two* or *the two first*. Some famous grammarians, notably Dean Alford and Jespersen, have supported *the two first*, but the majority of expert opinion is overwhelmingly against them. So *the first two* holds the field. But the point is not important. Everyone knows what you mean, whichever you say.

FOLLOWS (AS FOLLOWS)

Do not write *as follow* for *as follows*, however numerous may be the things that follow. "The construction in *as follows* is impersonal, and the verb should always be used in the singular" (O.E.D.).

GOT

Have got, for *possess* or *have*, says Fowler, is good colloquial but not good literary English. Others have been more lenient. Dr. Johnson said:

> "He has got a good estate" does not always mean that he has acquired, but barely that he possesses it. So we say "the lady has got black eyes", merely meaning that she has them.

And Dr. Ballard has written:*

> What is wrong with the word? Its pedigree is beyond reproach. If the reader will consult the Oxford English Dictionary he will find that Shakespeare uses the word. So does Swift; Ruskin uses it frequently, and Augustine Birrell in *Obiter Dicta* asks "What has the general public got to do with literature?" Johnson in his Dictionary gives possession as a legitimate meaning of the verb to get, and quotes George Herbert. Indeed he uses it himself in a letter to Boswell. The only inference we can draw is that it is not a real error but a counterfeit invented by schoolmasters.

When such high authorities differ, what is the plain man to think? If it is true, as I hold it to be, that superfluous words are an evil, we ought to condemn "the lady has got black eyes", but not "the lady has got a black eye". Still, in writing for those whose prose inclines more often to primness than to colloquialisms, and who are not likely to overdo the use of *got*, I advise them not to be afraid of it. The Americans have the handy practice of saying "I have gotten" for "I have obtained" and reserving "I have got", if they use the word at all, for "I possess." But I believe that the usual way for an American to express an Englishman's "I haven't got" is "I don't have".

---

* *Teaching and Testing English.* The same writer's *Thought and Language* contains an even longer and more spirited defence of *got*.

HARD and HARDLY

Hard, not *hardly*, is the adverb of the adjective *hard*. *Hardly* must not be used except in the sense of *scarcely*. *Hardly earned* and *hard-earned* have quite different meanings.

Hardly, like *scarcely*, is followed by *when*, not by *than*, in such a sentence as "I had hardly begun when I was interrupted". *Than* sometimes intrudes from a false analogy with "I had no sooner begun than I was interrupted".

HELP

The expression "more than one can help" is a literal absurdity. It means exactly the opposite of what it says. "I won't be longer than I can help" means "I won't be longer than is unavoidable", that is to say, longer than I *can't* help. But it is good English idiom.

> They will not respect more than they can help treaties exacted from them under duress. (Winston Churchill, *The Gathering Storm*.)

Writers who find the absurdity of the phrase more than they can stomach can always write "more than they must" instead.

INCULCATE

One *inculcates* ideas into people, not people with ideas; *imbue* would be the right word for that. A vague association with *inoculate* may have something to do with the mistaken use of *inculcate with*.

INFORM

Inform cannot be used with a verb in the infinitive, and the writer of this sentence has gone wrong:

> I am informing the branch to grant this application.

He should have said *telling* or *asking*.

LESS and FEWER

The following is taken from *Good and Bad English* by Whitten and Whitaker:

> *Less* appertains to degree, quantity or extent; *fewer* to number. Thus, *less* outlay, *fewer* expenses; *less* help, *fewer* helpers; *less* milk, *fewer* eggs.
> But although *few* applies to number do not join it to the word itself: a *fewer* number is incorrect; say a *smaller* number.
> *Less* takes a singular noun, *fewer* a plural noun; thus, *less* opportunity, *fewer* opportunities.

ORDER (IN ORDER THAT)

May or *might* are the words to follow "in order that". It is incorrect to write "in order that no further delay will occur" or "in order that we can have a talk on the subject". And it is stilted to write *in order to* where *to* will serve equally well. Jack and Jill did not go up the hill in order to fetch a pail of water. English idiom recognises *so as to* and *so that they might* as alternative ways of expressing purpose, but has not yet admitted the American *so* without *that* ("so they could fetch a pail of water").

OTHERWISE

Twenty-five years ago Fowler pointed out that this word was having "very curious experiences" in that, although an adverb, it was being used more and more both as an adjective and as a noun. These experiences have certainly not abated since then.

The adjective that *otherwise* dispossesses is *other*. This is exemplified in such a sentence as "There are many difficulties, legal and other-wise, about doing what you ask".

The noun that *otherwise* dispossesses is whatever noun has the contrary meaning to one just mentioned. This is exemplified in such a sentence as "I will say nothing about the reasonableness or other-wise of what you ask", where the word replaced is *unreasonableness*.

Fowler condemns both these as ungrammatical. Since it is just as easy in the first case to write *other* and in the second either to omit *or otherwise* or to substitute the appropriate noun, there is no reason why one should not be on the safe side and do the grammatical thing. But it would be wrong to leave the subject without quoting Dr. Ballard:

> A new pronoun is as rare a phenomenon as a new comet. Yet it dawned on me the other day that a new pronoun had insidiously crept into the English language. It was heard on everybody's lips, it was used on the platform and in the press, it figured prominently in blue-books and official papers. And yet I could find it in no dictionary—not, that is, as a pronoun—nor could I discover it among the lists of pronouns in any grammar, however modern. Still, if the current definition is correct, the word is beyond doubt a pronoun. The word is *otherwise*. A committee is appointed by an educational body *to report on the success or otherwise of the new organisation of schools.* What does *otherwise* stand for? Why *failure*, of course. And *failure* is a noun. Therefore *otherwise* is a pronoun. . . . I thought at first with Mr. H. W. Fowler that *otherwise*, so used, was not a pronoun but a blunder. But when I considered the people who used it so—school-masters and school inspectors, and ambassadors, and statesmen and judges on the bench—I could not accept Mr. Fowler's views. For I would rather wrong the dead—dead languages that is—and wrong myself and you than I would wrong such honourable men. There is no help for it. *Otherwise* is a pronoun.

Sometimes *other* gets its revenge, and supplants *otherwise*.

> It is news to me that a sheep improves the land other than by the food fed through it.

Prefer

You may say "He prefers writing to dictating" or "he prefers to write rather than to dictate", but not "he prefers to write than to dictate".

Prevent

You may choose any one of three constructions with *prevent*: *prevent him from coming*, *prevent him coming* and *prevent his coming*.

Purport (verb)

The ordinary meaning of this verb is "to profess or claim by its tenor", e.g. "this letter purports to be written by you". The use of the verb in the passive is an objectionable and unnecessary innovation. "Statements which were purported to have been official confirmed the rumours" should be "statements which purported to be official confirmed the rumours".

Regard

Unlike *consider*, *count* and *deem*, *regard* requires an *as* in such a sentence as "I regard it as an honour".

Require

Require should not be used as an intransitive verb in the sense of *need* as it is in:

> You do not require to do any stamping unless you wish (you need not) and
> Special arrangements require to be worked out in the light of local circumstances (special arrangements will have to be. . . .).

Substitute

To *substitute* means to put a person or thing in the place of another; it does not mean to take the place of another. When *A* is removed and *B* is put in its place, *B* is substituted for *A* and *A* is replaced by *B*. We may write:

> The Minister has substituted Jones for Smith as a member of the committee,

but we must not write:

> Jones has substituted Smith as a member of the committee.

or:

> Smith has been substituted by Jones as a member of the committee.

In the last two sentences the verb needed is *replaced*.

Such and So

> It will take some time to unravel such a complicated case.

There are those who say that this is unidiomatic, and that we ought to say "so complicated a case". But if we choose to regard them as pedants we shall have Fowler on our side, and so cannot be far wrong.

Unequal

> The idiom is unequal *to*, not *for*, a task.

Very

One of the most popular objects of the chase among amateur hunters of so-called grammatical mistakes used to be *very* with a past participle—"very pleased", for instance. It is true that *very* cannot be used grammatically with a past participle—that one cannot, for instance, say "The effect was very enhanced"; we must say *much* or *greatly*. But when the participle is no longer serving as a verb, and has become in effect an adjective, it is legitimate to use *very* with it as with any other adjective. There can be no objection to "very pleased", which means no more than "very glad", or to "very annoyed", which means no more than "very angry". But it will not do to say "very inconvenienced" or "very removed", and in between are doubtful cases where it will be as well to be on the safe side and refrain from *very*.

Worth

Worth has a prepositional force, and needs an object. This object may be either *while* (i.e. the spending of time) or something else. It is therefore correct to say "this job is worth while"; it is also correct to say "this job is worth doing". But one object is enough, and so it is wrong to say "this job is worth while doing".

Worth-while as an adjective ("a worth-while job") has not yet reached more than colloquial status.

SOME COMMON CAUSES OF CONFUSED EXPRESSION

Confusion between more and less

It is curiously easy to say the opposite of what one means when making comparisons of quantity, time or distance, especially if they are negative. A common type of this confusion is to be found in such statements as "Meetings will be held at not less than monthly intervals", when what is meant is that the meetings will be not less frequent than once a month, that is to say, at not more than monthly intervals.

M

Maximum and *minimum* sometimes cause a similar confusion, leading to one being used for the other. They have done so in the following sentence, which is taken from a passage deprecating the wounding of wild animals by taking too long shots at them:

> It would be impossible to attempt to regulate shooting by laying down minimum ranges and other details of that sort.

It would indeed.

Another correspondent sends, as an instance of ambiguity of a similar kind,

> On the mainland of Ross the population has been more than halved in the past twenty years.

Though not actually ambiguous, this is certainly not the clearest way of saying that the population has fallen to less than half.

Expression of multiples

We learn at an early age that if we want to declare one figure to be a multiple of another the proper way of doing so is to say that the first is so many times the second. "Nine is three times three." But in later life some of us seem to forget this and to say "Nine is three times greater (or three times more) than three". Not only is this an unnecessary distortion of a simple idiom, but a stickler for accuracy might say even that it was misleading: the figure that is three times greater (or more) than three is not nine but twelve. I was moved to these reflections by the following passage:

> The figure set for the production of iron ore in 1955 is 3,500,000 tons, more than twelve times greater than in 1936; for pig-iron it is 2,000,000 tons, ten times greater than in 1936; for cement 4,000,000 tons, twice as much as in 1936.

The writer of this seems to have forgotten the formula of his multiplication tables until reminded of it by finding himself up against the awkwardness of having to say "twice greater".

Overlapping

By this I mean a particular form of what the grammarians call *tautology*, *pleonasm* or *redundancy*. Possible varieties are infinite, but the commonest example is writing "the reason for this is because . . ." instead of either "this is because" or "the reason for this is that . . ." as in the first of these examples.

> The Ministry of Food say that the reason for the higher price of the biscuits is because the cost of chocolate has increased.
> The subject of the talk tonight will be about. . . . (A confusion between "the subject will be . . ." and "the talk will be about . . . ".)
> The reason for the long delay appears to be due to the fact that the medical certificates went astray. (A confusion between "the

reason is that the certificates went astray" and "the delay is due to the fact that the certificates went astray".)

The cause of the delay is due to the shortage of materials. (A confusion between "the cause of the delay is the shortage" and "the delay is due to the shortage".)

By far the greater majority. . . . (A confusion between "the great majority" and "by far the greater part".)

He did not say that all actions for libel or slander were never properly brought. (A confusion between "that all actions . . . were improperly brought" and "that actions . . . were never properly brought".)

An attempt will be made this morning to try to avert the threatened strike. (Those who were going to do this might have attempted to do it or tried to do it. But merely to attempt to try seems rather half-hearted.)

Save only in exceptional circumstances will any further development be contemplated. (A confusion between "only in exceptional circumstances will any further development be contemplated" and "save in exceptional circumstances no further development will be contemplated".)

The common fault of duplicating either the future or the past is a form of this error.

The most probable thing will be that they will be sold in a Government auction.

This should be "The most probable thing is that they will be".

The Minister said he would have liked the Government of Eire to have offered us butter instead of cream.

This should be "he would have liked the Government of Eire to offer . . .".

Qualification of Absolutes

Certain adjectives and adverbs cannot properly be qualified by such words as *more, less, very, rather,* because they do not admit of degrees. *Unique* is the outstanding example. When we say a thing is *unique* we mean that there is nothing else of its kind in existence; *rather unique* is meaningless. But we can of course say *almost unique.*

It is easy to slip into pedantry here, and to condemn the qualification of words which are perhaps strictly absolutes but are no longer so treated—*true,* for instance, and *empty* and *full.* We ought not to shrink from saying "very true", or "the hall was even emptier to-day than yesterday" or "this cupboard is fuller than that". But this latitude must not be abused. It is carried too far in this quotation

It may safely be said that the design of sanitary fittings has now reached a high degree of perfection.

Nor should we condone the expression *more or less wholly,* even though I found it in a book on style by an eminent contemporary man of letters. Nor does the comparative seem happily chosen in *more virgin*, which a correspondent tells me he has seen in an advertisement.

Repetition

Pronouns were invented to avoid the necessity of repeating nouns. The section on PRONOUNS (p. 143) deals with this subject, and also with the device known as "the polite alias" or "elegant variation".

Unnecessary repetition of a word is irritating to a reader. If it can be avoided in a natural way it should be. For instance, in the sentence "The Minister has considered this application, and considers that there should be a market in Canada", the repetition of "consider" gives the sentence a clumsy and careless air. The second one might just as well have been "thinks". It would have been easy also to avoid the ugly repetition of *essential* in the sentence "it is essential that the Minister should have before him outline programmes of essential works". But where the same thing or act is repeatedly mentioned, it is better to repeat a word than to avoid it in a laboured and obvious way.

Irritating repetition of a sound (assonance) is usually mere carelessness.

> The controversy as to which agency should perform the actual contractual work of erection of houses.
> Reverting to the subject of the letter the latter wrote. . . . (This is indefensible because it could so easily be avoided by calling "the latter" by name.)
> Since a certain amount of uncertainty still appears to exist.

This is not even true, for I feel sure that what really existed was an uncertain amount of uncertainty.

A FEW POINTS OF SPELLING

AUTARCHY

Autarchy means absolute sovereignty. *Autarky* (sometimes mis-spelt *autarchy*) means self-sufficiency. The difference in spelling reflects the different Greek words from which they are derived.

DEPENDANT

In the ordinary usage of today *dependant* is a noun meaning "a person who depends on another for support, position, etc. " (O.E.D.). *Dependent* is an adjective meaning relying on or subject to something else. Dependants are dependent on the person whose dependants they are.

ENQUIRY

Enquiry and *inquiry* have long existed together as alternative spellings of the same word. In America *inquiry* is dislodging *enquiry* for all purposes. In England a useful distinction is developing: *enquiry* is used for asking a question and *inquiry* for making an investigation. Thus you might enquire what time the inquiry begins.

FOREGO

To *forego* is to go before (the foregoing provisions of this Act). To *forgo* is to go without, to waive (he will forgo his right).

ISE or IZE

On the question whether verbs like *organise* and nouns like *organisation* should be spelt with an *s* or a *z* the authorities differ. The O.E.D. favours universal *ize*, arguing that the suffix is always in its origin either Greek or Latin and in both languages it is spelt with a *z*. Other authorities, including some English printers, recommend universal *ise*. Fowler stands between these two opinions. He points out that the O.E.D.'s advice over-simplifies the problem, since there are some verbs (e.g. *advertise, comprise, despise, exercise* and *surmise*) which are never spelt *ize* in this country. On the other hand, he says "the difficulty of remembering which these *ise* verbs are is the only reason for making *ise* universal, and the sacrifice of significance to ease does not seem justified". This austere conclusion will not commend itself to everyone. It does not do so to the authors of the *A.B.C. of English Usage*, who say roundly, "the advice given here is to end them all in *ise*", a verdict with which I respectfully agree.

X

Punctuation

That learned men are well known to disagree on this subject of punctuation is in itself a proof, that the knowledge of it, in theory and practice, is of some importance. I myself have learned by experience, that, if ideas that are difficult to understand are properly separated, they become clearer; and that, on the other hand, through defective punctuation, many passages are confused and distorted to such a degree, that sometimes they can with difficulty be understood, or even cannot be understood at all.

ALDUS MANUTIUS. *Interpungendi ratio,* 1566. From the translation in *Punctuation, its Principles and Practice* by T. F. and M. F. A. HUSBAND, Routledge, 1905.

THIS is a large subject. Whole books have been written about it, and it is still true, as it apparently was 400 years ago, that no two authorities completely agree. Taste and common sense are more important than any rules; you put in stops to help your reader to understand you, not to please grammarians. And you should try so to write that he will understand you with a minimum of help of that sort. Fowler says:

It is a sound principle that as few stops should be used as will do the work. . . . Everyone should make up his mind not to depend on his stops. They are to be regarded as devices, not for saving him the trouble of putting his words in the order that naturally gives the required meaning, but for saving his reader the moment or two that would sometimes, without them, be necessarily spent on reading the sentence twice over, once to catch the general arrangement, and again for the details. It may almost be said that what reads wrongly if the stops are removed is radically bad; stops are not to alter the meaning, but merely to show it up. Those who are learning to write should make a practice of putting down all they want to say without stops first. What then, on reading over, naturally arranges itself contrary to the intention should be not punctuated, but altered; and the stops should be as few as possible consistently with the recognised rules.

The symbols we shall have to consider in this chapter are the apostrophe, colon, dash, full stop, hyphen, inverted commas, question mark, semicolon. It will also be a suitable place to say something about capital letters, paragraphs, parentheses and sentences.

APOSTROPHE

The only uses of the apostrophe that call for notice are (*a*) its use to denote the possessive of names ending in *s* and of pronouns, (*b*) its use before a final *s* to show that the *s* is forming the plural of a word or symbol not ordinarily admitting of a plural and (*c*) its use with a defining plural (e.g. *Ten years imprisonment*).

(*a*) There is no universally accepted code of rules governing the formation of the possessive case of names ending in *s*, but the most favoured practice (especially with monosyllables) seems to be not just to put an apostrophe at the end of the word, as one does with an ordinary plural (strangers' gallery), but to add another *s*—Mr. Jones's room, St. James's street, not Mr. Jones' room, St. James' street.

As to pronouns, all these except the pronoun *one* dispense with an apostrophe in their possessive cases—*hers*, *yours*, *theirs*, *ours* and *its*, but *one's*, not *ones*. *It's* is not the possessive of *it* but a contraction of *it is:* the apostrophe is performing its normal duty of showing that a letter has been omitted.

(*b*) Whether an apostrophe should be used to denote the plural of a word or symbol that does not ordinarily make a plural depends on whether the plural is readily recognisable as such. Unless the reader really needs help it should not be thrust upon him. It is clearly justified with single letters: "there are two o's in woolly"; "mind your p's and q's". Otherwise it is rarely called for. It should not be used with contractions (e.g. M.P.s) or merely because what is put into the plural is not a noun. Editors of Shakespeare do without it in "Tellest thou me of ifs", and Rudyard Kipling did not think it necessary in:

> One million Hows, two million Wheres,
> And seven million Whys.

(*c*) Whether one should use an apostrophe in such expressions as "Ten years imprisonment" is a disputed and not very important point. The answer seems to be that if *ten years* is regarded as a descriptive genitive (like *busman's* in *busman's holiday*) we must write *years'*; if as an adjectival phrase there must be no apostrophe but the words must be hyphened (*see* HYPHEN). In the singular (*a year's imprisonment*) *year's* can only be a descriptive genitive.

In such phrases as *games master* and *customs examination*, *games* and *customs* are clearly adjectival, and need no apostrophe.

CAPITALS

Several correspondents have asked me to say something about the use of capital letters. The difficulty is to know what to say. No one needs telling that capitals are used for the first letter in every sentence, for proper names and the names of the months and days and the titles of books and newspapers. The only difficulty is with words that are sometimes written with capitals and sometimes not. Here there can be no general rule; everyone must do what he thinks most fitting. But two pieces of advice may perhaps be given:

(i) Use a capital for the particular and a small letter for the general. Thus:

> It is a street leading out of Oxford Street.
> I have said something about this in Chapter I; I shall have more to say in later chapters.
> In this case the Judge went beyond a judge's proper functions.
> Many parliaments have been modelled on our Parliament.

(ii) Whatever practice you adopt, be consistent throughout any document you are writing.

COLON

About the use of the colon there is even less agreement among the authorities than about the use of other stops. All agree that its systematic use as one of a series of different pause-values has almost died out with the decay of formal periods. But some hold that it is still useful as something less than a full stop and more than a semi-colon; others deny it. Into this we need not enter; it will be enough to note that the following uses are generally recognised as legitimate:

(*a*) To mark more sharply than a semicolon would the antithesis between two sentences.

> In peace-time the Civil Service is a target of frequent criticism: in war-time criticism is very greatly increased.
> In some cases the executive carries out most of the functions: in others the delegation is much less extensive.

(*b*) To precede an explanation or particularisation or to introduce a list or series: in the words of Fowler "to deliver the goods that have been invoiced in the preceding words".

> The design of the school was an important part of the scheme: Post Office counters with all the necessary stores were available and maps and framed specimens of the various documents in use were exhibited on the walls of light and cheerful classrooms.
> News reaches a national paper from two sources: the news agencies and its own correspondents.

For the second purpose the dash is the colon's weaker relative.

COMMA

The use of commas cannot be learned by rule. Not only does conventional practice vary from period to period, but good writers of the same period differ among themselves. Moreover stops have two kinds of duty. One is to show the construction of sentences—the "grammatical" duty. The other is to introduce nuances into the meaning—the "rhetorical" duty. "I went to his house and I found him there" is a colourless statement. "I went to his house, and I found him there" hints that it was not quite a matter of course that he should have been found there. "I went to his house. And I found him there". This indicates that to find him there was surprising. Similarly you can give a different nuance to what you write by encasing adverbs or adverbial phrases in commas. "He was, apparently, willing to support you" throws a shade of doubt on his bona fides that is not present in "He was apparently willing to support you".

The correct use of the comma—if there is such a thing as "correct" use—can only be acquired by common sense, observation and taste. Present practice is markedly different from that of the past in using commas much less freely. The fifteenth-century passage that heads this chapter is peppered with them with a liberality not approved by modern practice.

I shall attempt no more than to point out some traps that commas set for the unwary, and those who want to know more about the subject I would refer to Carey's *Mind the Stop*,* a little book which has the rare merit of explaining the principles of punctuation without getting lost in its no-man's-land. I shall first deal with some uses of the comma that are generally regarded as incorrect, and then with uses which, though they may not be incorrect, need special care in handling, or are questionable.

A. Incorrect uses.

(i) The use of a comma between two independent sentences not linked by a conjunction. The usual practice is to use a heavier stop in this position, usually a semicolon. (See also under SEMICOLON, p. 193.)

> We wrote on the 12th May asking for an urgent report regarding the above contractor's complaint, this was followed up on the 24th May by a telephone call.
> You may not be aware that a Youth Employment Service is operating throughout the country, in some areas it is under the control of the Ministry of Labour and National Service and in others of the Education Authorities.

There should be a semicolon after *complaint* in the first quotation and *country* in the second.

> The Department cannot guarantee that a licence will be issued, you should not therefore arrange for any shipment.

*Cambridge University Press, 1939.

> I regret the delay in replying to your letter but Mr. X who was
> dealing with it is on leave, however, I have gone into the matter. . . .

There should be a full stop after *issued* in the first quotation and
after *leave* in the second.

(ii) The use of one comma instead of either a pair or none.

This very common blunder is more easily illustrated than explained.
It is almost like using one only of a pair of brackets. Words that are
parenthetical may be able to do without any commas, but if there
is a comma at one end of them there must be one at the other end too.

> Against all this must be set considerations which, in our submission
> are overwhelming. (Omit the comma.)
> We should be glad if you would inform us for our record purposes,
> of any agency agreement finally reached. (Either omit the comma or
> insert one after *us*.)
> It will be noted that for the development areas, Treasury-financed
> projects are to be grouped together. (Either omit the comma or insert
> one after *that*.)
> The first is the acute shortage that so frequently exists, of suitable
> premises where people can come together. (Omit the comma.)
> The principal purpose is to provide for the division between the
> minister and the governing body concerned, of premises and property
> held partly for hospital purposes and partly for other purposes. (Omit
> the comma.)

(iii) The use of commas with "defining" relative clauses.

Relative clauses fall into two main classes. Grammarians give
them different labels, but *defining* and *commenting* are the most convenient and descriptive. If you say "The man who was here this
morning told me that", the relative clause is a defining one; it com-
pletes the subject "the man", which conveys no definite meaning
without it. But if you say, "Jones, who was here this morning, told
me that", the relative clause is commenting; the subject "Jones" is
already complete and the relative clause merely adds a bit of information about him which may or may not be important but is not
essential to the definition of the subject. A commenting clause
should be within commas; a defining one should not. This is not an
arbitrary rule; it is a utilitarian one. If you do not observe it, you
may fail to make your meaning clear, or you may even say something different from what you intend. For instance:

> A particular need is provision for young women, who owing to
> war conditions have been deprived of normal opportunities of
> learning homecraft. . . .

Here the comma announces that the relative clause is "commenting"; it is added by way of explanation why young women in
general had this need after the war. Without the comma the relative

clause would be read as a "defining" one, limiting the need for this provision to those particular young women who had in fact been deprived of those opportunities. Conversely:

> Any expenditure incurred on major awards to students, who are not recognised for assistance from the Ministry, will rank for grant. . . .

Here the comma is wrong. The relative clause must be "defining". The commas suggest that it is "commenting" and imply that no students are recognised for assistance.

> I have made enquiries, and find that the clerk, who dealt with your enquiry, recorded the name of the firm correctly.

The relative clause here is a defining one. The comma turns it into a commenting one and implies that the writer has only one clerk. The truth is that one of several is being singled out; and this is made clear if the commas after *clerk* and *enquiry* are omitted.

The same mistake is made in:

> The Ministry issues permits to employing authorities to enable foreigners to land in this country for the purpose of taking up employment, for which British subjects are not available.

The grammatical implication of this is that employment in general is not a thing for which British subjects are available.

An instruction book called "Pre-aircrew English", supplied during the war to airmen in training in a Commonwealth country, contained an encouragement to its readers to "smarten up their English". This ended:

> Pilots, whose minds are dull, do not usually live long.

The commas convert a truism into an insult.

(iv) The insertion of a meaningless comma into an "absolute phrase".

An absolute phrase (e.g. "then, the work being finished, we went home") always has parenthetic commas round it. But there is no sense in the comma that so often carelessly appears inside it.

> The House of Commons, having passed the third reading by a large majority after an animated debate, the bill was sent to the Lords.

The insertion of the first comma leaves the House of Commons in the air waiting for a verb that never comes. (*See* p. 156.)

(v) The use of commas in an endeavour to clarify faultily constructed sentences.

It is instructive to compare the following extracts from two documents issued by the same department.

It should be noted that an officer who ceased to pay insurance contributions before the date of the commencement of his emergency service, remained uninsured for a period, varying between eighteen months and two-and-a-half years, from the date of his last contribution and would, therefore, be compulsorily insured if his emergency service commenced during that period.

Officers appointed to emergency commissions direct from civil life who were not insured for health or pensions purposes at the commencement of emergency service are not compulsorily insured during service.

Why should the first of these extracts be full of commas and the second have none? The answer can only be that, whereas the second sentence is short and clear, the first is long and obscure. The writer tried to help the reader by putting in five commas, but all he did was to give him five jolts. The only place where there might have been a comma is after *contribution*, and there the writer has omitted to put one.

Another example of the same abuse of a comma is:

Moreover, directions and consents at the national level are essential prerequisites in a planned economy, whereas they were only necessary for the establishment of standards or for grant-aid and borrowing purposes, in the comparatively free system of yesterday.

The proper place for "in the comparatively free system of yesterday" is after *whereas*, and it is a poor second-best to try to throw it back there by putting a comma in front of it.

The most barefaced attempt I have come across to correct a slovenly sentence by a comma was perpetrated by a Colonial bishop, who wrote to *The Times* a letter containing the sentence:

I should like to plead with some of those men who now feel ashamed to join the Colonial Service.

After the publication of the letter the bishop wrote again to *The Times*, saying:

The omission of a comma in my letter makes one seem to suggest that men might feel ashamed of joining the Colonial Service. My typescript reads, "I should like to plead with some of those men who now feel ashamed, to join the Colonial Service".*

(vi) The use of a comma to mark the end of the subject of a verb, or the beginning of the object. (*See* also p. 123).

It cannot be said to be always wrong to use a comma to mark the end of a composite subject, because good writers sometimes do it deliberately. For instance, one might write:

---

*Quoted in Gowans Whyte, *Anthology of Errors*, Chaterson, 1947.

The question whether it is legitimate to use a comma to mark the end of the subject, is an arguable one.

But the comma is unnecessary; the reader does not need its help. To use commas in this way is a dangerous habit; it encourages a writer to shirk the trouble of so arranging his sentences as to make their meaning plain without punctuation.

> I am however to draw your attention to the fact that goods subject to import licensing which are despatched to this country without the necessary licence having first been obtained, are on arrival liable to seizure. . . .

If the subject is so long that it seems to need a boundary post at the end, it would be better not to use the slovenly device of a comma but to rewrite the sentence in conditional form.

> . . . if goods subject to import licensing are despatched . . . they are on arrival. . . .

In the following sentence the comma merely interrupts the flow

> I am now in a position to say that all the numerous delegates who have replied, heartily endorse the recommendation.

Postponement of the object may get a writer into the same trouble.

> In the case of both whole-time and part-time officers, the general duties undertaken by them include the duty of treating without any additional remuneration and without any right to recover private fees, patients in their charge who are occupying Section 5 accommodation under the proviso to Section 5 (1) of the Act.

This unlovely sentence obviously needs recasting. One way of doing this would be:

> The general duties undertaken by both whole-time and part-time officers include the treating of patients in their charge who are occupying Section 5 accommodation under the proviso to Section 5 (1) of the Act, and they are not entitled to receive additional remuneration for it or to recover private fees.

(vi) The use of commas before a clause beginning with *that*. A comma was at one time always used in this position:

> It is a just though trite observation, that victorious Rome was itself subdued by the arts of Greece. (Gibbon.)
> The true meaning is so uncertain and remote, that it is never sought. (Johnson.)
> The author well knew, that two gentlemen . . . had differed with him. (Burke.)

We are more sparing of commas nowadays, and this practice has gone out of fashion. "Indeed it is safe to say that immediately before the conjunction *that* a comma will be admissible more rarely than before any other conjunction."*

B. If we turn from uses of the comma generally regarded as incorrect to those generally regarded as legitimate, we find one or two that need special care.

(i) The use of commas with adverbs and adverbial phrases.

(*a*) At the beginning of sentences.

> In their absence, it will be desirable . . .
> Nevertheless, there is need for special care . . .
> In practice, it has been found advisable . . .

Some writers put a comma here as a matter of course. But others do it only if a comma is needed to emphasise a contrast or to prevent the reader from going off on a wrong scent, as in:

> A few days after, the Minister of Labour promised that a dossier of the strike would be published.
> Two miles on, the road is worse.

On the principle that stops should not be used unless they are needed, this discrimination is to be commended.

(*b*) Within sentences.

To enclose an adverb in commas is, as we have seen, a legitimate and useful way of emphasising it. "All these things may, eventually, come to pass" is another way of saying "All these things may come to pass—eventually". Or it may serve to emphasise the subject of the sentence: "He, however, thought differently". The commas underline *he*. But certain common adverbs such as *therefore, however, perhaps, of course*, present difficulties because of a convention that they should always be enclosed in commas, whether emphasised or not. This is dangerous; the only safe course is to treat the question as one not of rule but of common sense, and to judge each case on its merits. Lord Dunsany blames printers for this convention:

> The writer puts down "I am going to Dublin perhaps, with Murphy". Or he writes "I am going to Dublin, perhaps with Murphy". But in either case these pestilent commas swoop down, not from his pen, but from the darker parts of the cornices where they were bred in the printer's office, and will alight on either side of the word *perhaps*, making it impossible for the reader to know the writer's meaning, making it impossible to see whether the doubt implied by the word *perhaps* affected Dublin or Murphy. I will quote an actual case I saw in a newspaper. A naval officer was giving evidence before a Court, and said, "I decided on an alteration of

---

*Carey, *Mind the Stop*.

course". But since the words "of course" must always be surrounded by commas, the printer's commas came down on them . . . and the sentence read, "I decided upon an alteration, of course"!

The adverb *however* is specially likely to stand in need of clarifying commas. For instance, Burke wrote:

> The author is compelled, however reluctantly, to receive the sentence pronounced on him in the House of Commons as that of the Party.

The meaning of this sentence would be different if the comma after *reluctantly* were omitted, and one inserted after *however*.

> The author is compelled, however, reluctantly to receive, etc.

(ii) The "throw-back" comma.

A common use of the comma as a clarifier is to show that what follows it refers not to what immediately precedes it but to something further back. William Cobbett, in the grammar that he wrote for his young son, pointed out that "You will be rich if you be industrious, in a few years" did not mean the same as "you will be rich, if you be industrious in a few years". The comma that precedes the adverbial phrase *in a few years* indicates that that phrase refers not to "if you be industrious" but to the whole clause "you will be rich if you be industrious". As usual, the device is clumsy. The proper way of writing the sentence is "You will be rich in a few years if you be industrious". If words are arranged in the right order these artificial aids will rarely be necessary. Examples of the dangers of the "throw-back" comma will be found on p. 151 under the heading *which*.

(iii) Years in commas.

Printers and typists are apparently taught that, in dates, the year must be encased in commas. ("On the 2nd August, 1950, a committee was appointed; on the 6th December, 1951, it reported"). I know of no usefulness that could be claimed for this practice to offset its niggling and irritating appearance. There are signs of an incipient revolt against it. At least one official publication has been issued lately that discards this use of the comma almost ostentatiously. But I expect that House Rules and Secretarial Colleges will put up a successful resistance to so revolutionary an idea.

(iv) Commas in series

(*a*) Nouns and phrases.

In such a sentence as:

> The company included Ambassadors, Ministers, Bishops and Judges

commas are always put after each item in the series up to the last but one, but practice varies about putting a comma between the last but one and the *and* introducing the last. Neither practice is wrong. Those who favour a comma (a minority, but gaining ground) argue that, since a comma may sometimes be necessary to prevent ambiguity there had better be one there always. Supposing the sentence were:

> The company included the Bishops of Winchester, Salisbury, Bristol, and Bath and Wells.

the reader unversed in the English ecclesiastical hierarchy needs the comma after *Bristol* in order to sort out the last two bishops. Without it they might be, grammatically and geographically, either (*a*) Bristol and Bath and (*b*) Wells, or (*a*) Bristol and (*b*) Bath and Wells. Ambiguity cannot be justified by saying that those who are interested will know what is meant and those who are not will not care.

(*b*) Adjectives.

Where the series is of adjectives preceding a noun, it is a matter of taste whether there are commas between them or not:

> A silly verbose pompous letter, and
> A silly, verbose, pompous letter

are equally correct. The commas merely give a little emphasis to the adjectives. Where the final adjective is one that describes the species of the noun, it must of course be regarded as part of the noun, and not be preceded by a comma. Thus:

> A silly, verbose, pompous official letter.

DASH

The dash is seductive; it tempts the writer to use it as a punctuation-maid-of-all-work that saves him the trouble of choosing the right stop. We all know letter-writers who carry this habit to the length of relying on one punctuation mark only—a nondescript symbol that might be a dash or might be something else. Moreover the dash lends itself easily to rhetorical uses that may be out of place in humdrum prose. Perhaps that is why I have been tempted to go to Sir Winston Churchill's war speeches for examples of its recognised uses.

(*a*) In pairs for a parenthesis.

> No future generation of English-speaking folks—for that is the tribunal to which we will appeal—will doubt that we were guiltless.

(*b*) To introduce an explanation, amplification, paraphrase, particularisation or correction of what immediately precedes it.

> They were surely among the most noble and benevolent instincts of the human heart—the love of peace, the toil for peace, the strife for peace, the pursuit of peace, even at great peril.
> Overhead the far-ranging Catalina air-boats soared—vigilant protecting eagles in the sky.
> The end of our financial resources was in sight—nay, had actually been reached.

(*c*) To indicate that the construction of the sentence, as begun, will be left unfinished (what the grammarians call *anacoluthon*).

> But when you come to other countries—oddly enough I saw a message from the authorities which are most concerned with our Arab problem at present, urging that we should be careful not to indulge in too gloomy forecasts.

(*d*) To gather up the subject of a sentence when it is a very long one; after the long loose canter of the subject you need to collect your horse for the jump to the verb.

> The formidable power of Nazi Germany, the vast mass of destructive munitions that they have made or captured, the courage skill and audacity of their striking forces, the ruthlessness of their central war direction, the prostrate condition of so many people under their yoke, the resources of so many lands which may to some extent become available to them—all these restrain rejoicing and forbid the slightest relaxation.

Similarly with the jump from the verb.

> I would say generally that we must regard all those victims of the Nazi executioners in so many lands, who are labelled Communists and Jews—we must regard them just as if they were brave soldiers who die for their country on the field of battle.

(*e*) To introduce a paradoxical, humorous or whimsical ending to a sentence.

> He makes mistakes, as I do, though not so many or so serious—he has not the same opportunities.

(*f*) With a colon to introduce a substantial quotation or a list (e.g. *as follows:*—). This, though common, is unnecessary since either the colon or the dash can do all that is needed by itself.

Full stop

The full stop is an exception to the rule that stops should be few. I have no advice to give about it except that it should be plentifully used: in other words to repeat the advice I have already given that

N

sentences should be short. I am not, of course, suggesting that good prose never contains long ones. On the contrary, the best prose is a judicious admixture of the long with the short. Mark Twain, after advising young authors to write short sentences as a rule, added:

> At times he may indulge himself with a long one, but he will make sure that there are no folds in it, no vaguenesses, no parenthetical interruptions of its view as a whole; when he has done with it, it won't be a sea-serpent with half of its arches under the water, it will be a torch-light procession.*

If you can write long sentences that you are satisfied really merit that description, by all means surprise and delight your readers with one occasionally. But the short ones are safer. I have said more about this on pp. 22/3 and 194.

Always use a full stop to separate into two sentences statements between which there is no true continuity of thought. For example, *and* is too close a link in these sentences.

> There are 630 boys in the school and the term will end on April 1st.
> As regards Mr. Smith's case a report was made on papers AB 340 and I understand he is now dead.

Hyphen

In *Modern English Usage* Fowler makes an elaborate study of the hyphen. He begins engagingly by pointing out that "superfluous hair-remover" can only mean a hair-remover that nobody wants, and he proceeds to work out a code of rules for the proper use of the hyphen. He admits that the result of following his rules "will often differ from current usage". But, he adds, "that usage is so variable as to be better named caprice". The author of the style-book of the Oxford University Press of New York (quoted in Perrin's *Writer's Guide*) strikes the same note when he says "If you take hyphens seriously you will surely go mad".

I have no intention of taking hyphens seriously. Those who wish to do so I leave to Fowler's eleven columns. If I attempted to lay down any rules I should certainly go astray, and give advice not seemly to be followed. For instance, the general practice of hyphening *co* when it is attached as a prefix to a word beginning with a vowel has always seemed to me absurd, especially as it leads to such possibilities of misunderstanding as *unco-ordinated* must present to a Scotsman. If it is objected that ambiguity may result, and readers may be puzzled whether *coop* is something to put a hen in or a

---

*Quoted in Earle's *English Prose, its Elements, History and Usage*, 1890.

profit-sharing association, this should be removed by a diaeresis (*coöp*) not a hyphen (*co-op*). That is what a diaeresis is for.

I will attempt no more than to give a few elementary warnings.

(i) Do not use hyphens unnecessarily. If, for instance, you must use *overall* as an adjective (though this is not recommended) write it like that, and not *over-all*.

But if you do split a word with a hyphen, make sure you split it at the main break. Though you may write *self-conscious*, if you wish to have a hyphen in the word, you must not write *unself-conscious* but *un-selfconscious*.

(ii) To prevent ambiguity a hyphen should be used in a compound adjective (e.g. *well-written, first-class, six-inch, copper-coloured*). The omission of a hyphen between *government* and *financed* in the following sentence throws the reader on to a false scent:

> When Government financed projects in the development areas have been grouped. . . .

But remember that words which form parts of compound adjectives when they precede a noun may stand on their own feet when they follow it, and then they must not be hyphened. "A badly-written letter" needs a hyphen, but "the letter was badly written" does not. There must be hyphens in "the balance-of-payment difficulties" but not in 'the difficulties are over the balance of payments".

(iii) Avoid as far as possible the practice of separating a pair of hyphenated words, leaving a hyphen in mid-air. To do this is to misuse the hyphen (whose proper function is to link a word with its immediate neighbour) and it has a slovenly look. The saving of one word cannot justify writing

> Where chaplains (whole- or part-time) have been appointed

instead of "where chaplains have been appointed, whole-time or part-time".

Inverted Commas

I have read nothing more sensible about inverted commas than this from the *A.B.C. of English Usage*:

> It is remarkable in an age peculiarly contemptuous of punctuation marks that we have not yet had the courage to abolish inverted commas. . . . After all, they are a modern invention. The Bible is plain enough without them; and so is the literature of the eighteenth century. Bernard Shaw scorns them. However, since they are with us, we must do our best with them, trying always to reduce them to a minimum.

I have only two other things to say on this vexatious topic.

One is to give a warning against over-indulgence in the trick of encasing words or phrases in inverted commas to indicate that they are being used in a slang or technical or facetious or some other unusual sense. This is a useful occasional device; instances may be found in this book. But it is a dangerous habit, as I have pointed out on p. 5.

The second question is whether punctuation marks (including question and exclamation marks) should come before or after the inverted commas that close a quotation. This has been much argued, with no conclusive result. It does not seem to me of great practical importance, but I feel bound to refer to it, if only because a correspondent criticised me for giving no guidance in *Plain Words* and accused me of being manifestly shaky about it myself. The truth is that there is no settled practice governing this most complicated subject. Pages were written about it by the Fowlers in *The King's English*, but their conclusions are by no means universally accepted.

There are two schools of thought. Most books on English advise that stops should be put in their logical positions. If the stops are part of the sentence quoted, put them within the inverted commas. If they are part of a longer sentence within which the quotation stands, put them outside the inverted commas. If the quotation and the sentence embracing it end together, so that each needs a stop at the same time, do not carry logic to the lengths of putting one inside and one out, but be content with the one outside. To give three simple examples of the application of this advice to question marks:

> I said to him "Why worry?"
> Why did you say to him "Don't worry"?
> Why did you say to him "Why worry"? (Strictly "Why worry?"?)

Many publishers will not have this. They dislike the look of stops outside inverted commas if they can possibly be put inside. Here is an extract from a publisher's House Rules:

> Commas, full stops, etc., closing matter in quotation marks may be placed before the final quotation marks, whether they form part of the original extract or not, provided that no ambiguity is likely to arise as to exactly what is quoted and what is not; this rule may not be as logical as that which insists on placing the punctuation marks strictly *according to the sense*, but the printed result looks more pleasing and justifies the convention.

But we need not concern ourselves here with questions of taste in printing. The drafter of official letters and memoranda is advised to stick to the principle of placing the punctuation marks according to the sense.

PARAGRAPHS

Letters, reports, memoranda and other documents would be un-readable if they were not divided into paragraphs, and much has been written on the art of paragraphing. But little of it helps the ordinary writer; the subject does not admit of precise guidance. The chief thing to remember is that, although paragraphing loses all point if the paragraphs are excessively long, the paragraph is essentially a unit of thought, not of length. Every paragraph must be homogeneous in subject matter, and sequential in treatment of it. If a single sequence of treatment of a single subject goes on so long as to make an unreasonably long paragraph, it may be divided into more than one. But you must not do the opposite, and combine into a single paragraph passages that have not this unity, even though each by itself may be below the average length of a paragraph.

PARENTHESIS

The purpose of a parenthesis is ordinarily to insert an illustration, explanation, definition, or additional piece of information of any sort, into a sentence that is logically and grammatically complete without it. A parenthesis may be marked off by commas, dashes or brackets. The degree of interruption of the main sentence may vary from the almost imperceptible one of explanatory words in appo-sition,

> Mr. Smith, the secretary, read the minutes,

to the violent one of a separate sentence complete in itself:

> A memorandum (six copies of this memorandum are enclosed for the information of the Board) has been issued to management committees.

Parentheses should be used sparingly. Their very convenience is a reason for fighting shy of them. They enable the writer to dodge the trouble of arranging his thought properly; but he does so at the expense of the reader, especially if the thought that he has spatch-cocked into the sentence is an abrupt break in it, or a long one, or both. The second of the two examples just given shows an illegitimate use of the parenthesis. The writer had no business to keep the reader waiting for the verb by throwing in a parenthesis that would have been put better as a separate sentence. The following examples are even worse:

> . . . to regard day nurseries and daily guardians as supplements to meet the special needs (where these exist and cannot be met within the hours, age, range and organisation of nursery schools and nursery classes) of children whose mothers are constrained by individual cir-cumstances to go out to work. . . .

If duties are however declined in this way, it will be necessary for the Board to consider whether it should agree to a modified contract in the particular case, or whether—because the required service can be provided only by the acceptance of the rejected obligations (e.g. by a whole-time radiologist to perform radiological examinations of paying patients in Section 5 beds in a hospital where the radiologists are all whole-time officers)—the Board should seek the services of another practitioner. . . .

These are intolerable abuses of the parenthesis, the first with its interposition of 21 words in the middle of the phrase "needs of children", and the second with its double parenthesis, more than 40 words long, like two snakes eating each other. There was no need for either of these monstrosities. In both examples the main sentence should be allowed to finish without interruption, and what is now in the parenthesis, so far as it is worth saying, should be added at the end:

> . . . to regard day nurseries and daily guardians as supplements to meet the special needs of children whose mothers are constrained . . . and whose needs cannot be met. . . .
>
> . . . or whether the Board should seek the services of another practitioner, as they will have to do if the required service can be provided only. . . .

Here is a parenthesis that keeps the reader waiting so long for the verb that he has probably forgotten what the subject is:

> Close affiliation with University research in haematology—and it may be desirable that ultimately each Regional Transfusion Officer should have an honorary appointment in the department of pathology in the medical school—will help to attract into the service medical men of good professional standing.

In former days, when long and involved periods were fashionable, it was customary after a long parenthesis to put the reader on the road again by repeating the subject with the words "I say". Thus the writer of the last example would have continued after "medical school" with the words "close affiliation with University research in haematology, I say, will help to attract, etc.". Now that this handy device has fallen into disuse, there is all the more need not to keep the reader waiting. There was no necessity to do so here. What is said as a parenthesis might just as well have been said as an independent sentence following the main one.

It is not only the reader who may forget where he was when the parenthesis started. Sometimes even the writer does, as in the letter quoted on p. 24.

> . . . Owing to a shortage of a spare pair of wires to the underground cable (a pair of wires leading from the point near your house back to the local exchange, and thus a pair of wires essential to the provision of a telephone service for you) is lacking. . . .

The writer thought he had entered the parenthesis with the words "Owing to the fact that a spare pair of wires to the underground cable" and he continued conformably when he emerged.

Question Marks

Only direct questions need question marks; indirect ones do not. There must be one at the end of "Have you made a return of your income?" but not at the end of "I am writing to ask whether you have made a return of your income".

It is usual to put question marks at the end of requests cast into question form for the sake of politeness. "Will you please let me know whether you have made a return of your income?"

For the position of question marks in relation to inverted commas *see* p. 190.

Semicolon

Do not be afraid of the semicolon; it can be most useful. It marks a longer pause, a more definite break in the sense, than the comma; at the same time it says "Here is a clause or sentence too closely related to what has gone before to be cut off by a full stop". The semicolon is a stronger version of the comma.

> The scheme of work should be as comprehensive as possible and should include gymnastics, games, boxing, wrestling and athletics; every endeavour should be made to provide facilities for swimming.
> If these arrangements are made in your factory you should take any difficulty which you may have to these officers when they call; you need not write to the Tax Office or call there.

These two sentences illustrate the common use of the semicolon. Each consists of two clauses. If these had been linked by the conjunction *and*, a comma would have been enough after *athletics* and *call*. But where there is no conjunction a comma is not enough; the stop must be either a semicolon or a full stop. (*See* p. 179.) The writers of these sentences felt that the clauses were not closely enough linked to justify a conjunction but too closely linked to admit of a full stop. They therefore rightly chose the middle course of a semicolon.

Examples of the use of a comma in such a position could be found in good writers, but a stronger stop is generally regarded as more suitable. Certainly each of the following sentences needs a semicolon in place of the comma.

> The Company is doing some work on this, it may need supplementing.
> If it is your own pension please say what type it is, if it is your mother's then it need not be included in your income.

The semicolon is also useful for avoiding the rather dreary trailing participles with which writers often end their sentences:

> The postgraduate teaching hospitals are essentially national in their outlook, their geographical situation being merely incidental.
> An attempt to devise permanent machinery for consultation was unsuccessful, the initial lukewarm response having soon disappeared.

There is nothing faulty in the grammar or syntax of these sentences, and the meaning of each is unambiguous. But they have a tired look. They can be wonderfully freshened by using the semi-colon, and rewriting them:

> The postgraduate teaching hospitals are essentially national in their outlook; their geographical situation is merely incidental.
> An attempt to devise permanent machinery for consultation was unsuccessful; the initial lukewarm response soon disappeared.

SENTENCES

A sentence is not easy to define. Many learned grammarians have tried, and their definitions have been torn in pieces by other learned grammarians. But what most of us understand by a sentence is what the O.E.D. calls the "popular definition": "such a portion of composition or utterance as extends from one full stop to another". That definition is good enough for our present purposes, and the question we have to consider is what general guidance can be given to a writer about what he should put between one full stop and the next.

The two main things to be remembered about sentences by those who want to make their meaning plain is that they should be short and should have unity of thought. Here is a series of 84 words between one full stop and another, which violates all the canons of a good sentence. In fact it might be said to explode the definition, for it would be flattering to call it a "sentence". "This is not a sentence", said a friend who was good enough to look through this book in proof. "This is gibberish".

> Forms are only sent to applicants whose requirements exceed one ton, and in future, as from tomorrow, forms will only be sent to firms whose requirements exceed five tons, and as you have not indicated what your requirements are, I am not sending you forms at the moment because it is just possible that your requirements may be well within these quantities quoted, in which case you may apply direct to the usual suppliers, of which there are several, with a view to obtaining your requirements.

If we prune this of its verbiage, and split it into three short sentences, a meaning will begin to emerge.

Only firms whose requirements exceed five tons now need forms. Others can apply direct to the suppliers. As you do not say what your requirements are I will not send you a form unless I hear that you need one.

The following is an even worse example of a meandering stream of words masquerading as a sentence:

Further to your letter of the above date and reference in connection with an allocation of . . ., as already pointed out to you all the allocations for this period have been closed, and I therefore regret that it is not possible to add to the existing allocation which has been made to you and which covers *in toto* your requirements for this period when originally received, by virtue of the work on which you are engaged, a rather higher percentage has been given to you, namely 100 per cent of the original requirements and at this stage I am afraid it is not practicable for you to increase the requirement for the reasons already given.

The fault here is excessive verbiage rather than of combining into one sentence thoughts that ought to have been given several. The thought is simple, and can be conveyed in two sentences, if not in one:

Your original application was granted in full because of the importance of your work. I regret that the amount cannot now be increased, as allocation for this period has been closed.

XI

Epilogue

He that will write well in any tongue, must follow this counsel of Aristotle, to speak as the common people do, to think as wise men do; and so should every man understand him, and the judgment of wise men allow him.

ROGER ASCHAM

A BOOK designed as a guide to officials in the use of English runs the risk of giving a false impression. It cannot help being concerned mainly with faults to be corrected, and so may make the picture look blacker than it is. The true justification for such a book is not so much that official English is specially bad as that it is specially important for it to be good. The efficiency of government, central and local, depends to an ever-increasing extent on the ability of a large number of officials to express themselves clearly. At present there is a popular idea that most of them cannot—or will not—do so. The term *officialese* has been invented for what is supposed to be their ineffective way of trying. I do not know exactly what that word means, and, for once, the Oxford English Dictionary is not illuminating. It defines *officialese* unhelpfully as "the language characteristic of officials or official documents". The 1933 supplement carries us a step further by giving a recent example from *These men thy Friends* by E. Thompson (1927):

"Who are these noble Arabs?" asked Kenrick. "It's officialese for beastly Buddoos", explained Edmund Candler.

Even with the illustration we are left in some doubt about the true characteristics of officialese. But that it is not ordinarily used as a term of praise is certain.

I should be sorry to be thought to support the popular notion that officials write a language of their own of a uniquely deplorable kind. Undoubtedly they have their peculiar faults of style. So have journalists theirs. It is reasonable to attribute those of officialese in the main to the peculiar difficulties with which official writers have to contend. As we have seen, much of what they write has to be devoted to the almost impossible task of translating the language of the law, which is obscure in order that it may be unambiguous, into terms that are simple and yet free from ambiguity. And our system of government imposes on officials the need always of being cautious

196

and often of avoiding a precision of statement that might be politically dangerous. Moreover, they do not easily shake off the idea that dignity of position demands dignity of diction. But it is certainly wrong to imagine that official writing, as an instrument for conveying thought, is generally inferior to the lamentably low standard now prevalent except among professional writers. It is not only the official who yields to the lure of the pompous or meretricious word, and overworks it; it is not he alone who sometimes fails to think clearly what meaning he wants to convey by what he is about to write, or to revise and prune what he has written so as to make sure that he has conveyed it. From some common faults he is comparatively free. Most officials write grammatically correct English. Their style is untainted by the silly jargon of commercialese, the catchpenny tricks of the worst sort of journalism, the more nebulous nebulosities of politicians, or the recondite abstractions of Greek or Latin origin in which men of science, philosophers and economists often wrap their thoughts. Sometimes it is very good, but then no one notices it. Occasionally it reaches a level of rare excellence.

The fact is not that officials do uniquely badly but that they are uniquely vulnerable. Making fun of them has always been one of the diversions of the British public. The fun sometimes has a touch of malice in it, but the habit springs from qualities in the British character that no one would like to see atrophied. The field for its exercise and the temptation to indulge in it are constantly growing. *De facto* executive power, which during the seventeenth and eighteenth centuries moved from the King to Ministers, is being diffused lower still by the growth of social legislation. The theory that every act of every official is the act of his Minister is wearing thin. The "fierce light that beats upon a throne and blackens every blot" is no longer focused on the apex, but shines on the whole pyramid. So many people have to read so many official instructions. These offer a bigger target for possible criticism than any other class of writing except journalism, and they are more likely to get it than any other class, because a reader's critical faculty is sharpened by being told— as we all so often have to be nowadays—that he cannot do something he wants to, or must do something he does not want to, or that he can only do something he wants to by going through a lot of tiresome formalities.

So it is natural enough that official writing, with its undeniable tendency to certain idiosyncrasies of style, should have been worked up into a stock joke. The professional humorist, in print or on the stage or on the air, can always be sure of a laugh by quoting or inventing bits of it. It is a way of getting one's own back. It is pleasantly flattering to the critics' sense of superiority. Bagehot once pictured the public of his day as saying to themselves with unction:

> Thank God *I* am not as that man; *I* did not send green coffee to the Crimea; *I* did not send patent cartridge to the common guns and common cartridge to the breech-loaders. *I* make money; that miserable public functionary only wastes it.

So we may imagine the critic of today saying: "Thank God *I* am not as that man; when *I* write a letter I make my meaning plain; this miserable public functionary only obscures his, if indeed he ever had any". He may be right about the functionary, but he is probably wrong about himself.

Though the spirit that still moves us to mock our officials may be healthy, the amusement can be overdone. One or two recent critics of so-called officialese have indulged in it to excess, deriding without discrimination, putting in their pillory good as well as bad, sometimes even mistaking the inventions of other scoffers for monstrosities actually committed. That is regrettable. It is a curious fact that attempts to teach "good English" often meet with resistance. Probably the explanation is that an exaggerated importance was for so long given to things that do not greatly matter; the conviction still lingers that instruction in good English means having to learn highbrow rules of no practical usefulness. It will take a long time to put the truth across that "good English" consists less in observance of grammatical pedantries than in a capacity to express oneself simply and neatly. Unfair criticism arouses reasonable resentment, and increases the difficulty of creating an atmosphere receptive of the new ideas. Even the notion that *officialese* in its derogatory sense is encouraged by authority has not wholly disappeared. The truth is, on the contrary, that great pains are now taken to train staffs to write clear and straightforward English. There may not yet be much to show for it in results, but that is another thing.

It does not seem to me to be true to say that the language itself is in decay. Its grammatical and syntactical usages are carefully preserved, perhaps too carefully. It is constantly being invited to assimilate new words, and seems capable of digesting many of them without any great harm, some indeed with profit. Some of the changes that have taken place in the meaning of words have weakened the language, but others have strengthened it, and on the whole there is no great cause for disquiet here. The language remains as fine and flexible an instrument as it was when used by Shakespeare and Bacon; in some respects it has been enriched. There are some alive today, and some recently dead, whose exact and delicate English would bear comparison with the outstanding writers of any generation. What is wrong is not the instrument itself but the way we use it. That should encourage us to hope that we may do better. When we are tempted to say that we have fallen away from the high standard of our forefathers, we must not forget the vast increase in the part played by the written word in our affairs. With such an increase in quantity it would be surprising if there were not some deterioration in quality. The field in which these faults are most readily noticed—the writings of officials for the guidance of the public—is almost wholly new. We cannot say whether the crop that grows there is better or worse than it was a hundred years ago, for no crop then grew there.

However unfair it may be that official English should have been singled out for derision, the fact has a significance that the official must not forget. The reader is on the look-out for the tricks of style that he has been taught to expect from official writing. Shortcomings are magnified, and the difficulties that every writer has in affecting his reader precisely as he wishes are for the official wantonly increased. All the greater is his duty to try to convert *officialese* into a term of praise by cultivating unremittingly that clarity of thought and simplicity of expression which have always been preached by those who have studied the art of writing. Thus he may learn, in the word of the 400-year-old advice that heads this chapter, by thinking as wise men do, and speaking as the common people do, to make every man understand him.

Bibliography

ALFORD, Henry. *The Queen's English.* George Bell & Co., 1889.

ALLBUTT, Sir T. Clifford. *Notes on the Composition of Scientific Papers.* Macmillan, 1925.

BALLARD, P. B. *Teaching and Testing English.* University of London Press, 1939. *Thought and Language.* University of London Press. 1934.

BELL, Vicars. *On Learning the English Tongue.* Faber & Faber, 1953.

BERG, P. C. A. *A Dictionary of New Words in English.* Allen & Unwin, 1953.

BRADLEY, H. *The Making of English.* Macmillan, 1904.

BROWN, Ivor. *A Word in your Ear.* Cape, 1942 (and sequels to 1953).

CAREY, G. V. *Mind the Stop.* Cambridge University Press, 1939. *American into English.* Heinemann, 1953.

Chambers's Shorter English Dictionary. Chambers, 1949.

CHASE, Stuart. *The Tyranny of Words.* Methuen. 7th edition, 1950.

COBBETT, William. *A Grammar of the English Language.* Oxford University Press, 1906.

COLLINS, V. H. *The Choice of Words.* Longmans, Green, 1952.

DAVIES, H. Sykes. *Grammar Without Tears.* J. Lane, 1951.

DUNSANY, Lord. *Donwellian Lectures,* 1943. Heinemann, 1945.

EDUCATION, MINISTRY OF. *Report of the Departmental Committee on the Teaching of English in England.* H.M. Stationery Office, 1921.

EVANS, B. Ifor. *The Use of English.* Staples Press, 1949.

FLESCH, R. F. *The Art of Plain Talk.* New York. Harper, 1946.

FOWLER, H. W. *A Dictionary of Modern English Usage.* Oxford University Press, 1926.

FOWLER, H. W. and F. G. *The King's English.* Oxford University Press. 3rd edition, 1930.

GRAVES, R. and HODGE, A. *The Reader over your Shoulder.* Cape, 1943.

HARTOG, Sir P. *Words in Action.* University of London Press, 1947.

HERBERT, Sir A. P. *What a Word!* Methuen, 1949.

JESPERSEN, Otto. *Growth and Structures of the English Language.* Blackwell, 1946. *Essentials of English Grammar.* Allen & Unwin, 1953.

JOHN O'LONDON. *Is it Good English?* Newnes, 1924.

KAPP, R. O. *The Presentation of Technical Information.* Constable, 1948.

LOUNSBURY, T. R. *The Standard of Usage in English.* New York. Harper, 1908.

MENCKEN, H. L. *The American Language.* 3 volumes. Rowtledge, 1948.

MONTAGUE, C. E. *A Writer's Notes on His Trade.* Penguin Books, 1949.

OGDEN, C. K. and RICHARDS, I. A. *The Meaning of Meaning.* Kegan Paul, 1946.

ONIONS, C. T. *Advanced English Syntax.* Kegan Paul, 1905.

ORWELL, George. *Shooting an Elephant and Other Essays.* Secker and Warbing, 1950.

Oxford English Dictionary. Clarendon Press. 2nd edition, 1933.

PARTRIDGE, E. *Dictionary of Clichés.* Routledge and Kegan Paul. 4th edition, 1950. *Usage and Abusage.* Hamish Hamilton. 4th edition, 1948. *You Have a Point There.* Hamish Hamilton, 1953.

PARTRIDGE, E. and CLARK, J. W. *British and American English Since* 1900. Andrew Dakers, 1951.

PERRIN, P. G. *Writer's Guide and Index to English.* New York. Scott, 1942.

QUILLER-COUCH, Sir A. *The Art of Writing.* Cambridge University Press, 1916.

ROSSITER, A. P. *Our Living Language.* Longmans, Green, 1953.

SMITH, Logan Pearsall. *The English Language.* Williams & Norgate, 1912. *Words and Idioms.* Constable, 1949.

SOCIETY FOR PURE ENGLISH. *Tracts.* Oxford University Press. 1919-45.

TREBLE, H. A. and VALLINS, G. H. *An A.B.C. of English Usage.* Oxford University Press, 1936.

VALLINS, G. H. *Good English: How to Write It.* Pan Books, 1951. *Better English.* Pan Books, 1953.

WARNER, G. T. *On the Writing of English.* Blackie, 1940.

Webster's New International Dictionary. Bell & Son, 1928.

WEEKLY, E. *The Romance of Words.* British Publishers Guild, 1949. *Words and Names.* Murray, 1932.

WESEEN, Maurice H. *Words Confused and Misused.* Pitman, 1952.

WHITTEN, W. and WHITAKER, F. *Good and Bad English.* Newnes. 2nd edition, 1950.

WHYTE, A. Gowans. *An Anthology of Errors.* Chaterson, 1947.

YOUNG, G. M. *Daylight and Champaign.* Hart-Davis, 1948. *Last Essays.* Hart-Davis, 1950.

Index

o

1392. Wt. 3030. K.287. 8/54. S.P. & S. S.O. Code No. 63-137*